The House with Round Windows

The House with Round Windows

A Memoir

by
Richard Snodgrass

Carnegie Mellon University Press
Pittsburgh 2022

Acknowledgments

The story "Tunnels of Love" appeared in a slightly different version, in *Pittsburgh Quarterly*, Winter 2017.

W. D. Snodgrass, excerpts from "Home Town" from *Heart's Needle* (Knopf, 1959), "The Survivors" from *Remains* (Perishable Press, 1970). Excerpts from "Ten Days Leave," "The Mother," and "To a Child" from *Not for Specialists: New and Selected Poems*. Copyright © 1959, 1970, 2006 by W. D. Snodgrass. All reprinted with the permission of The Permissions Company, LLC on behalf of BOA Editions, Ltd., boaeditions.org and the Estate of W. D. Snodgrass.

Book design by Connie Amoroso

Library of Congress Control Number 2021947137
ISBN 978-0-88748-680-7
Copyright © 2022 by Richard Snodgrass
All rights reserved
Printed and bound in the United States of America

10 9 8 7 6 5 4 3 2 1

for Helen and DeWitt,
and, as with everything,
for Marty

Contents

O quickly disappearing photograph

In my more slowly disappearing hand.

—Rainer Maria Rilke

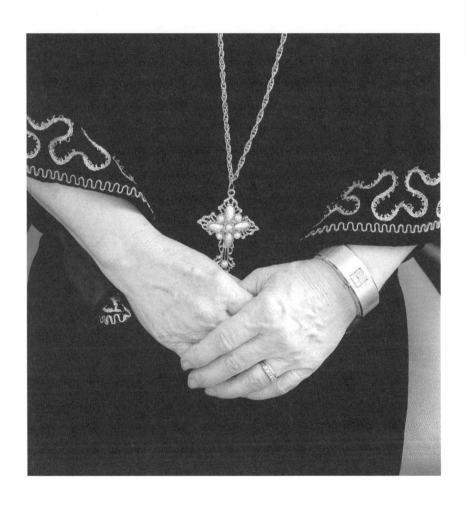

Prelude

I went back later to show her—the elderly woman, Helen; my mother—the photographs I had taken of the house. I told her of the stories I had written about us, that they talked about some of the same things that were at the heart of my brother's poetry, though from a different perspective.

"You don't have to worry," she said. "I've read all of his poetry. Even the ones under a pseudonym. I know he wasn't very complimentary to us. To me."

I was taken aback. I knew my brother had tried to hide some of his strongest poems from her; we had discussed how confident we were that she didn't know about them. Now she was telling me that she knew about them all along. That she knew his image of her as a dark sun with her feckless children orbiting about her, his likening her to an old sow who could smother her own sucklings, devour her own farrow. Yet she had said it without rancor or sadness, simply matter-of-fact.

I told her that the book I wanted to write wasn't always complimentary to the family, either, that I was hard on us, hard on myself. That it often showed us at our worst. In a bad light, so to speak.

She smoothed the wrinkles from the tablecloth in front of her, cocked her head just slightly. "Well, everything we did was human, wasn't it?"

The Stories

Part One

Home Is Where

1975

There is a head, the top of a head, moving above the floor in the hallway outside my room. I close my eyes and wait. Surely she wouldn't do that, would she? In a moment I peek over the edge of the bed again. Yes. She would. The head is still there, the gray hair rolled into rows of sausage curls, the tear-shaped glasses perched on her nose. She is on the steps coming up from the second floor, peering through the spaces between the balusters outside my bedroom door. Shifting her head, first one eye, then the other, like the dance of an owl trying to adjust its perspective.

Sigh. A deep breath. My first attempt to say something comes out as a croak.

"What is it, Mother?"

The head says something unintelligible. I am naked under the sheet with my usual morning erection. I consider jumping up and going over to the banister, to the top of the stairs, giving her something to think about.

"I'll be down in a little while."

The eyes shift back and forth between the posts. She speaks again, a dull murmur, her lips drawn tight together as though she is chanting a silent prayer. Then she clomps back downstairs, landing flat-footed on each tread. Jingling the bell on the wall outside my door that she used to call me with when I was a teenager, the long cord dangling down the stairwell to the first floor. I roll over on my back. Reflections of the cars passing in the street travel across the ceiling of my attic room, stretching across the angles of the slanted walls. The dormer window glows in the alcove. The curtains stir with the slight breeze. Though I have not seen it for nearly two decades, I recognize the light of eight o'clock on a spring morning in Beaver Falls, Pennsylvania.

From the open window comes a crash, almost like an explosion—the sound of a flatbed truck speeding around the corner, its wheels jumping in and out of the potholes in the street, hitting the sections where the pavement is worn down to the bricks. The diesel revs as the driver downshifts for the corner, then the mufflers rack off as the truck coasts downhill toward the lower leg of the S curve; the trailer creaks and groans as it is pulled against its own momentum, its own inertia, the brakes sing. Another truck is coming up the hill, engine straining. I can hear the cars pulling into the parking lot across the street, the crunch of the tires in the loose gravel, the chatter of the faculty members and students as they head down the block toward Geneva College. The chimes at McCartney Library strike the quarter hour, with one of the notes missing. I pull up the sheet over my head. In front of my eyes is a large blue embroidered *M*, marking it as part of the linen that Mother salvaged from her parents' home in Nebraska. The pigeons stomp around outside the rear window, on their side of the air conditioner, talking things over.

The room is just as I left it nearly twenty years earlier, complete to the collection of toiletries on top of the dresser from the 1950s—shaving lotion, talcum powder, deodorant—and the eight-by-ten handpainted color photograph of my high school sweetheart. Every time I come for a visit the photograph is sitting out in the room; every time I put it away again under some magazines on a shelf. It might not be so bad, but Mother didn't even like the girl. And consider myself lucky. The rest of the house is in total chaos, as always, like a junk store gone mad, or as if a cellar had erupted. Every surface in the downstairs—dining room, front hallway, living room, sunporch, kitchen—every table, chair, sofa, divan, window seat, footstool, ottoman, coffee table, bookcase, mantel, shelf—is covered with things. Everywhere: things. Old magazines, clothes, newspapers, towels, toys, boxes of screws, dishes, glasses, tools, empty bottles, trinkets—total visual overload. This year there is an added wrinkle. The floor in every room of the downstairs is taken up with large green plastic trash bags. When I arrived from the airport, I took a few steps inside the front door and stopped. There was no place to move, no place to sit down, no place to put my luggage. I stood transfixed.

Mother bustled around me and began kicking clear a path into the dining room.

"You'll have to excuse the way things look. I know everything's in an awful mess. I've been trying to sort out some of these things, but I just haven't been able to get much done since I had the flu this year. I've got some good medicine for it, though, the doctor gave me. You'll just have to fight your own way. Now then, my sweet patootie, can I get you something to eat?"

Eating was the last thing on my mind. Besides, it seemed doubtful that there was anyplace to set a dish, much less attempt to prepare a meal, in all of this. My immediate concern was to find a space large enough to set down my bag and camera gear and still be able to find them again.

Mother took off her imitation leopard-skin cape and her white satin pillbox hat and threw them on a chair that was already piled with newspapers. As I looked more carefully I could discern a kind of path that wound its way through the downstairs, hitting the important spots in each room—the big red plastic rocking chair, the dining room table, the several television sets. Mother worked her way further into the dining room, bending over with her knees spread far apart and her bottom to the wind, to pick up a crumpled napkin and an empty lipstick tube. When she stood up again and tried to move forward, her feet were attacked by several light cords. She kicked them into submission beneath the dining room table, then looked at me and giggled.

"Why don't you put down your things and stay awhile?"

I saw an open space in the living room and pushed my way in that direction, knocking over a stack of *Time* magazines with my tripod in the process. The room was just as cluttered as the others, except there were fewer green trash bags. Two card tables were set up in the middle of the room, side by side, each one piled with bank statements, letters, stationery bearing the official seal of the Daughters of the American Revolution, newspaper clippings. The overstuffed chairs and the couch were barely visible underneath their own allotments of stuff. On top of the baby grand piano, among everything else, was a large cross made of egg containers, the tits covered with small paper flowers like pasties.

Behind me was a large mirror that covered one wall. The room doubled in size, the clutter doubled in quantity. In the middle of this mess stood a rather tall man in his mid-thirties, dressed in a Brooks Brothers suede sport coat, green turtleneck, brown Levi's, boots, and a summer Stetson. He did not look happy.

I stuck out my tongue at him and retraced my steps back to the dining room. Mother was standing in one of her paths, stuffing rags and the parts of several electric motors into one of the plastic bags. When it was full, she trussed it up with a plastic tie and hefted it out of the way. Then she began filling up another one.

"Your sister Shirley lets one or two of her girls come down and help me once in a while. They're a big help and I pay them for it."

She held up the cord from an appliance to see if she recognized it, shook it at me as though it were alive, and tossed it into another bag.

"Can I help you?" I offered.

"No, no, dear, this is fine. I just want to get a few of these things out of the way." She smiled absently in my direction. "After all, we'll have to have a place to eat."

I looked at the mess on the dining room table. It looked as though every drawer in the kitchen had been dumped on it, but through the doorway the kitchen appeared to be as full of junk as the other rooms. I couldn't imagine where it all came from.

"Isn't it amazing?" Mother grinned, reading my thoughts. "I don't know where it all comes from, either."

"I don't know where it's all going to go."

"What?"

"It certainly is a lot of stuff," I yelled.

"It is, it is indeed, my young son."

She looked around, then reached across a pile of cardboard boxes and almost toppled over. I was afraid if she fell when no one was here, they'd never find her again.

"Is there something . . . anything I can do?" I said, looking around the room and feeling desperate.

She was leaning the other direction now, her knees braced against the side of a chair, rummaging through the piles of things on the buffet.

"Here it is!"

She gave a little laugh, pleased with herself, and pulled a flashlight from underneath a pile of handkerchiefs, a *TV Guide*, and an imitation Amish trivet. She fumbled with the switch, then snapped it on and pointed it at me, her face full of glee.

"I knew there was one around here somewhere."

She wiggled the light and the dim beam danced over my body. She laughed. Then she began to sweep the room with the light. It was late afternoon; outside it was still a sunny day. But sunlight barely penetrated into the house, and the light that did was quickly absorbed into the dark wood paneling and became lost in the shadows. The faint beam from the flashlight ranged over the room, up the wall to the mantel over the closed-in fireplace, picking up the color snapshots of my sister's children, a plaster statue of a bear, a small basket, several pewter candlesticks, a vase; down the built-in bookcases now filled with dusty goblets and plates decorated with a large lotus flower; across the dining room table; over stacks of the *News-Tribune* and *Pittsburgh Press*, coffee cups, an empty cottage cheese container, crumpled Kleenex, a cluster of pens and pencils thrown like pickup sticks. As I followed the beam across the table, one of the piles of cloth blinked, stretched, stood up, and came over toward me. I jumped back.

"I'm not going to hurt you."

I thought she was talking to me, but she was addressing the cat, Merry Anne. The animal tried several routes to where we were standing but had trouble finding her footing and almost slid off a plastic sheet onto the floor. She finally found a path through the attachments for the vacuum cleaner.

"That's remarkable," Mother said.

"It's more than that."

"She never stays around when there are men in the house. She must remember you."

The cat looked at me, the tip of its tongue sticking out between the lips, and looked away. It was a long thin gray tabby with eyes like a Disney caricature and a grizzled chin. For years Mother had said it was dying of cancer, but when I asked about it on the phone a few months earlier, she said, "Oh, that? It must've gone away."

Merry Anne sat on the edge of the table, trying not to fall off, watching

Mother play with the flashlight. Mother rubbed the flashlight against the animal's chest.

"She's my girl, that's what she is."

The cat looked surprised but tolerant of the roughhousing, and spoke once. Mother whispered something to the animal that seemed to interest it quite a bit. Then they both leaned forward and touched foreheads.

I had to sit down. San Francisco, where my home was now, was beginning to seem more than a continent away. But the red plastic rocker was heaped with blankets, and the dining room couch was a sorting area for dishes. I finally sat on a stack of *Cosmopolitans* and *Redbooks* on one of the dining room chairs. Mary Tyler Moore peeked up at me from between my legs.

Mother put down the flashlight and started to carry one of the green plastic trash bags toward the kitchen.

"Mother!"

"Yes?"

"Where are you going?"

"You just take it easy. I've got some things to do."

I blew air through my lips, cast my eyes to the heavens asking for strength, and followed her.

"I'm not going to sit here while you lug these things around."

"I don't do too badly for an old woman."

I tried to reach around her to take the bag but she poked me in the chest with her elbow. It felt like I had been prodded with a nightstick. She chuckled.

"Go get your own bag. This one's mine."

She carried the bag in front of her with two hands, as though she had a dead animal around the neck, pushing things out of her way along the narrow path, out through the kitchen and back door. I looked around. There were at least a dozen bags within reach.

"Which one?" I called after her.

"Oh, any one that looks full."

The screen door banged behind her. I grabbed the nearest one and followed her. I was curious as to what I was carrying, but I couldn't make out any distinguishing shapes through the heavy green vinyl. I imagined severed heads, parts of delivery boys, the leg of a mailman.

We spent the next couple of hours carrying the green bags from the house to an empty stall in the garage. Between trips she demonstrated one of her new white plastic garbage cans—there were half a dozen scattered around the house and the backyard—rolling it along on its built-in wheels; and called my attention to points of interest around the yard: the area where she wanted to plant new rosebushes later this year; the azalea bushes where the neighborhood boys gathered at night to do unspeakable things. I learned Mr. Funkhauser across the alley had died, and that his middle-aged unwed daughter had learned to drive. I learned that Mrs. Majors across the street didn't have much longer to live, but that Mrs. Mulroy was thriving. I learned that the college still wanted to buy our house, but that she was holding out for more money.

And she told me again the stories about the break-ins to the house. Of the boys who rang the front doorbell, then the back doorbell, and when she left the door unlocked would run through the house and out the other side. And the morning she came back from church and heard the glass break in the kitchen door and found an arm reaching inside trying to find the doorknob. She hit the arm with a cast-iron skillet and thought she broke it—the arm, not the skillet—but the police never checked the hospitals. At other times the cellar doors were found open; locks had been tampered with; keys were missing.

"I've found things missing all over the house where they must have broken in."

And I thought: *How could she tell anything was missing?* Wondered: *How could a burglar find anything of value in all this mess?*

"They always pick a house like this, you know. They can tell by just looking at it that there are valuables inside."

And I imagined: a burglar, his shoulder bruised from breaking in the cellar door, his knuckles skinned and bleeding from forcing the antiquated locks, sitting in the middle of the downstairs hallway, surrounded by green plastic trash bags, tears rolling down his cheeks. Or laughing hysterically.

"I had the man from the college come over and put bigger locks on all the doors and steel bars across the cellar windows. But there's no telling when they'll try again."

Imagined: walking upstairs and opening one of the closed-off rooms to find two young men standing there among the piles of cardboard boxes and old furniture, their eyes wide with terror, their faces drawn from hunger, saying, *Hey, man, we didn't mean nothing, we just want to find a way out of here!*

It was dusk by the time we carried the last bag from the house. She carefully locked the garage, and I followed her along the concrete walk toward the house. Then she stopped, took a deep breath, and flapped her arms a couple of times. She looked up at the back of the tall brick house, the branches of the trees moving gently overhead.

"Isn't it good?" she said.

"What's that?"

"Oh. Everything."

Then she continued bustling along the walk, head down and whistling to herself, into the house. The spaces between the furniture were open now, you could walk around easier, but after all our work I still couldn't see that it made much difference.

The bells from the college library sound the hour: nine o'clock. I scrunch down in the bed, stretch, flap the covers several times to see my body appear and disappear and feel the air circulating against my skin. Then I throw back the covers and swing out of bed. Standing in the middle of the room, I can only see a part of the street, so I pull on a T-shirt and stand in the alcove at the window.

The day is bright though the valley is still filled with a morning haze. From this height I look down on the roofs of the stores catty-cornered across the street, the neighbors' houses, the trees. Directly across from me, a block away, is the Gothic bell tower at the college, and beyond, across the river, the solid mass of the valley's hills. I had forgotten the green of an eastern spring, the lushness of the bushes and trees that break the hard edges of the buildings, and the soft though full quality of the light. It seems a full camera stop less than the light I had grown used to in the West.

I look at the pile of camera cases and gear on the floor, lenses, light meters, tripod. I take the light meter to the window, aiming it first at the sky to prime the cell, then put it to my eye and pan the room. The first days here were overcast, and worse, broken clouds with the sun ducking in and out, the light never constant. If I'm going to photograph in the house I'll need all the sunlight I can get, unless the exposures are going to be hours long.

I walk around the room, sighting through the meter, trying different angles, compositions. The room is interesting in a way, though mainly from the viewpoint of its architecture. There is the three-quarter wood paneling on the walls, the angles formed by the pitch of the roof. The alcove with the dormer window facing the street, the smaller window at the back. One wall is crowded with empty wardrobes, lined up side by side like upended oversized coffins. But the furniture for the most part is stark, as though no one lives in the room anymore. No one does.

There are few decorations in the room. On the wall near the front dormer window are two pictures, one large, one small, hanging side by side so their frames touch, their arrangement determined by the existing hooks in the wall. The large one is a color lithograph of a Scottish castle, fronting a loch and the Highlands. The smaller one is a copy of a painting by John Singer Sargent entitled *Corfu Lights and Shadows*. How it came to be in the house, much less in my room, I haven't a clue; perhaps my brother brought it when he lived here with his first wife, while he went to the local college for a year. The painting is of a small cottage—growing up, I thought it must be an adobe hut in Mexico; I had never heard of John Singer Sargent. I had always thought the scene uninteresting except for the shadow on the wall of the hut, perhaps from a tree, perhaps from a cloaked figure that appears to be edging toward the black open doorway. The only other picture hanging on the walls is a crayon and charcoal caricature of De, my older brother, in his late teens. It was said that we looked the same at the same age, but when I lived in this room I spent countless times comparing his image with mine in the mirror and never found the similarities. The similarities are even fewer now.

For a while, I considered De the main reason for these visits home. I had the idea to photograph the house to illustrate its relationship to my brother's poetry. In fact, De never lived in the house for any length of time. A few years at the end of high school; later, for a year or so after he came back from the Navy. But in the poetry of W. D. Snodgrass, the house became the embodiment of all he deplored and condemned about his family, and the world in general—the root of his ethics and his poetics.

His first book, the Pulitzer Prize–winning *Heart's Needle*, introduced the family and the house in the very first poem and established the themes that followed throughout the book and, for that matter, the rest of his work: the unquenchable desire for—and the unspeakable deadliness of—love. In *Remains*, written under the pseudonym S. S. Gardons, the house became the embodiment of a family's decay and smother love. Later, that oppression became the father figure of Hitler in *The Fuehrer Bunker*, driving the inhabitants to extremes of behavior, destroying themselves and those around them. The betrayal of loved ones cavorted through *W. D.'s Midnight Carnival*. He spent decades writing poems in an adapted nursery-rhyme style about the buried terrors of childhood.

My brother's early work started what came to be known as the Confessional school of poetry—highly autobiographical examinations of self, in plain language, that had a kind of confessional air, an opening up of secrets that paid homage to and sought redemption from the god of psychotherapy. In time, others became more famous at it; others perhaps had a broader scope—Robert Lowell in *Life Studies*, Anne Sexton, Sylvia Plath—but no one else reached W. D.'s heights of lyricism and poetic form. Or, for that matter, his depths of insights into the self's darker, baser motives. In his later work, he worked hard to wrench himself free of the confessional label, to broaden his range with larger, even historical subjects. But his basic ideas just wouldn't go away. Underlying all was the thought that sanctuary of any sort, whether it's home or family, bunker or farmhouse, is a scary place.

In photographing the house, I hoped to reveal something of my brother's torment and intent. At one time it seemed worthwhile, even an important thing to do. But now I wasn't so sure. After working on the project for a couple of years, the series had grown into something more. Something different. The experience of exploring the imagery of the house had proven to be an object lesson of its own; though the premises were often the same as in my brother's work, I sometimes came to different conclusions. As a result, my brother and I disagreed increasingly about the family over the last few years. The latest disagreement, a few months earlier during a visit to his home in Erieville, New York, had sent my brother storming out of his own house in a blind fury, howling into the woods. I was learning that for De the family was a subject you could talk about but not discuss.

All things considered, there seems enough lunacy in the house to go around. Downstairs, on the second floor, I can hear Mother moving about, on the pretense of looking for something, waiting for me to come down. Degas said the dancer is just the pretext for painting. Maybe my desire to photograph the house is nothing more than my desire to photograph. An occasion to make images. To be sure, the rooms are awash with imagery, changing daily like flotsam and jetsam cast ashore on a deserted beach as the old woman, my mother, moves things about.

I look in the mirror, at the disheveled figure in a T-shirt with long white legs. I remembered my father looked like this when he went to the bathroom in the middle of the night, holding his underpants against his genitals. I remembered he looked like this the morning when he stood grieving in the upstairs hallway, the morning my sister died. When I photograph here, memories surface on the luminous ground glass like the faces of the drowned, remembrances of long ago. Or maybe not so long ago. Thomas Wolfe was wrong, of course. The melancholy truth is that you can go home again. I wondered how many of us, no matter how far we travel, have never been away.

Killing the Wabbits

It started to snow in the afternoon and continued on through the evening. An hour or so before I was supposed to leave, I took the family car and drove downtown, in several inches of snow, to cruise the main street one last time, a farewell tour as it were, as if I thought it would be my last time, even though I was only going to visit my brother for a couple of days. At eight o'clock in the evening, the town was deserted in the storm. No one was driving, and the cars parked along the curbs were turning into white mounds. The Christmas decorations were still up over Seventh Avenue, though not turned on in February, and the snow squalls drove against the garlands of imitation pine boughs and unlit electric candles.

I wanted to stop at my girlfriend's house, but we had already said our good-byes after school, a tearful farewell. I usually took every opportunity to see her, even inventing opportunities if I had to, but for once I decided to leave well enough alone. Reluctantly, I headed back through the silent town, following the cinder truck up the long grade to College Hill, the shovelfuls of cinders thrown by the workmen in the back of the dump truck fanning out in front of me, the unburned carbon in the cinders from the mills glimmering like cheap jewels under the streetlights, to my family's house, the big house on the corner at the top of the hill. The lights spilled out over the snow-covered terraced lawn, the curved windows on the corners giving glimpses of the life within, the chandelier in the living room where my father would be watching his cowboy programs, my mother in the kitchen cleaning up after dinner. Shortly after nine, my mother drove me back through town to the train station. She wanted to wait to see that I got on the train okay, but I sent her back home; I was an adult now, or at least I thought I was, almost eighteen, a young adult certainly, not a child, I could do it on my own. The train was full of skiers, college kids in expensive sweaters, carrying on among themselves, heading north. It continued to snow through the night. I sat for hours with my feet propped up on the seat across from me, above the cold floor, reading the dirty parts of *Peyton Place*, feeling very adult indeed.

I left the book stuffed between the cushions when I changed trains at Buffalo. My connection was late with the storm, and I waited most of the dark hours of the morning in a tile cavern, wishing I hadn't been so hasty with the book. I got to Rochester a little after six a.m. and woke my brother from a sound sleep. He told me to grab a taxi, that it would be easier on account of the snow. I rode through the white-clogged streets of a new world, my arrival heralded by rhe flashing red lights of salt trucks and road scrapers.

I slept most of the day, curled on a mattress on the floor of the living room. I woke once, sometime around noon, and found Kathy, Jan's daughter by her first marriage, standing in the middle of the room, staring down at me. Jan called her away. When I woke again at four, she was staring at me again, this time sitting on another mattress at right angles to me, eating a cookie.

"Do you know what I did in school today?"

"What?" It was more a moan than a question.

"We had to draw a picture of our favorite animal. I drew a picture of you."

"What?"

"I drew you all curled up like that. I called it Uncle Mole."

"What?"

"Kathy, come away. Let him sleep."

Jan came in from the kitchen. She wore a peasant skirt, her long dark hair trailing down her back, and furry moccasins. She smiled warmly.

"How are you doing?"

"Okay. I guess. Sorry I slept so long."

"Nonsense. We'll leave you so you can get dressed." She herded the little girl away.

The only times I had ever been in apartments was when I visited my brother at various universities—Iowa, Cornell—and this was the first time I ever visited him on my own. His apartments were always an adventure for me, very different from anything I knew before, very different from my home in Beaver Falls. Instead of beds or chairs, there were mattresses on the floor; instead of bookcases, there were bricks and boards; instead of family photographs on the walls, there were reproductions of paintings with strange shapes and colors. I pulled on my clothes and went out to the kitchen to join Jan and Kathy.

De got home from the university after five and went out again right away to help the black man upstairs dig out his car after the snowplow went by. The radio was playing classical music. Jan moved about the kitchen fixing dinner in a sort of dance; Kathy worked on a new drawing of Uncle Mole. There were candles on the table for light. I must have looked bewildered, because Jan laughed sympathetically at me.

De came in, stomping snow across the kitchen. Jan turned away from the stove and kissed him full on the mouth; I turned away. The fact was I hardly knew my brother. He was in high school when I was born and was drafted into the Navy during World War II before I could remember him much. After he returned from the service, he lived with the family for brief periods, including a few months with his new wife, Lila, before they left for him to start graduate school at Iowa, but we rarely had anything to say to each other. I remember him playing the timpani, his kettledrums set up in a corner of the living room, practicing for auditions that never came, playing to records of the prelude to act three of *Lohengrin* and the final movement of Berlioz's *Symphonie fantastique*; I remember him making theater maquettes out of cardboard boxes for productions Geneva College had neither the time nor the money nor the inclination to produce; I remember my parents at his request buying him a cello at Volkwein's in Pittsburgh—the same place when I was a junior in high school they bought me the most beautiful Gretsch pearl-gray drum set you ever saw in your life—but he gave it up a few months later.

I knew my brother only as an older guy with a mustache and beard; he could have been an uncle, a family friend (if we had any), or a passing stranger. And though I nearly had a fight on account of him once—in the schoolyard in the third grade, when Gary Javens didn't believe me when I said my brother could be as great as Shakespeare, something I had heard my mother say; it didn't matter, of course, that neither Gary Javens nor I knew anything about Shakespeare—I actually thought De was a little weird. Okay, more than a little.

But the previous summer, during his visit for our sister's wedding, he took a new interest in me. The family was sitting around the dining room table one evening. I don't remember how it started, but De was trying to tell Mother that our house wasn't the same as other people's, that other people didn't live this way. To help him make his point, I broke in with a ten-minute description of every object in the room, a running commentary on the seemingly endless clutter and multitudinous knickknacks that covered every flat surface, ending with my description of a particularly bulbous pannier that I referred to as a pregnant basket. Mother looked hurt; Father tried not to laugh; and De and Jan gazed at me as though Christ had just taught the elders. Later that night they invited me out for a pizza and asked me leading questions about my feelings about the house and the family, but I couldn't come up with anything to equal the pregnant basket and we rode home in silence. But before they left, for reasons I didn't understand, they took me aside and invited me to visit them in Rochester. And for reasons I didn't understand, I decided to.

De was shuffling about the apartment, having replaced his outside boots for a pair of moccasins, making small talk about my trip and the snow. Kathy watched him expectantly. On one of his trips through the room she took an empty paper bag, opened it, and threw it in his path. He looked at her in mock indignation and kicked it. She kicked it back. He kicked it again and the game was on, a kind of soccer, in and out of the kitchen, dining room, bedroom, until the bag was torn to bits. He hugged her and clapped her on the bottom and sent her giggling back to Jan. I wondered if their life was always like this.

I don't recall what we had for dinner, but during my visits over the following six or seven years they introduced me to exotic dishes that I had never heard of before—curries, stuffed grape leaves, sweet and sour sauces. After dinner, Kathy went to bed, having been directed by De to give me a hug. Jan did dishes while De sat at the kitchen table with his manuscripts of poems, asking us for rhyme words while he made lists in the margins. I wandered from room to room, wondering why I had come.

I leaned against the refrigerator, looking at a reproduction of Picasso's *Pierrot* tacked on the wall without a frame.

"Are you dating anyone?" Jan asked as she stacked dishes on the drainboard.

I said yes but it came out funny. She laughed.

"You don't sound too sure about it."

"I didn't mean it that way. She's a beautiful girl. Italian."

"You still don't sound very sure about it."

"Oh, there's nothing wrong with her. I guess . . . I don't know, sometimes I have trouble believing she really likes me, you know?"

Jan stopped doing the dishes and looked at me. De looked up from his poems.

"You mean she doesn't show you how she feels about you?"

"Oh no, she tells me she does. It's not her. I guess it's me. You know, I guess I have trouble believing that anyone could really like me that way, you know?" I laughed a little to each one of them in turn.

"Do you have any idea why you might feel that way?" De said.

"Oh, I've thought about it. A lot. I guess something must have happened to me when I was younger to make me feel that way. You know?"

As revelations and epiphanies go, there undoubtedly have been more significant ones in the history of the world. But this one was enough to change my life. I don't know how much I believed what I said, or how much I sensed what they wanted me to say. It was probably a combination of both. But I did say it, and a whole lot more. We talked through the night, sitting around the kitchen table, De and Jan alternately asking me questions about my childhood, what it was like to live in the house, how I felt about my life in general, playing the role of analysts to me as the patient. And I poured out all the suspicions and fears and hatreds, real and imaginary, that I could think of against my parents and the family. That night talking to De and Jan, everything about my life seemed false and self-destructive; worse, everything about my family and the way I was raised seemed geared to intentionally destroy me, forcing me into a way of life that would in time drain the life from me.

"Is that what happened to Barbara?" I asked at some time in the middle of the night.

De said, "Whew!" looked to the heavens, and got up to start pacing. Jan looked at him, looked at me. She reached over and took my hand. De came back and sat down.

"What do you think happened to her?" he said, leaning his elbows on the table, one leg folded under him on the chair.

"I don't know."

"I'll bet you do. If you think about it. You said as much already."

"I found her. I was the last one to talk to her. Or she talked to."

"Why do you think somebody would die, just like that?"

"They said it was a heart attack. A blood clot."

"Who said?"

"Mother. Father. I don't know."

De and Jan looked at each other. Jan lowered her head.

"We discussed this a lot before you got here," De said, "trying to decide whether to talk to you about this or not. But I think you already see everything there is to it."

"They don't know exactly how she died," Jan said.

De nodded. "They were going to do an autopsy, but somebody prevented it."

"Who?"

De shrugged. He looked pained.

"You mean somebody killed her?" I said.

"In a way. Yes."

I was bewildered, confused. My body was trembling uncontrollably.

"Or do you mean she killed herself?"

He nodded again. "That, too." De set his jaw and looked at me over the tops of his glasses. "And I think you already know about this."

"I don't understand." I looked from one to the other in a kind of terror.

"Sure you do. Think about it. What would happen if you didn't have anything to live for?"

"I guess you'd die."

"And who do we know that could prevent you from having anything to live for? Anything you really wanted for yourself? Remember, Barbara died on Independence Day. I don't think that's coincidence."

They looked at me sympathetically, as if understanding my desperation at the hideous logic. A great emptiness opened in front of me, inside of me. And I saw my parents as monsters, killers, who had destroyed my sister's life with smother love, and who were trying to do the same to me. Everything I had once believed in fell away, home and family, and I would never see the world the same way again. I broke down totally into uncontrollable sobs. De and Jan cried, too, and they embraced me across the table, sharing in the pain and joy of my enlightenment.

Through the rest of the night we recounted all the emotional tricks my parents, especially my mother, used to trap me in their way of life—the disapproving looks, the hurt stares; the offers of endless gifts that stopped as soon as you asked for something specific; the ethic that would rather see you sick than healthy, would rather have you needy than able to stand on your own two feet. There was the house itself that my mother kept dark and cluttered, choking life; there was the big car they let me drive, making me dependent upon their money, getting me used to luxury and privilege, the expensive things of life. All of them were tricks in my brother's book, playing with my emotions, multiplying like rabbits everywhere you turned. After he said it, De howled with laughter at the idea. They had seen a Bugs Bunny cartoon the night before I arrived where Elmer Fudd stalks through the woods, singing "Kill the Wabbit" to the tune of Wagner's "Ride of the Valkyries." It became our battle cry. We joined hands around the table at dawn, chanting "Kill the Wabbits, Kill the Wabbits, Kill the Wabbits," and I knew the Wabbits were my family, my mother and my father somehow in collusion with her, and I was filled with hatred and hope and dread. I collapsed on my bed in the living room and slept again through the day.

I don't remember much else that happened during the remaining hours of the visit. When I finally awoke that second day, it was with an overwhelming loneliness, and I wished none of it had happened, that it all would go away. But it had happened, it would not go away, and I felt a new sense of purpose. The purpose was to get out of the house, to change my way of life, to overcome what my parents were trying to do to me. The rest of the visit consisted mostly of sitting around the table clarifying the things we talked about the first night. I entertained them with my newfound theory that the house actually contained the nine basements of Dante's *Inferno*, each level devoted to such things as decayed newspapers, dirty dustrags, used Band-Aids. It was a big hit. In turn, De explained how he had discovered a central image in his poetry, the ability and necessity of people to either accept or reject their own breath, and therefore their lives. It became a matter of whether one wanted to win or lose, live or die.

"We've been trained by the family that losing is better," he said across the table, a few hours before I was to leave.

"How did they do that?"

"When you lose, you get comforted. When you get sick, you get waited on. That's what happened to Barbara. But she played it so far, there was no place left for her to go. She bought into it, and she paid for it with her life."

"It's the same thing that people would much rather have you think badly of them than nothing at all," Jan said.

De threw her a look as if she didn't know what she was talking about and went on.

"You have to keep in mind now that only you can decide if you're going to win or lose."

"I want to win."

"Good, good. But it's not going to be easy. You're going to have to fight them every step of the way, because they're going to do everything they can to derail you."

"We're with you," Jan said.

The three of us embraced again and chanted the cry, "Kill the Wabbits! Kill the Wabbits!" They wondered if it would be possible for me to stay with them, to not go back at all, but we decided I'd have to return, if only to finish high school. Then it would be away to college and a better life.

They drove me to the train station and I rode again through the night, back to Beaver Falls, but this time with new eyes. I felt older, more than an adult now, mature, gifted with new intelligence, touched with the grace to see the phoniness and manipulations of human existence. I watched the other passengers, pitying them for their lack of self-awareness, feeling almost holy.

As the scattered lights of the farm towns slid past the windows, I wrote soapy and tearful poems about casting aside veils.

The train that I arrived on was the train Father took to his office in Pittsburgh. As we pulled into the station, I saw him standing on the platform, in his dark wool overcoat and gray hat, his briefcase tucked under his arm. There was no way to avoid him. I climbed down the steps and he waved.

"How's it going, fella?" He clapped me on the shoulder.

I mumbled something about being tired.

"I'll bet you are. Well, Mother's waiting for you on the other side. You can tell me all about it tonight when I get home."

He kidded with the conductor and waved again from the doorway of the coach as the train pulled out. I walked along the cold breezy platform and down the stairs into the tunnel to the other side of the tracks. I was the only one who got off the train. The morning was still blue-black and filled with smoke. The snow of a few days earlier remained as slush.

Mother was sitting in the car in the turnaround in front of the station, looking anxious. She was wearing her good wool coat with the square shoulder pads like a linebacker, as if it were a special occasion. She smiled when she saw me.

"I was afraid you missed it or something," she said as I climbed in. She patted me on the knee before putting the car in drive. "How was the trip?"

I sat as close to the window as I could and stared straight ahead.

"It was okay."

Album I
The Setting

The House with Round Windows. *The title, you should know from the onset, is wrong. Or rather, incorrect. The windows of the house weren't round at all; in point of fact they were curved. In the same way that the corners of the big orange-brick house were round—or curved. Though no question they were unusual, the house unusual, to say nothing of the stained-glass windows, the dormers of the mansard roof, the stunted umbrella trees on the front lawn. The very presence of the three-story house, sitting back from the corner on its terraces, in a neighborhood of smaller frame houses and a small shopping district, in a Western Pennsylvania mill town, was out of the ordinary. Strange.*

But it was the windows that identified the house to people in my hometown. Growing up, I heard the same story all the time. "Snodgrass? Oh yes, you must be DeWitt's boy. You live up there on College Hill don't you, in that big house with the round windows?" In Beaver Falls, Pennsylvania, round *was close enough. I was twenty years older and three thousand miles away before it occurred to me to question it.*

The house wasn't built for us. Originally, I'm told, it was built for a prominent attorney in town who planned to use it as a clubhouse—"a place for alcohol and gambling," so the story went: a gaming house, as it were—rather than as a private residence. A place for trysts, as a matter of fact. An early Playboy *mansion, if you*

can believe it. But his deals in town, such as they were, fell through and he had to head for the comparative safety of Ohio.

This was a few years before the start of World War I. For a time after that, the house sat pretty much to itself, near Geneva College, at the top of the S curve on Route 18 where the trolleys climbed out of the main part of town toward the amusement park at Morado. Sam Beagly, the barber in the neighborhood when I was growing up, once told me that most of the land around the area was originally an apple orchard, and they used to have horse races up and down the dusty roads.

In time, the amusement park burned down, the trolley tracks were torn up, small stores—including Sam Beagly's barbershop—clustered around the corners as the town spread up the hill from the valley floor. When my parents bought the house in 1940 for $7,000, the grounds had been reduced to two corner lots, and the apple orchards replaced with the small frame houses of mill hands and merchants.

Beaver Falls was the last in a chain of small mill towns that ran north from Pittsburgh along the Ohio River and its tributary, the Beaver River. Was, because the mills are closed now since the decline of the American steel industry in the 1980s. In the day, the mills were a little lighter, a little cleaner, in Beaver Falls than the ones farther down the valley, closer to Pittsburgh, say, in Aliquippa and Ambridge and Monaca. But it was still a factory town, and most of the talk in the place was about the tube mill, Union Drawn, and the cork works.

In contrast to the mills, however, are the hills of the valley, a wall of nature sitting at the end of the side streets, a backdrop for the small frame houses and the old brick factories. The hills set the horizon, brace the sky, and help establish the color of the days—the white of winter, the brown of late fall or early spring, the reds and yellows of autumn, the green of summer.

Among the valley towns, Beaver Falls was considered one of the better places to live. In Beaver Falls, College Hill was considered a better part of town. And on College Hill, our house was considered one of the better homes.

My mother was never one to leave well enough alone. That was certainly true of the house. The wood paneling stayed pretty much as it was; no one would have dared touch the beamed ceilings in the dining room or downstairs hall, the woodwork of the banisters and the staircases. But I grew up with carpenters dividing bedrooms, opening doors from solid walls, partitioning off one end of the sunporch for a den my father never used.

Then there were the appliances. The end of World War II was marked with a steady stream of servicemen trooping through our house, but they weren't from the armed forces. They came bringing washing machines, clothes driers, dishwashers. I converted the shipping crates into houses of my own. And outside, my mother added stone lions and a tiered planter on the lawn crowned with a gazing ball (that we had to take in each night so it wasn't stolen). In all of the transformations, I never saw my father lift a hammer or set a screw. A man who could tend the finances of multimillion-dollar corporations, he couldn't even change a fuse. His world was at his office in Pittsburgh. The house was my mother's domain. Her world.

In the course of things, the house took on another life. A life of its own, as it turned out. As a presence, a backdrop, a metaphor in my brother's poetry. To him it was the personification of the subterfuges of our mother, the manipulativeness of our father, and all that was deadly in our family—a house that embodied the darker side of love. When I first read my brother's poetry, it was like reading words that were already engraved in my consciousness, that already existed in my mind, expressing feelings I already knew from personal experience:

> . . . But he comes, wide awake,
> A tourist whispering through the priceless rooms
> Who must not touch things or his hand might break
> Their sleep and black them out.

Later, when I understood more of his principles and what he was talking about in his work, his poems became cautionary tales of what to avoid in this world as exemplified by our family and the house:

> The Venetian blinds are drawn;
> Inside, it is dark and still.
> Always upon some errand, one by one,
> They go from room to room, vaguely, in the wan
> Half-light, deprived of will.

Most of all, his work became the expression—the touchstone; the Bible, really— of the terrors and delusions, the imperatives and pitfalls, of human relationships:

> Without love we die;
> With love we kill each other.

Once in a seminar at Berkeley, a graduate student referred to my brother as a "kitchen poet." When asked, I responded without saying who I was that I thought ol' W.D. would say that kitchens are pretty important. And I knew from our shared experience which kitchen he would have in mind. Though not in a positive light.

I came into the family about the same time as the house. And the link between the two was probably intentional. My parents were approaching forty—not a bad time to be buying a house, to be sure, but a bit problematic, if not downright chancy, when it came to having a child—and it was a time when they were establishing their future. My father was a successful certified public accountant in Pittsburgh and was preparing to start his own firm. As for my mother, her oldest child, De, was fifteen and in a few years would be leaving home for college. The same for my sisters. The purchase of the house represented my father's growing success and status in the

business world. And in the town, his hometown, whose impression of him was always important to him—it was proof that Doc Snodgrass' boy had made good. To make the dream complete, they needed a boy to round out the perfect family. They also may have needed something to reaffirm or at least shore up the marriage. And after seven years without one to look after, my mother simply may have needed a baby.

It was the only house I ever lived in growing up. It was the only house I ever knew. I left when I was nineteen and returned only for short visits. But whenever I returned I found myself wandering through the rooms, as if I had lost or misplaced something, though I could never determine exactly what it was I was looking for.

The house lasted longer than the family. Almost. One by one, we moved away, started families of our own, died. At the end, only Mother was left. In her seventies, a collector of mementos, a keeper of memories. A funny old woman, a town character, sifting through the junk-filled rooms of the old house. She talked of selling the house, getting a smaller place, but first she had to clean it up a bit, sort out the things she needed, fix it up so she'd get a better price. She talked of selling it, but everyone knew she never would.

When I left to go into the world, before my parents drove me to my new life as a freshman in college, she pressed a key in the palm of my hand and told me teary-eyed that the front door would always be open for me. I carried that key with me for years, through college and my new life in San Francisco; but the morning I tried to use it, at six o'clock, before anyone was up, after hitchhiking across the country, the key, wouldn't you know, didn't work. Not that she had changed the locks. It turned out she had simply given me the wrong key.

I suppose I could have thrown the key away after that. But I kept it with me. It seemed like a good thing to keep in mind.

The Stories

Part Two

Tunnels of Love

1949

First, you had to pull the red wicker settee with its circus-striped cushions a few feet away from the wall. Then you put the Army-surplus table Mother sometimes used for the sewing machine next to that, in front of the closed-in fireplace; and if Father wasn't using them for the work he brought home from the office, you put the two card tables side by side next to that. This section ended under the curve of the rear window, in the little cave-like area behind the antique serving cart.

The big overstuffed chair with the blue slipcover went on the other side of the settee, making a solid base at the front corner, while along the short side of the room, you lined up as many of the dining room chairs as you could get away with, the minimum being three, tilted back against the window seat over the radiators. The entrance had to be Father's chair, standing upright and turned sideways, so that the straight back and the chair arms formed a sort of portico. Then you covered the whole thing with every blanket, spread, and comforter in the house, stretching them between the furniture and walls and holding them in place with Scotch tape. There. A tunnel that extended around two sides of the dining room, the perfect hiding place for an eight-year-old boy and, occasionally, Gabriel the cat.

I lay there in the darkness of my tunnel. Behind me the radiators ticked softly inside the shelter of blankets and furniture. It was early in the winter morning. Outside it was still dark and there was the threat of snow later in the day. Every light was on in the downstairs of the house, as lit up as though it were evening. But it was dark inside the tunnel, and warm from the heat of the radiators. I was lost in the smell of old wool. It was probably a bit suffocating, too, but I didn't seem to mind.

I looked out at the world, my cheek resting on the rug, through the bars at the base of the settee. My father's shoes appeared at the bottom of the stairs. They were expensive shoes, he told us: Florsheims, a businessman's shoes. He had close to a dozen pairs, and he stopped every morning in the lobby of his office building in Pittsburgh to have the pair he was wearing that day shined. The shoes hesitated for a moment, then came toward me across the hall rug, the bare floor of the doorway, and into the dining room. They stopped in front of the settee, a few feet from my nose.

Mother's shoes came from the kitchen and stood beside the Florsheims. They were an old pair of open-toed wedgies, a faded green suede, with a torn strap on one and a buckle missing on the other—house shoes. Her big toe waved at me.

"How long is he going to have the house torn up like this?" Father didn't sound angry, just inquisitive.

"Shh. He's in there."

"He's in there now? It's so early. Well, I didn't say anything wrong. I was only wondering."

Mother's shoes turned around and went to the table. "I thought I'd keep him home the rest of the week. He's still not very strong."

"What did the doctor say?"

"I didn't ask him. But I'm sure he'd think it was a good idea."

Father's shoes paced up and down in front of the settee.

"If this isn't the darnedest thing . . ."

"Sit down and have your coffee. We'll miss your train."

"How can I sit down? He's got my chair somewhere in this thing."

I thought if I used that tone of voice, Mother would say I was whining. Mother's voice was soft and matter-of-fact.

"You can sit on one of the others this time. It won't hurt you. I let him use yours because you haven't been home for supper the last couple of nights."

Father didn't have anything to say to that. The shoes went over to the table and he sat down. He crossed his legs and the left shoe dangled in the air in front of his right leg, the toe pointed downward. With his pant leg carefully pulled up so he wouldn't lose his crease, I could see his white silk stockings—he insisted on a particular brand that he bought by the box at Kaufmann's—and the buckles of his garters. I thought of crawling out to see him but decided to stay where I was.

There was a flurry of activity on the stairs, and Nanki Poo, the black Pekingese, came bounding into the hall after helping to wake my older sisters upstairs. He shuffled across the room and pressed his face against the wicker bars to say hello. I touched his tongue with my fingertips. Then he went to Father's chair, his tail wagging so violently that he could hardly stand up.

"Helen, you better bring some bacon for Nanki."

"He already had his breakfast a little bit ago."

Father's hand appeared and ruffled the dog's ears.

"I know, fella. I know. We're working on it."

To press the point, Nanki sat up on his hindquarters, a furry upright log, and begged, his front paws pressed together and waving in the air. He glanced over at me to see how he was doing.

Mother's shoes appeared from the kitchen.

"You spoil him terribly."

"He's such a good fella."

Her shoes took their place at the table. Bits of bacon began to drop from Father's place at the table. Nanki Poo lapped them up from the hair-covered rug.

There were different kinds of darkness in the tunnel, and different kinds of light. The light shone in between the bars of the settee, between the edges of the tables and chairs and the gaps in the cloth. Overhead, the blankets and comforters glowed blue and green and red. My favorite was the white tufted spread, stretched across the opening behind the settee—a soft gentle white that shone above me like the nave of a chapel. When the late afternoon sunlight came through the back window, the tan and gold coverlet spread over the serving cart became as radiant as a treasure room.

There were also dozens of nooks and crannies in which to hide things— under the bases of the chairs, in the folds of the blankets, beneath the settee. I crawled backward on my hands and knees to the corner behind the overstuffed chair, where there was a space big enough to turn around in, and headed back toward the entrance. Hidden in the rungs of one of the upturned chairs was a box of animal crackers. I sat up, my head touching my ceiling of blankets, and munched a lion and two bears, washing them down with sips of day-old water from my Cub Scout canteen.

They must have heard me stirring about.

"Don't you want some breakfast?" Mother called.

I debated with myself whether to answer or not. "I've got some crackers."

"Doesn't he want some bacon?" Father said.

"I'll get him some milk." I leaned over and watched Mother's shoes disappear into the kitchen.

"Are you feeling better?" Father said.

"I'm all right."

"Don't you want to come out and see your poor old father? Your dear old dad?"

I was glad I didn't have to answer him, the way I would have had to answer him if I was looking at him. In a moment, Mother's shoes came back into the room and a glass of milk descended in front of the opening.

"Can you get this okay? Don't spill it."

I crawled forward and found I could just reach it with my outstretched hand. Father laughed a little, trying to be jovial.

"Seems like a strange way to raise the boy."

"At least I know where he is. And he rests a lot in there."

"You know what's best."

I hadn't felt sick at all that first Monday morning, three weeks earlier, even though I told Mother I did. Maybe a little tired, but mostly I simply didn't want to go to school that day. So I whined a little and put on my sick face and generally acted pitiful, and she let me lie on the couch all day and listen to the radio. By that night, however, I really was sick. And getting sicker. Vomiting, diarrhea, fever and chills. The doctor came and officially proclaimed me ill, though no one ever came up with a good reason why. Lacking anything better, they said it was some kind of flu. I was better now, of course, and actually could have gone back to school a week earlier. But every time Mother asked me how I was feeling I talked in a small voice and said I still felt woozy and she kept me in. If I played it right, I was sure I could stretch it out for the entire month.

"We have to go!"

Chairs were pushed back from the table, shoes began to move. Nanki Poo got out of the way. I finished my milk, put away the crackers, and crawled on hands and knees down the tunnel and around the corner behind the settee. Lying once again with my face against the rug I could see Father standing in the hallway, running his hands over his hair to make sure it stayed flat. He adjusted his tie, pulled his suit coat down; he put on his heavy blue topcoat and his gray hat with the tall crown. His briefcase was tucked under his arm. Mother took her coat from the banister, patted her pockets to make sure she had Kleenex, and called up the steps.

"It's almost seven thirty. I'm taking Father to the train."

My older sisters yelled something from far away. Mother turned in my direction though I was sure she couldn't see me. "I'll be right back."

She led the way out the door. Father stood there for a moment, looking helpless at the settee. Then he ducked his head and followed Mother to the car. Once the front door was closed, Nanki ran around the downstairs, whimpering, making sure they were actually gone. Then he ran upstairs to find my sisters.

I knew I didn't have much time; Mother only had to drive Father to the station at the bottom of the hill. I crawled back down the tunnel, collected my dirty glass and canteen, and climbed out into the room. For a moment the light hurt my eyes and I was a little stiff. The knees and elbows of my pajamas were about worn through. I picked at the remains of bacon on Father's plate, then wandered out to the kitchen and found some whole strips on the stove. I filled my canteen in the sink and grabbed a couple handfuls of vanilla wafers and Ritz crackers. After dumping my day's provisions inside the entrance to the tunnel, I went to the foot of the stairs and listened for sounds of my sisters.

Someone was in the big bathroom; someone else was on the third floor. That left the smaller bathroom free. I crept up the stairs on all fours, keeping close to the side of the staircase, and looked around the newel-post at the top. The coast was clear, the door to the smaller bathroom at the end of the hall was open. Still on hands and knees, I scurried down the hall, standing up only when I was in the bathroom, and closed the door.

It was Shirley in the bathroom next door, I could hear her singing to herself. I peed along the side of the bowl so I wouldn't make any noise. The water didn't look yellow, I didn't have to flush. I turned the knob quietly and tiptoed back down the hall. I just made it to the top of the stairs when the door to the big bathroom opened and Shirley came out. I dropped down and pressed against the side of the banister until she went up the stairs to her room on the third floor. Then I hurried back downstairs. Mother was just pulling up in front of the house. I dropped to the floor and was safely inside the tunnel before she came in the door.

I popped a vanilla wafer in my mouth and crawled along, rounded the corner and came face-to-face with Gabriel. To make sure I stopped, he placed a paw without needles on my nose. I lay down and he carefully stepped over me, jumping up on the arm of the overstuffed chair where he fit nicely under the folds of the blanket. Mother, still in her overcoat, stood at the foot of the stairs.

"You're going to be late for school, Shirley!"

"No, I'm not," came the faraway reply.

Mother frowned; she took off her coat, draped it over the banister, and came into the room. Her shoes moved to the dining room table, then pointed my direction.

"Can I get you anything?"

"No. I'm okay."

"Are you sure you're warm enough?"

"I'm sure."

The shoes continued to aim my direction for a few moments, then turned away. I looked up in the darkness. Gabriel's eyes blinked at me sleepily.

Then the eyes widened as Shirley came galloping down the stairs. Her saddle shoes and bobby sox danced across the floor to the table.

"You're going to be late for school," Mother repeated.

"No, I'm not. I'm ready."

Shirley's shoes were pointed at Mother's, but Mother's were pointed away.

"Is Barbara up?"

"Yeah." Shirley was chewing something. "I think she's going to be sick again."

"That's not a nice thing to say."

"She's starting to breathe heavy again."

"That doesn't mean she's going to be sick. It will help her if you don't always talk about her like that."

"All I said was that she was breathing heavy."

"And don't take that tone of voice with me."

"Aw, Mom! What did I do?" Her shoes shifted uneasily. Mother's shoes remained solid and pointed away. It was a full minute before Mother spoke again.

"You know very well what I mean."

"What?" Shirley whined, a downward curve. I smiled to myself. Shirley moaned a little and walked into the hall, the spring gone from her step. I watched her pretty, soft legs between her sox and the edge of her poodle skirt as she put on her coat. Mother's shoes didn't move, hadn't shifted. Shirley was ready to go; I could see her shoes in the doorway, looking to Mother.

"Is there anything I should get at the store on the way home?"

Mother's reply was barely audible, and her shoes gave no indication that she'd said anything at all. Shirley's shoes continued to wait in the doorway several minutes. I heard her give another little moan, almost a cry, as she turned and left the house.

Mother remained where she was. I could hear her turning the pages of a magazine. In a few moments she began humming to herself. Then she began whistling softly, not a whistle really, just dry air between her lips in a little tune. "When I Grow Too Old to Dream." The shoes turned and went into the kitchen.

There was the sound of scurrying down the steps, and Nanki Poo leapt once more into the downstairs, turning around to make sure that Barbara was still following him. Barbara's footsteps were slow and labored on the stairs. At the sound of all this activity, Gabriel jumped down from his perch and stepped through the rungs of a chair to see what was going on. Barbara's shoes were high heels, shiny brown-and- white leather, almost new. Nanki Poo danced around her ankles, then bounded ahead to tell the good news of Barbara's arrival. Gabriel swatted him on the head, able to see for himself.

Barbara's shoes came across the room and stood at the table for a moment. Her hands appeared and caressed the dog's face as she told him he was a good boy. Gabriel walked passed the two, as if he didn't care for such emotional displays, but when Barbara stroked his back he arced to her touch.

Then she sat down wearily in the same chair Father had used, her ankles crossed. I could hear her breath as it whistled through her lungs. Gabriel sniffed at the pointed toes of her shoes, then headed for the kitchen, giving only a passing glance at Mother's wedgies as they came into the room.

"There you are!" Mother said cheerfully. "Ready for some breakfast?"

"I don't think so. . . . Maybe just . . . some coffee."

Mother's shoes stood beside my sister's chair. For a moment no one spoke as the three of us listened to my sister struggle for her breath.

"You shouldn't try to go to the office if you're not feeling well." Mother's voice was suddenly sad, grave.

"Oh, I can't . . . let Father down again. I've missed so much. . . ."

"He'd want you to stay home if you're sick. You know that."

"I know. . . ."

The shiny shoes pulled together back under the chair as Barbara leaned forward to put her head on the table. Her ankles were still crossed, as if they were tied together. I wondered if she was crying. Mother's old house shoes remained beside her.

"You know you could never let your father down. You know he loves you."

"I know. . . ."

"That's the good thing about working for your father. He understands these things. He wouldn't want you to do anything that you weren't able to do."

Barbara was crying. Nanki sat up and rested a paw on her leg. Barbara's hand dropped to pet him but remained motionless on his fur.

"You know we only want whatever will make you happy."

Mother's shoes stood a long time beside Barbara's chair. I raised up and looked through a small hole in the blankets. Barbara's head was bowed on her arms. Mother rubbed the back of her older daughter's neck, her hand working slowly and methodically under the rim of black curls. But Mother was gazing out the back window, staring at something or nothing at all, her face calm and almost smiling, her thoughts far away. Then she looked down at the girl, the young woman. She began to sing softly: "Bye-lo-bye, bye-lo-bye, bye-lo-baby-bye . . ." Then she broke off suddenly from the massage and went out to the kitchen. Barbara raised up slightly, dazed as though someone had hit her.

Barbara had her coffee and a half slice of toast and got ready to leave. Mother chirped around her, straightening her collar, fluffing her hair, smoothing out the wrinkles of her dress. Nanki, Gabriel, and I kept watch from the floor. When Mother finally had her dressed and out the door, she sighed heavily. Her old green shoes crisscrossed the room a couple of times, redding up; then she plopped down in the overstuffed chair at the corner of my tunnel. The blankets trembled, the walls shook.

"I'm sorry. I hope I didn't disturb anything."

"No, it's okay."

"Can I get you anything?"

"I'm all right."

Her shoes rested, tilted on their heels. Her ankles were thick, without definition, and rolled slightly over the straps of the shoes. The shoes rocked back and forth for a few minutes, then grew still. Across the room, Nanki lay with his chin on the floor; Gabriel curled on the chair Father and Barbara had used under the edge of the tablecloth, his head hanging over the edge like a furry gargoyle. Mother's breath grew deeper and slower; soon she was snoring lightly. I lay behind her on the floor, in the shadows of my tunnel, face turned toward the dark wood of the baseboard. Glad that everyone had gone and we were alone in the house again.

Lament

1950

The bands of the Coldstream Guards and the Black Watch were massed in front of the gates of the castle. The slow scream of the pipes, the tattoo of the drums, sounded through the hot afternoon; the slanting sunlight caught the glint of bayonets, the flash of swords. The regiments of foot soldiers, dressed in red tunics, were in formation on either side of the ramp leading to the gate. Detachments of hussars and lancers were positioned on the plains beyond the walls. The sentries in the turrets and along the balustrades were alert. The colors flew from the highest tower.

All eyes were turned down the walls of the great canyon, down the towering cliffs toward the river. There was no wind; the banners and guidons were motionless on their standards. At last the relief column of light cavalry came into view as they gained the bank of the river, the mounted figures slowly growing larger as they worked their way up the valley toward the battlements. Behind them came units of engineers, mounted artillery. The vanguard was nearing the parade ground, ready to pass in review and receive the salute of the colors, when the needle reached the end of the record and clicked maddeningly on the end grooves. I jumped up and ran across the room to flip over the record, in the process wiping out a detachment of Gurkha Rifles.

I lay down again on the floor of my bedroom, stretched out beside the bed, and tried to reenter the small world spread out in front of me. I put my face on the dusty floor, feeling the cracks of the varnished hardwood against my cheek, and closed one eye to see the triumphant entrance of the cavalry into the walls of the castle. Then I opened both eyes and lay on my back. The walls of the canyon were my bed again; the river was the edge of the runner in the upstairs hallway. The sunlight came through my bedroom window at the back of the house, and I still didn't know what to do with myself.

This side of the record was slower, more melancholy. Lone pipers on the faraway slopes of the lochs, knee-deep in heather, playing for fallen comrades. I rolled over on my stomach, my chin on my hands. I recently had grown to like the feel of pressure against my groin, but I didn't as yet know why. Spread on the floor in front of me was close to a thousand dollars' worth of metal figures of British soldiers, paid for by my parents, of course, but disguised as payments for mowing the grass or shoveling snow. The grass needed cut right now, but I was too lazy. Mother was just beginning to complain about it; if I let it go too long, we both knew I'd do it if she gave me her hurt look. Or worse, if she started to cut it herself. But there was no hurry yet. I was already a couple of hundred dollars ahead in the game; I could get more soldiers whenever I wanted them.

The soldiers had returned only recently from a display downtown at the Carnegie Library. For a month they were locked up in lighted cases at the rear of the main room, underneath the wall-sized painting of Christ instructing the elders, with typewritten cards explaining the different regiments. There was even a picture of me in the *News-Tribune*, my plump, pimply face looming over models of the coronation coach and the throne with the sacred rock, the Stone of Scone. For a month I was a celebrity in Beaver Falls. But I had missed the soldiers, missed the pleasure of the long afternoons in solitude playing with them on the floor, waging imaginary battles against Indian lancers and rebellious Zulus. I realized my mistake the moment I saw them locked up behind glass. I didn't collect the soldiers to display them. I collected them to people my special world. But now that they were back, something was changed about them, something was spoiled. The intimacy was gone, and for the first time I began to feel foolish playing with them.

Gabriel the cat looked in from the doorway, wondering what I was doing down on his level. He looked things over briefly and continued down the hall. I called after him and went on all fours to the doorway, but he had disappeared. I crawled back, churning my knees against the slippery floor like a locomotive fighting for traction. Then I stood up and went to the window.

Outside the day was green. The green of the sycamores in the backyard, the weeping willow and the elms next door; the green of the bushes, green of the lawns. I could hear the voices of my friends playing somewhere in the neighborhood, but I couldn't see them. Mrs. Beuliah was in her backyard, hanging sheets to dry and propping up the clothesline with long forked sticks. The Beuliahs didn't have any children, and she was my special friend. She used to invite me in for cookies, and one day she showed me all the rooms in their house, but I was very young then and Mother didn't like me to go over there. Next door to her, Mrs. Kindermann was cranking water from the pump outside their back door, while a couple of the neighborhood "little kids" in their bathing suits, Linda and Waynie, splashed and danced in the runoff.

I picked my way back through the frozen regiments and out into the hall. Gabriel had finished his survey of the second-floor bedrooms and, not finding anything of interest, was on his way upstairs to the third floor. He walked through my ankles but didn't care for any fuss and moved away when I tried to scratch his ears. He sat down out of reach, took a few swipes at his side with his tongue, then bounded up the steps three at a time.

I made my own survey of the second-floor rooms and couldn't come up with anything more than the cat did. Mother was downstairs, working in the kitchen; my sisters were out of the house. I thought of taking the opportunity to follow Gabriel upstairs and explore my sisters' rooms again, the dresses in the closets and the drawers of underwear, but I decided it was better to wait until everyone was out of the house. I rested my weight against the banister and slid one-step, one-step down the stairs and out the front door.

Traffic was busy on the hill from town, heading toward the swing shift at the tube mill. A truck crane stopped cars in both directions as it made the corner and headed down toward the main part of town, the boom missing the telephone wires by inches. I angled across the street to Jake's house. Jake was sitting in the strip of dirt between the curb and the sidewalk in front of his house, spread out over the body of a wooden jeep his father made for him years earlier but had never been able to find suitable wheels. His sister Tootsie was sitting on the front stoop, reading.

"What're you doing?"

"Nothing. Sitting."

"That's all he ever does. Nothing," Tootsie said.

"Shut up," Jake said.

Tootsie stuck out her tongue.

They were all older than I was by several years. Jake had been my best friend while we were growing up; we had pedaled wagons and toy cars up and down every sidewalk in the neighborhood. But since Jake and his sisters started to go downtown to junior high school, they weren't as friendly and we didn't do things together anymore.

"Jake, you didn't clean up your room!" Barb called from inside. She was the oldest of the three and was put in charge while their parents were at work. Her voice had become identical to their mother's. She stood at the rusty screen window, holding a dustrag.

"Oh, hi, Tex." She smiled at me, then looked back at Jake. "Why don't you clean your room, Dumbo?"

"Why don't you mind your own business?" Jake said. He sprawled out even further over the wheelless jeep.

"You think you're so smart. Wait till Mom gets home." Barb disappeared into the house.

I was Tex because of my love of cowboy boots. There was Jake, Tootsie, Barb, Michigan Mike, Earl, Stewie, Twig, Chicken, Snevaj (Javens spelled backward), Goodie, Mulzie, Bork, Gur-Gur (he stuttered), Toes, and Gidge. The College Hill Kids. Or to be more precise, the 32nd Street College Hill Kids. I sat down on the steps below Tootsie. She was wearing shorts and her bare thighs formed a platform for her book. She looked at me and smiled. She was knock-kneed, stringy, and sometimes walked as though she was trying to kick her feet away. I was totally in love with her.

Earl came up the street, snapping the belt he used to carry newspapers on his route against the sidewalk. Earl didn't like me. He was an athlete and four or five years older; I was an overweight, pimply-faced rich kid. When Earl walked, he lifted slowly on the balls of his feet, like the senior high football players did when they strolled down the street, and he kept the sleeves of his T-shirts rolled up to his armpits. He stepped over me and sat down beside Tootsie in the open doorway. He rubbed her bare leg a couple of times.

"Cut it out, Earl!"

"What are you reading?"

She held up the cover for him to see. Dickens: *A Tale of Two Cities*. He shrugged. Barb came to the screen door, said, "Hi, Earl," and went back inside.

Waynie in his swimming trunks came running from playing at the Kindermanns' across the street. He was six years old, a red-haired brat that nobody liked.

"Hey, Waynie, come here a minute," Earl said.

"Why?" Waynie said.

"I got something to show you."

"What?" He wanted badly to see what it was, but he knew Earl.

Earl laughed into his shoulder.

"What are you going to do?" Tootsie said.

"Come here, Waynie."

"No! You're going to do something to hurt me!"

"I'm not going to hurt you."

"You're going to hurt me!" He started walking toward his house next door, crying.

"Why'd you do that?" Tootsie said.

"What I'd do?"

Waynie picked up something off the sidewalk and came back toward us. When he got close enough he threw a stone. The stone flew straight up into a tree and landed in the street, six feet away from any of us. Earl was up and running after him, Waynie screaming, Earl swinging his paper belt. As Waynie disappeared around the far side of his house, Waynie's father opened their front door and stuck out his head. Earl pulled up short.

"Why don't you pick on someone your own size, tough guy?" Waynie's father said.

"Waynie threw a stone." Earl walked slowly back to the stoop but kept an eye over his shoulder, ready to run if the man started after him.

"What did you do to him first?"

"Nothing." Earl sat down again.

"Waynie threw a stone," Tootsie said.

"You kids leave him alone, you hear?" He came out the door and Earl was ready to hurdle Tootsie if he had to. But the man went down the alley on the other side of his house. We could hear Waynie crying as his father beat him and dragged him in the back door.

Earl raised his middle finger in that direction. We laughed but I didn't know what it meant. Earl and Tootsie giggled and leaned against each other, their bare arms touching. Jake yawned from the wheelless wooden jeep. I thought of my soldiers, spread out over the floor in my room.

"There's nothing to do," Earl said.

"We could play ball," I said.

"That's dumb."

Earl put his tennis shoe against my shoulder.

"Don't."

"Why not?"

"I don't want you to."

"I want to."

"Leave me alone."

"Tell us all about it." That was his latest favorite phrase. He laughed to Tootsie.

"Leave Tex alone," she said.

"Tell us all about it, Tex-ass. Tex-ass, Tex-ass."

He took the shoe away. He grabbed the back of my neck and tried to squeeze it but I wiggled away.

"Let's do something," Barb yelled from inside.

"We're trying to think of something," Tootsie yelled back.

"Well, let's do something," Barb yelled back.

Tootsie made a face and shook her head.

"We could go play with Tex-ass' little tin soldiers," Earl said, shaking my shoulders. I moved away a little further. Earl laughed.

Barb came to the open door, drying a dish. She pushed the side of her foot against Tootsie's bottom.

"Move!"

"Don't!"

"I want to come out!"

"You're drying dishes."

"You were supposed to."

Barb pushed against her again. Tootsie pushed back.

"Tex, why don't you go home and get your Monopoly," Barb said.

"Yeah, Tex, why don't you go home?" Earl said.

"That's not nice," Tootsie said.

"Tex knows I'm only kidding. Don't you, Tex? Tell us all about it."

"I don't want to play Monopoly," Jake said.

"You never want to do anything," Barb said.

"What can we do?" Tootsie said.

"I know something we can do," Earl said.

Earl flicked his tongue and grinned at Tootsie. She hit him on the upper arm, but not very hard. Barb giggled—"Hey," she said, as if she had an idea—and looked at her sister, at Jake. Jake straightened up and grinned, raised his eyebrows. They shared something I didn't understand.

"Like I said, go home, Tex," Earl said. "This doesn't include you." The others laughed.

The crab apple hit the sidewalk a few feet from the steps, splattering across the pavement and showering us with pulpy fragments.

"Hey!" Earl said.

"What was that?" Tootsie said.

"Look out!" Jake cried, spilling off the jeep and onto the dirt as another crab apple came sailing across the street toward us. It was followed by a barrage of crab apples, some shattering on the sidewalk, others hanging up in the branches of the trees along the curb and falling into the street. Twig came running down the sidewalk from the corner, crab apples hitting around him like shrapnel.

Across the street near the corner of the block, using the parked cars for cover, were half a dozen guys—from Locust Street, near the Chinese graveyard. They were carrying burlap sacks full of crab apples. They only raised up long enough to heave a couple of the missiles, then ducked down again. Earl was the first one to grab the apples that didn't splatter and start winging them back again, hitting the protective cars with a heavy thunk.

The attackers laughed at the misses, Earl laughed back at them, but the crab apples kept coming, harder, skipping across the pavement with increased accuracy and slamming into the curb or the side of the Munteans' house. Tootsie ran inside with Barb and closed the door. Jake and Twig joined Earl in throwing the apples back. A crab apple hit Twig on the side of the leg and sent him to the ground, howling. Jake ran around the side of the house and came back with handfuls of one-inch gravel from the Mitchells' new driveway. Earl grabbed one of the rocks and threw it. The rock pinged off a metal fender.

"Hey, watch out!" came the cry behind the cars.

"Eat shit!" Earl said and threw another rock, denting the door of my family's Olds.

My family's big brick house sat on its terraces at the corner of the block like the neighborhood castle. I ran, as fast as I could, past Earl and Jake, across the street. Earl yelled at me, "Hey! Get back!" A rock missed my head by inches; the boys behind the cars were yelling, "Get him! Get him!" A rotten apple hit me on the arm; my sleeve was wet and smelled acrid. I kept running. The crab apples and stones were coming at me from both sides now, in front of me and behind, as I ran diagonally up the terrace of our front lawn, almost losing my footing in the tall grass, and over to the front steps. A new wave of panic swept over me when I thought the door might be locked. I struggled with two hands on the handle and pushed inside and bolted it behind me. I could hear the missiles hitting the steps outside, and shouts from the boys on both sides. An apple splattered against the window of the sunporch but the glass didn't break.

I hurried through the quiet house, afraid they might find some way to get in, afraid that there was nothing to stop them. I ran upstairs, down the hall, frantic, finding Mother at last on the third floor, on a stepstool, changing a light bulb in my sister's room.

"There's a bunch of guys outside and they're throwing rocks and crab apples!"

Mother squinted at the bulb, shook her head. Fiddled with the fixture. "Why are they doing that? What started it?" She looked unpleasant, tired. Uninterested. I hadn't explained it right. This wasn't what I wanted.

"We were just sitting there on Jake's front step and they started throwing things! Somebody's going to get hurt!"

"Then you better stay inside until they go away." She tossed the empty carton for the new bulb onto the bed, climbed down from the stool, and went over to the light switch, flicking it on and off, on and off, to make sure it worked.

"But aren't you going to stop them?"

She sighed wearily. "I can't fight your battles for you all your life, my young son."

"But they hit me!" I held up the sleeve of my shirt. I didn't understand. She had always defended me before, had called me into the house when things started to get too rough, had gone out herself if anyone started to pick on me. I didn't understand.

She looked at me crossly. "You're a big boy now, too big to be tied to my apron strings. Do you want everyone to think you're a momma's boy? You'll have to learn to take care of yourself."

She left the light on and turned away and began digging in a closet. I went back downstairs to the second floor, to the front bedroom. The sun was behind the house now, lost in the trees, the rooms here in the front of the house in shadow, gloomy, the air heavy, oppressive. Through the windows the afternoon glowed like a bright panorama, a luminous screen. Below in front of our house, the pavement was littered with the remains of crab apples, but the kids from Locust Street were gone. Across the street, Tootsie was walking around the side of her house, yelling something to Barb inside. Jake and Earl were on the sidewalk throwing a softball back and forth, while Twig sat on the front steps rubbing his leg. I stood in the second-floor window of my house, in the window curved like a turret, at the level of the branches of the trees, watching.

Safekeeping

I

The bicycle was sitting on the sunporch when I came down to go to school on my birthday morning. A Schwinn Black Phantom. Morning sunlight leveled through the windows, glinting off the chrome fenders. It was the most beautiful bike I had ever seen. And not at all what I wanted.

"I hope you like it," Mother said. "It's the most expensive one they make. We went all the way to Pittsburgh to get it."

"We had a dickens of a time putting it together, too," Father said. "I'll bet I took two pounds of flesh off my knuckles, ha ha."

I stared at the bicycle, still too flabbergasted to say anything. They took my silence to mean I was pleased.

"You better not ride it until we can get a lock for it," Mother said. "And you'll have to spend some time getting used to it. And absolutely, you're not allowed to ride it on the main street."

"But all the guys ride on the main street."

She closed her eyes and shook her head. "You heard me. Absolutely not. You'll fall off and kill yourself."

"You listen to your mother," Father said. "I've found it's easier in the long run."

"We'll keep the bike up here on the sunporch at night," Mother said.

"How'll I get it up and down the steps?" I was big for my age—on the fat side, to be honest—but I never thought of myself as particularly strong.

"I guess I'll have to carry it for you. It's too big for you to do it yourself. At least until you're older."

"What about keeping it in the garage?" Father said.

Mother looked resigned. "No, I'll manage."

I continued to stare at the bike. It was beginning to seem less and less of a good idea. The bike I actually wanted was an English racing bike, a Raleigh with three gears, very thin and built for speed. But Mother was afraid that they weren't safe, or that we couldn't get it fixed if something went wrong with it. In truth, at this point I would have been happy with any bike that I could call my own. When I first learned to ride, I was only allowed to ride my sisters' bikes because Mother thought they were safer without the crossbar. But now that I was older, I wouldn't be caught dead on a girl's bike. The summer before, Mother painted my brother's old bike an eggshell blue, with the hope that I'd be content with that. But the bike was almost twenty years old, it was built funny with an enormous tank around the crossbar, and besides it had twenty-four-inch wheels. Only little kids rode less than a twenty-six-incher.

For the next couple of weeks, my twenty-six-inch beauty got no further than sitting in all its glory in the protection of the sunporch, and I had to content myself with sitting on it after school, balanced at a tilt on the kickstand, watching the traffic out the windows while pedaling furiously up and down imaginary streets. The problem was, first of all, the lock—she couldn't find one that she thought strong enough. Then there was the question of batteries for the horn and light, and reflective tape for the handlebars. Then she thought she should paint the chrome fenders with protective varnish so they wouldn't rust, but that only resulted in giving the chrome a permanently dull finish. I was beginning to think I would be too old to ride the bike before I got it on the street.

But I didn't dare complain too much. My impatience to get a full-sized bike nearly cost me the chance to get one at all. A month before my birthday, Billy Gurvin let me ride his twenty-six-incher. It didn't seem so difficult and I couldn't understand what all the fuss was about. I sailed down 32nd Street hill and around the corner where Mother was working in the yard. I was already safely past her when she looked up and saw me; she let out a scream and I panicked and went up the side of the terrace and flopped over with the bike on top of me. I was grounded from all bikes for a week after that, but I had taken so much skin off my leg after tangling with the chain that I couldn't ride anyway.

There was no question that mine was the most beautiful bike anyone had ever seen on College Hill. My friends would file into the sunporch to admire it, sit on the seat, turn on the light, beep the horn, then climb on their own old beat-up bikes and pedal away without me. The body was jet black, with chrome fenders and trim. There were thin red accent lines on the center tank and along the tubes of the frame, and the name *Schwinn* was written in script between my thighs. But the most unusual and distinctive feature of the bike was the large chrome spring situated above the front fender, a shock absorber between the wheel and the frame. You could stand on the pedals and jump up and down and watch the spring work in and out.

"You're going to wear it out before you get it outside," Mother said.

"I just want to get it outside," I whined.

"Pretty soon. You better wait until the weather gets a little better, dear."

It was nearly a month after my birthday before I finally got to ride the bike around the neighborhood, avoiding of course the main street. In the evenings after school, Michigan Mike and I would chase each other on our bikes through the back streets of College Hill, creating contests to see who was the fastest—he always was—and who was the best at jumping curbs—my specialty. Our favorite sport, however, was mock dogfights, following each other around in slow clenched circles in the middle of the street, trying to stay on the other's tail, touching tire to fender to unbalance the other without falling off yourself, then swooping away to start over. We would twist and turn in ever-tightening circles until it was dusk and the only light came from the streetlamps, and Mother called me home. I would holler in return, make one last reckless dive at my friend, then charge up the driveway and across the front lawn to the front steps. I held the screen door open while Mother picked up the bike and carried it to safety.

But riding it around the neighborhood was not the same as riding it to school. It took nearly a full week of cajoling before I got her permission, but when the great day arrived I almost wished I hadn't. I was scared to death.

My bowels turned to water; I gagged on my Wheaties. All I could think of were all the things that could go wrong along the way, all the dangers that suddenly loomed between home and school. The bike might fall apart under me; the tires go flat; my pant leg wind irretrievably in the chain and I'd be eaten alive by the sprockets. I wanted to leave as early as possible, to allow plenty of time for all the trouble I anticipated, but Mother was busy with other things and delayed taking the bike off the sunporch.

"It's time to go!" I moaned, pacing around the dining room.

"Don't be silly. You don't have to leave for another fifteen minutes."

"But I want to go early."

"I'll take it down the steps when it's time."

She went back to the kitchen. I went out on the sunporch and made a last-minute check of the bike, surprised to find it was even standing in one piece. I rubbed as much shine as I could into the varnished fenders, tested the horn. Then, on a whim, I tried lifting it. The bike didn't seem as heavy as Mother made out; I seemed to be able to manage it okay. I tried it again, then opened the front door, propped open the screen, and wheeled it down the first step. No problem. I eased it down the second. Now the weight came to me, and the bike was all handlebars and pedals, poking me in the chest and trying to trip me. For a second I had the feeling that it was taking me down the steps, not the other way around. But I held on and fought back and bumped it down to the sidewalk.

I let out a whoop of triumph and headed for the house to tell Mother. But she was standing in the doorway above me, her eyes hurt, her mouth set. I started to chirp that I had made it all right without her, but she turned and walked back into the house.

2

The sun was still low in the morning sky, as low as it could be when it made its appearance above the valley's hills. The sunlight angled between the houses and the trees, sheets of warmth and brilliance broken by the flickering shadows. Overhead the branches of the sycamores and maples were full in the late spring; the rushing air cooled my sweaty face. I pedaled along standing up, setting the rhythm with the kick of my right leg, listening to the new tires sing on the pavement and the tick of metal touching metal. I coasted down the long slope of Fifth Avenue, jumping up and down to watch the coil spring work to absorb my sudden weight, and was thoroughly delighted with myself.

As I neared the school at 37th Street, I passed other kids walking along the sidewalks and was certain everyone was watching me, admiring my new bike. I made large sweeping S curves in the street and rode proudly past the groups standing on the front steps of the school. I half expected a crowd to follow me into the bike shelter while I parked it, but nobody followed, nobody said anything, nobody seemed to notice the bike at all. I wasn't sure if I was disappointed or relieved. I walked across the playground and sat in the first level of the open squares of the jungle gym.

"What's the matter, can't you climb any higher?" a voice said over my head. I knew there was someone on top, but I hadn't realized it was a kid in my class named Boggs.

"I don't want to go any higher."

He laughed. "Chickenshit. You can't climb any higher, you're too fat."

I liked the way my mother put it: I wasn't fat, I was just husky. Really, really husky.

"I could if I wanted to."

"So why don't you?"

"I don't want to."

Boggs laughed again sarcastically. I was hoping he'd leave me alone, but he leaned over and let strings of spit fall from his mouth, dropping them between the bars, coming closer to me. I shifted my position, but he followed me overhead. I swung down and walked away. He laughed again. The singsong went: "Fatty, fatty, two-by-four, can't fit through the kitchen door."

As I approached my friends on the steps of the school, Ralph called out, "Here he is!" He was standing with Alex and Johnny Allen. "Here he is! Here's Teela! Up, Teela, up, boy!"

Ralph was Sabu the Elephant Boy; I was Teela, the bull elephant—characters from the Saturday morning *Buster Brown Show* on our recently acquired TV sets. It started, undoubtedly, from my size as well as my dubious ability to imitate an elephant cry from the television series. When the joke started I enjoyed it, encouraged it, but lately I had grown weary of the game. However, I learned it was easier to start playing the fool than it was to end it. Alex liked to kid around as much as Ralph, but Johnny Allen never said much since his mother died.

"Elephan-tine! Elephan-tine!" Ralph cried as he jumped off the steps and galloped across the school lawn. I didn't know where he was going.

"Was that your new bike?" Alex said.

"Did you get a new bike?" Johnny Allen said.

I was embarrassed for Johnny Allen, everyone knew his family was on hard times, but Alex kept on talking.

"Didn't you see it? It looks like it's all chrome. When the sun hits it, it'll be as bright as a mirror, vroom-vroom-vroom!"

I didn't want to talk about my bike. I longed for the time when the newness would be over and nobody would talk about it and I wouldn't have to think about it anymore.

"Elephan-tine! Elephan-tine!" Ralph came running back across the lawn in the hobbling gait children use to simulate riding a horse. He was carrying a branch from one of the dogwood trees.

"Teela! Here, Teela!" He trimmed the excess leaves from the stick and stood in front of the steps, switching it against his leg. "Teela! Come to Sabu!"

"Go away, Ralph," Johnny Allen said.

"Go play in traffic," Alex said.

I shook my head. "I don't want to, Ralph." Joyce, Lois, and Mary Louise were standing on the steps near the door to the school watching the proceedings. Ralph and I had played the game for months and it always got a laugh, but today I wasn't in the mood.

"We've got time," Ralph said.

"I said I don't want to."

"Why not?"

"I just don't."

"Come, Teela! Come, boy!"

Grudgingly I moved off the steps, hunched over, and put my arm to my nose to form a trunk. I followed Ralph around the sidewalk, shaking my head to ward off flies, blowing masses of air, and doing my elephant call as he guided me with the stick. Part of the performances were special tricks, rearing up with one leg raised, or taking imaginary peanuts from the girls and feeding them into my mouth, trumpeting loudly. The girls laughed. I curled my trunk-arm around Mary Louise's stacks of books and carried them about.

"Up, Teela!" Ralph cried.

Alex was the circus band:

> *Dancing in the dark,*
> *Something's funny I just heard you bark.*
> *You sounded just like a cocker spaniel*
> *Named Daniel. . . .*

Alex always got that far before collapsing in laughter at his own silliness. Boggs came from the playground and stood at the edge of the grass. I did my stalled elephant routine, leaning rhythmically against an imaginary chain, hoping that the bell would ring soon to call us in for class. I straightened up.

"Here, Teela!" Boggs said. He held out his books. "Take these."

I waved him away. "That's enough. I'm tired."

Ralph tossed the stick out into the street and rubbed his hands against his pants. But Boggs wasn't satisfied.

"How come you'll take the girls' books and you won't take mine?"

"The game's over. It's almost time for the bell."

"You're a turd." He pushed me in the shoulder.

I tried to ignore him and went over toward Johnny Allen. Boggs started to follow but the bell rang and everybody pushed forward inside the building.

I hoped Boggs would forget about it. We had been friends once, he used to play at my house, but he changed after he moved to Sunrise Dwellings, a row of bungalows built after World War II along the bluff above the river. He glared at me from across the room all morning and said something to me under his breath at recess that I didn't understand. I was afraid of him, even though I was taller and heavier. He was a short, square kid, and kind of crazy; his face was always flushed, his skin dry and flaky as if he were burning up inside. He fit in with the kids from the Dwellings, who were all a little older, more inclined to get in trouble, than the other College Hill kids.

When I went to my bike at noontime, he was waiting on his own bike at the curb and followed me down the street, pedaling around me and taking a couple of sideswipes. I told him to cut it out but he just laughed. He finally left me alone when he had to turn off at 35th Street to go home. I tried to stay out sick that afternoon, but Mother said there was nothing wrong with me and wouldn't write me an excuse. There was no way out of it.

In the afternoon Boggs seemed to forget about me and I hoped the trouble was over. After school he wasn't around. Alex lived only a block and a half from the school and I kept him company as he walked along, turning lazy circles on my bike in the middle of the street as we discussed whether the Navy or the Coast Guard was better. Ralph rode past, pedaling frantically, shouting "Elephan-tine! Elephan-tine!" at the top of his voice as he headed toward the ball field.

We were stopped in front of Alex's house when Boggs rode up. At first I thought he was going to pass us by, but he turned around and pulled in along the curb where I was, his bike facing mine. He didn't seem unfriendly, and laughed along with us as we decided that *Semper paratus* meant "Always keep the beach clean." But as we stood there, each one straddling his bike, Boggs began twisting his front wheel to hit mine, slapping it sideways, rubber to rubber.

"Come on, Boggs, cut it out."

He did it again, harder. I tried to back up but he pursued me and slapped the wheel harder, the strut of his front fender hitting mine. The vibrations shuddered up the handlebars.

"There's going to be a fight, there's going to be a fight!" Alex laughed.

Boggs hit the wheel again. I lost my balance and had to lay my bike down on the parking so I wouldn't fall off. Boggs got off his bike and pushed me.

I hit him, in the mouth, as hard as I could, the sudden blood covering his chin and my fingers. The surprise on his face, I'm sure, mirrored my own. But I didn't stop. I hit him again, again on his mouth, then aimed for his nose, his eyes, sending him backward over the curb and the sidewalk until he tripped and fell against the terrace of Alex's front yard and rolled over, covering his head, crying. Alex stood beside me, no longer laughing.

"Why'd you do that?" Boggs said. Alex and I bent over him, trying to see the damage. I gave him my handkerchief to stop the bleeding.

"You started it."

He got up and pushed me away and threw the handkerchief at me. It lay red and white on the grass. Still crying, he got on his bike and rode toward home.

Alex was jumping up and down, feigning punches, reliving the scene. I was suddenly overwhelmingly tired. I left him and headed up the long hill toward home, turning into the side street at the corner and into the alley beside Johnny Allen's house. I peddled over the bumpy paving bricks, the potholes in the sections of old concrete, watching the bike's shock absorber work in and out, past backyards, garages, fences, barking dogs, clothes hanging out to dry, children playing children's games. At the end of the alley at each street, I waited until I was sure no one was coming, no one would see me, afraid of I didn't know what, then sped across to the seclusion of the next alleyway, keeping close to the garage doors and the protective cover of the bushes, until I saw ahead over the low roofs the gables of my family's house, the orange brick through the leaves of the trees, the curve of the corner windows like battlements, standing on the pedals as I swooped down the last little grade and up the back driveway past the standing planter boxes and stone lions into the confines of the yard. Safe again.

Lair of the Baldy Sturber

1975

My eyes are receding back into my head. It has happened before, though I never understand how. Or always why. The lids appear to grow their own lids, folds of skin diagonally across the existing folds of skin, and the eyeballs themselves seem to become narrower, smaller. The openings, instead of being oval, are flattened at the top and bottom so that they are narrow cuts, open only wide enough to expose the pupil.

It has happened before. I am never aware of any impingement to my vision, any limitation to my depth of field. Nor am I ever aware of any physical discomfort, such as a headache. No, the only sensation might be a certain heaviness over the sockets, a sort of brooding, as if my forehead is in the process of turning to stone. But my wife, back when I had a wife, always recognized the symptoms.

"What's the matter?" she'd ask, looking at me suspiciously.

"What's the matter that you're asking 'what's the matter'?"

"Your eyes. They're becoming slits."

A good description: slits. And looking in the bathroom mirror I can see they are becoming slits again—indeed, already are slits. My eyes are in retreat, diving deeper into my skull, taking refuge as it were at the far ends of their sockets, letting the cheekbones and temples and forehead close in around them. I use to wonder sometimes—back home in San Francisco, if *home* is the right word; back in San Francisco where I made my new life, where I first noticed my eyes sometimes in retreat—if my eyes might keep on going, back into the cranium, hiding away among the soft gray folds of my brain, my eyelids flapping uselessly on empty holes. Or if I would sometime become aware of looking at the world as if through a pair of tubes. As it is, my eyes now are moist as if I have been crying, and they appear slow, dull, like eyes staring out from behind a mask that does not quite fit. Or eyes that are fixed to the opening of a bunker.

I turn away from the mirror, weary of me, and come face-to-face with the same image directly behind me. The twin mirrors hang five feet away from each other across the smaller of the two bathrooms, an attempt to open up the narrow room, my image reflected back and forth. As a kid I could never understand why I couldn't see myself multiply to infinity, why my head was always in the way. I find myself now leaning back and forth, ducking down, trying to catch a glimpse of me in perpetuity, caught up in the same old mysteries. Ridiculous. I wash my hands and spring out into the hall.

My Rollei Single Lens Reflex is sitting on its tripod by the steps to the third floor, waiting for me. I wander up and down the hall, looking for images that I think relate to my brother's poetry, the poems he wrote about the family, my mother, and the house:

> . . . . *Things can decay, break,*
> *Spoil themselves; who cares? She'll gather the debris*
> *With loving tenderness to give them; she*
> *Will weave a labyrinth of waste, wreckage*
> *And hocus-pocus; leave free no fault*
> *Or cornerhole outside those lines of force*
> *Where she and only she can thread a course.*
> *All else in her grasp grows clogged and halts.*

The hallway is certainly dark enough to suit my brother's point of view. It had been that way since I was thirteen years old and was given the task of refinishing the oak woodwork and redwood wainscoting, which I chose to do with dark mahogany varnish. High-gloss varnish at that—I recall proudly picking it out at Davidson's hardware. The once beautiful woodwork came out almost black, shiny enough to reflect your face. I find it more than a little uncomfortable now, trying to blame the family, blame my mother, for living in such darkness, condemning them for ruining the beauty of the house, when I was responsible for part of it. Except for the little light that spills in from the side rooms, most of the illumination in the hall comes from the stained-glass window at the top of the second-floor stairs. When the sun hits it in the late afternoon, the window glows green and yellow and blue—a peaceful valley at sunset with stylized evergreens in the foreground and the towers of a distant castle across a winding river. But most of the day the window is dull and lifeless, and the hallway as somber as a chapel. The two electric lights on either side of the window, knights holding spears topped with lampshades, are almost always turned on.

As I think about it, it seems a good part of my life as a boy growing up in the house has been centered around this upstairs hall. Whenever the family left the house, or I knew they were safely occupied downstairs, I prowled this corridor, wandering from room to room, opening dresser drawers and closets, lying on the different beds, trying to find some clue to the secrets that everyone seemed to be keeping from me. It isn't all that different now, I decide, except that now I prowl it with a camera.

I look at myself in the full-length hall mirror, do a little shuffling dance in my honor. Then I sit down on the steps to the third floor. It was in this hall, sitting on these steps, that I used to peek through the balusters for glimpses of my sisters naked. A few years later, I sat on these same steps to listen to the dragging footsteps overhead, and Vic Damone singing over and over "Vagabond Shoes," as my sisters pushed each other around to practice their latest steps from Arthur Murray's. It was in this hallway that Jean Brown, my sister Barbara's best friend, ran up and down in the middle of the night dressed only in her nightgown, shouting, "The war is over! The war is over!" and scared us all half to death. Later that same night, Barbara took me outside to see my first dawn; we sat together on the front steps watching the orange street sweeper do its crazy pirouettes along the curb.

And this hallway was the province of the Baldy-Sturber. After Father was thwarted in his attempt to name me Quinton—Quinton Snodgrass, definitely a name to conjure with; but my mother was right, the neighborhood kids in a steel town would have had a field day with that—he always had trouble calling me by my given name. His most popular variation was

Ditty-Witty—I'm afraid to think why. He did not give up on it easily; his final words to me on the phone as he lay on his deathbed were "Good-bye, Ditty." I am thankful that he gave up on Baldy-Sturber earlier.

I am told the name derived from Bald Disturber, because when I was two or so I was blond enough to appear bald, that and I had a predilection for running around naked through the upstairs hallway after my bath. I grew up hearing of my exploits of hiding bobby pins and hairbrushes, buttons and cuff links, while Mother chased me around trying to capture me in a towel. I don't remember any of that, of course, but I like to think it was true.

I stand at the camera and try to frame a couple of images—a pile of laundry about to engulf a doorway, a closet full of useless clothes. On a small table is a lamp made from a model of a covered wagon, along with several grimy water glasses, a bow from a little girl's hair, and a ceramic ashtray shaped like the face of a beagle that holds several dozen thumbtacks. But the images don't work, and the problems aren't just graphic. The voice is my brother's, not my own. There is craziness in the house, all right—this is definitely not your average house. But over the years I have spent photographing the house, it is the other images I discovered on my proof sheets, images that aren't of condemnation or blame, that disturb me the most. That speak in my voice.

I clap the viewfinder closed and rub my eyes. I'm getting tired and stale. I check the backward progress of my eyes in the hall mirror—they appear the same. Maybe I am making too much out of it, maybe it is a family trait. I walk around the hallway looking at the rogues' gallery of family portraits that Mother has hung on the walls above the wainscoting. There are the high school graduation portraits of the four children; color snapshots of her own father and stepmother in their rocking chairs; a grandson jumping a horse over a hurdle; granddaughters at play; a large study done at the turn of the twentieth century and printed on canvas of two little boys leaning against each other. But none of these images show anything peculiar in the eyes.

I stop in front of an enlarged snapshot of my father. I can remember the trip on which it was taken—a driving trip down through Virginia and Tennessee to visit Civil War battlefields. He is standing on top of a small stone wall, at a turnout on the highway, overlooking a deep valley. He is dressed in his sport clothes; his hands are in his back pockets. The film is too grainy, the figure too far away, to get a good look at his eyes. But it wasn't the eyes that interested me. He looks tired, and a bit perturbed at having his picture taken. Nevertheless, he is smiling.

My father always smiled. To distraction, really. I can't remember him any other way than smiling. Tolerant; nonplussed; imperturbable as a wall. I saw him troubled, of course, such as the night he tried to talk to my brother after dinner, the summer De and his second wife lived with us for a few months. I don't know what the discussion was about, other than it was about money, but it ended with De storming through the downstairs of the house calling Father a son of a bitch and a fucking bastard, throwing dining room chairs right and left before he ran up the stairs to their room. Father continued to sit there at his card table, covered with balance sheets from his office, looking innocently at Mother. And he smiled.

I can remember him laughing, at Sid Caesar and Jackie Gleason on television, though cowboys were always his favorite. I can remember him pleased, when the dogs sat up and begged from him at the table. I can remember him flirty and attentive with waitresses in coffee shops, as he asked for a warm-up for his coffee or for apple pie with "rattrap" cheese. But whatever other expressions or emotions were involved, they always incorporated the Smile. I can even remember him sincere, one evening when we were in the living room together talking—I have no idea now how that came about, we never sat together talking, maybe it was after *Gunsmoke* or *Have Gun—Will Travel*. He confided to me that he didn't like our house, that he was ashamed of the way Mother kept it, and he wished they could move to an apartment in Pittsburgh. When I asked him if he had ever discussed it with her, he said "your mother" always turned him down. But the next evening, when I was helping Mother with the dishes after dinner and I asked her about it, she seemed agreeable to the idea, if that was what Father wanted. I called him into the dining room to join us.

"Mother says she'd be willing to move to Pittsburgh and into an apartment if you want to. She says the only reason she wanted the house is because you did."

Mother's face was drawn and hurt. "I didn't know you wanted to move," she told her husband.

"What are you talking about?" Father said, looking at me.

"You told me you wanted to move to Pittsburgh, but you said you didn't think Mother wanted to. Well, Mother says—"

"I never said that." He looked from me to Mother and back again, shaking his head.

"If that's what you want . . ." Mother said.

I didn't understand what was going on. "Last night . . . in the living room . . . you said . . ."

"I never said anything of the kind. We couldn't move from here. How could you ever get such an idea? This is our home."

Mother looked at him heavily. Father stood with one hand in his pocket, jingling his change, looking back and forth at his wife, at his youngest son. And he smiled.

I leave the hallway and go into Mother's bedroom. Once, my parents' bedroom. A forbidden place when I was growing up, sacrosanct, for reasons I never understood. The clutter that has slowly dissipated in other parts of the house since my arrival is too much in evidence here. On the floor are stacks of cardboard boxes, children's toys, piles of winter clothes, an upended rowing machine. A Barcalounger covered with a sheet is tilted back in its reclining position in front of a floor-model television set. One side of the modern double bed is covered with cans of hair spray, cosmetics, toiletries; the covers on the other side are pulled back where she slept.

I find what I'm looking for on top of the dresser, among a couple of stuffed lions, a cigarette lighter in the shape of a gold Cadillac, a run-down alarm clock. They are the last studio portraits of Father, taken on the occasion of his admittance to the exclusive Duquesne Club in Pittsburgh. In one picture he stands full-length in front of dramatically shaped curtains, his hands at his sides. The other picture is a close-up, tight on his head and shoulders. Either they were taken during the same photo session, seconds apart—my father demonstrating an uncanny ability to hold a pose and expression—or one is a blow-up of the other. It doesn't matter, the smile in both photos is the same.

It is the same smile as in the picture in the hall, the same smile I remember when I was a child, only now it shows signs of weariness, a tiredness beyond tired. At this point he had begun to hear the whispers of his body, the bad news that all was not well within. (It occurs to me that perhaps at this point of the man's life, on some basic metaphysical level of being, he was simply growing tired of smiling.) It was the smile that people in town thought of when they found out I was DeWitt's boy. The smile that assured them I was fundamentally a good boy, from good people, as the saying went, no matter what I did. It was the smile he gave my mother when he sat down to dinner after his day in Pittsburgh, after having lunch at the William Penn Hotel or the Oliver Cork & Bottle, and confronted meat fried black and potatoes the consistency of cardboard. It was the smile he gave me when I asked for, and he said I could have, a $300 train set, a $1,000 drum set, an $1,600 used Jaguar.

The man smiled a lot. And I think the smile eventually wore him out. At the end, he no longer wore the smile, the smile wore him. The smile took over his life, though I don't know how much he realized it, presenting its own image to the world, independent of the intelligence or feelings behind it, dominating the man who bore it. It was the smile of the Cheshire cat, only tight-lipped, without joy or humor. And he knew when it was getting ready to leave him. The smile could leave the man, but the man couldn't leave the smile. And when Father died, or possibly because of it, the smile packed its bags and starting hitching rides across the country, flitting across the faces of truck-stop waitresses and bus drivers, farmers in their cornfields and ranchers with their herds, children in schoolyards and salesmen on a business call, across the Midwest and the mountain states, the deserts of Utah and Nevada, wandering through the foggy streets of San Francisco, looking up at thousands of apartment windows, until the smile found its way to me.

It was a nice fantasy. I wished that it was true. And knew that it wasn't. Only wishful thinking. I had my own smile to contend with, the smile I gave when salespeople ignored me in stores, when the company I worked for gave me projects I didn't want, when I helped my wife move out of our apartment into an apartment of her own. It was the smile I find on my face when I stand in the cluttered remnants of the place I once called home, the house I grew up in, and look at a picture of the smile frozen on my father's face.

I go back to the hallway. Pushed off into a corner is a tall, stand-up ultraviolet lamp. The lamp huddles against the wall like a grieving figure; its head is bent on the gooseneck stalk like a dying sunflower. I have considered several times photographing it as a metaphor of the state of the house, of its inhabitants, living and dead:

Pale soul, consumed by fear
Of the living world you haunt. . . .

But the lamp has other meanings for me, too. It was once a central figure in the lair of the Baldy-Sturber. Each night, after my bath, Mother turned on the crackling, purplish light, and I stood for precise seconds under its fearful rays, my eyes shielded by heavy dark goggles that converted the deadly tube into a luminous green worm. Then on signal I ran to the safety of the shadows, and Father stepped into place. He never wore goggles but trusted himself to keep his eyes closed. We watched him expectantly as he stood there, his head tilted slightly to one side as he thought his private thoughts, his delicate features as washed-out as in death. But on his face, patient, tolerant, self-contained, he always wore the smile in the sickly glow.

I take the goggles from where they hang on the handle. I stretch them to put them on, but the old elastic snaps under the strain and the straps hang useless. I look across at the figure in the mirror, but the hallway is too dark to see. Only time will tell if the smile on my face will consume me the way that Father's consumed him. For now, it is enough to know that, despite whatever similarities, the smile is my own. And so are my eyes.

Album II
Helen and Dewitt

Her story begins, or picks up from its own earlier beginnings, in large measure with the story that came to dominate her life: that she was responsible for her own mother's death. Helen Jessie—or maybe it was Jessie Helen; she never would say which—was born on the first of May 1901, and everyone said her mother was never the same afterward. She knew her mother only as a stern, disapproving woman who was sick all the time. She didn't know what they meant when they said the birth had torn her mother apart; she only knew she was somehow the cause of it. The talk didn't get any better when she was eight years old and her mother died.

She was the youngest daughter of Reverend William Murchie, a United Presbyterian minister in Red Oak, Iowa. Dad, as he was known within the family, kept the girls with him and did for them what he could, which included getting married again right away. But that only seemed to put him further from her. She had always been her father's favorite, but she was smart enough to know that it might just be his Christian charity to a homely child. As her father became more engrossed with his new wife, Helen (or Jessie) could only wish she was as pretty as her older sister Alfleda, or Flee, who even at a young age it seems was out in the bushes with anything that moved.

Flee knew how to get what she wanted from people. And she knew how to get

what she wanted from Helen. She'd threaten to hold her breath until she died. It never failed to work with my mother.

My father, on the other hand, was a small-town child of privilege. Born June 1, 1901, christened Bruce DeWitt, later known as just DeWitt, he was the first son of a respected physician in Beaver Falls, Pennsylvania. The family was well-known; comparatively speaking, well-to-do. When I had my paper route, it seemed that everybody on College Hill was brought into the world by Doc Snodgrass.

But Father had his problems, too. His mother wished he were a girl. Frail and spindly, he had to do his sister Catherine's work around the house—sweeping the floors, ironing the sheets and handkerchiefs. In a mill town, that made him a sissy. Still, he was better off than his baby brother, Stewart. Grandmother kept Stew in girls' clothes until he was eight.

In spite of all this, or because of it, Father worked summers on the ice wagon. Working on the ice wagon in those days meant learning to fight for the best blocks of ice at the icehouse. It also meant learning how to lift a three-hundred-pound block of ice off the wagon and into an icebox. Father explained to me once that it was

all a matter of balance, of learning how to go with the weight. It became one of his principles to live by.

The problem was that, when he started college, he was told to wear a beanie. Father went along with wearing the green beanie—to be a "Greenie"—when he was up at Geneva, the college on the hill above the town; but the football team, most of whom were from someplace else, told him he had to wear it even when he was away from the campus. Well, he wasn't going to do that, not Doc Snodgrass' son, not in his own hometown. One day when the team found him without it, they beat him till he couldn't walk. Somebody called a taxi and got him to the pool hall, where his friends laid him out on one of the tables. My grandfather just happened by the window and saw him lying there and got him home.

Father was a long time recovering, and the doctor swore out a warrant and the boys were fined. But going back to Geneva was out of the question, and he wasn't even safe in town. His father gave him a choice of schools he could go to, good

Presbyterian schools that were recommended by a friend. As it turned out, there were only two schools in the country that met Doc Snodgrass' standards.

In the spring of 1922, DeWitt arrived in Tarkio, Missouri, to go to Tarkio College. He was better dressed than the other fellows, had more money to spend, liked to hang around the bars and pool halls in town. He was a dude. The story goes that he proved himself to the locals by lifting a three-hundred-pound block of ice into a bar's icebox

when the regular iceman threw out his back. It's a good story but I don't necessarily believe it. What I do believe is that he was a thousand miles from home. And lonely.

In the dining hall at Tarkio, there was a senior at the head of each table to act as monitor and serve the food. The first day of her senior year, Helen Murchie took her seat at the head of her table. By chance, DeWitt Snodgrass—two years behind her but the same age—took the seat next to her, to her left. By custom, they kept those same seats for the rest of the school year. By someone else's arrangement, he asked her to a party in town. And they were together after that for the rest of their lives.

In Tarkio, the big thing to do on a Sunday—actually about the only thing to do—was to go out and walk the section, the square mile between the roads that divided the rich farmlands of Missouri. For the occasion my mother and father always wore their Sunday clothes. DeWitt was a dandy by Midwest standards, in tight pants and tailored jackets; Helen spent every penny she could get hold of for clothes good enough to be with him. They were an affectionate couple, I'm told, and delighted themselves when they scandalized the school administration by holding hands on campus—a daring thing to do in those days for United Presbyterians.

They were very much in love. And they tried not to think about what would happen to them when she graduated.

My mother was given to flights of fancy. Always was. She once worked for the Murphy Calendar Company, writing inspiring and dreamy verses for calendars and greeting cards. Intelligent, determined, a preacher's daughter, she dared to dream and thought herself strong enough to make her dreams come true.

When my future mother and father realized that circumstances were pulling them apart, they met in Chicago and were secretly married on August 30, 1923. While they honeymooned at the Morrison Hotel, it turned out her sister, Alfleda, was shacked up with a drummer in the hotel across the street. Afterward, Helen and DeWitt got on separate trains, Helen heading west, DeWitt heading east. She had a job that year as the principal of the high school in Burchard, Nebraska, where she taught algebra, Latin, and history. She also found herself coach of the girls' basketball team. She had never played basketball in her life, but under her guidance the team took the state championship that year. DeWitt, meanwhile, went back to Beaver Falls to live at home while he attended the University of Pittsburgh. He had become interested in accounting, and Tarkio didn't have the courses, or the prestige. Besides, she wasn't there anymore.

The following year the plan was for her to come east so they could live together; accordingly, my mother quit her job. But the Snodgrass family found out about it and was against the idea, and my father told her not to come. Without a job, she had to move back home—her father had recently been selected for a church in Wichita, Kansas—to live on her savings and dreams.

Grandmother Snodgrass had thinks of her own. About everything. Early in their marriage, she decided her husband should do all the shopping so she wouldn't have to leave the house. She decided she wanted to see her parents up in Sharon every other week, and that her husband should take her. When Grandfather decided he needed a new all-white doctor's office, in keeping with people's growing concern for cleanliness and sanitation, Grandmother decided he didn't. She said it would be too hard to keep clean. If people needed reassuring, she'd sit in the waiting room—which she decorated—and keep them company. About the same time, Grandfather noticed a steady decline of illness around town. Or at least in the number of illnesses he treated.

Grandmother was a lady. And she was determined to live like one.

When Grandfather wanted to smoke, Grandmother sent him downstairs to his office. There is no record of how Grandfather felt about the banishment, but he never stopped smoking. He sat in the quiet of his empty office, puffing away, and wrote short stories for his own amusement. I wish I could say he was an undiscovered American Chekhov, but I can't. The stories aren't very good. But one is sort of interesting: it's about a scientist sitting in his lonely laboratory one night who discovers a minute world under his microscope.

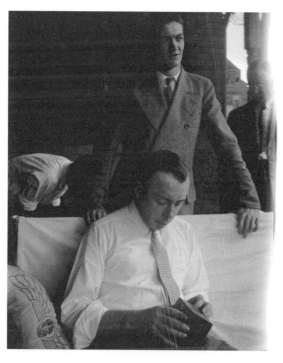

When Grandmother learned, through a misplaced letter, that her son had married a girl from Kansas, she had thinks about that, too.

It was a proud family tradition: Snodgrass men had their choice of only three occupations in life: doctor, preacher, or farmer. My father decided that he wanted to be an accountant.

It's hard for me to realize that Father and his generation believed that business—or rather, Business—would save the world. There would be no more hardship, no more injustice, no more hunger. Free enterprise would make the world a better place, a place where people could be anything they wanted to be, happy and fulfilled. He believed in the sanctity of Business, the same way I believed forty years later in civil rights, the Summer of Love, the Beatles.

Except DeWitt thought he could go one step farther. His would be a business for Business. He would be a businessman to businessmen. A certified public accountant, a man businessmen depended on, relied on. The one who balanced the figures, kept the books.

At one time Father just about gave up. If going to school meant doing without his new wife—stuck out there in Kansas—he was ready to give up school. When Grandfather Murchie heard about DeWitt's discouragement, he wrote a friendly letter to the Snodgrasses of Beaver Falls, saying isn't it a shame to keep these nice kids apart? Consequently, the Snodgrasses of Beaver Falls agreed to have Helen come for a visit for a couple of weeks during the spring. For a time my mother and father were very happy. But that time only served to make the eventual separation harder.

DeWitt kept on at Pitt, but his grades fell. He lost weight; he had constant diarrhea; he grew pale and sallow. Grandfather, Doc Snodgrass, probably afraid of what he might find, had his good friend in town, Dr. Boyd, make the examination. The prognosis was worse than he'd feared: his son wasn't sick, he was in love. Dr. Boyd said, "Bruce, if you want to save the boy's education, you better get that girl back here."

The Snodgrasses of Beaver Falls brought my mother to live with them in the fall of 1924. My parents lived in a small room in the middle of the second floor, between

the large master bedroom in front and my father's sister Catherine's equally large room in the back. Their window was filled with the wall of the house next door, and Mother always remembered that it was a long walk to the bathroom.

Helen wasn't sure how to set a table. She got confused as to which direction the knife was supposed to face, and which fork went where when there was more than one. Offhand, that doesn't sound too serious to me. But to Grandmother Snodgrass it showed a definite lack of character and breeding and upbringing.

The Snodgrasses saved all their grievances for the dinner table. It was probably the only time Grandmother could get them all together in one place to listen to her. A favorite topic of conversation seems to have been the morality of my mother's father marrying again after his wife died. The Snodgrasses also wondered what chance their son had in the world now that he was married to a Kansas farm girl. The family talked about it as though Helen wasn't sitting there. But she didn't budge.

The family might have forgiven my mother and father for being in love. After all, everyone suffers from their baser instincts. They might have forgiven my parents for wanting to be with each other. Everyone wants something, and at least they still had DeWitt at home. But they could never forgive my parents for having fun. In the

evenings, my parents walked hand in hand along Seventh Avenue, the main street, for heaven's sake; on the weekends they went on picnics by themselves. Scandalous! And there were the unspeakable things that went on in their tiny bedroom. Even their fights weren't proper. When my mother said something my father didn't like, he picked her up and set her giggling on top of the dresser.

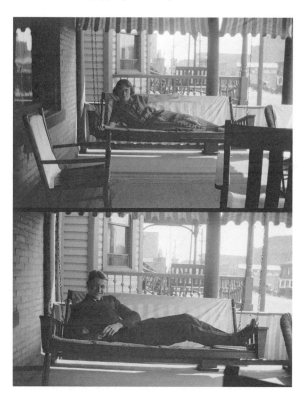

My father was not so much a proper man as he was a precise man. His handwriting was easier to read than most people's printing. And he wanted his clothes just so. He wore his pants so tight that sometimes he had trouble getting them up his legs. When they didn't fit the way he wanted, he had his wife rip out the seams to take them in a quarter of an inch. Though his hair was naturally curly, he wouldn't permit it to be so; all his life he plastered it down with Wildroot Cream Oil.

He knew what he wanted to look like. And he knew what he wanted to do. But he found out the world doesn't always cooperate. When he graduated from Pitt in the spring of 1925, he applied to more than fifty places for a job. (Family legend has the number to be fifty-seven, but that always sounded too much like Heinz's famous varieties to be true.) He finally found an opening in the cost accounting department at Westinghouse in East Pittsburgh. It was a long way from being a certified public accountant, and in terms of Beaver Falls, it was a long way from home.

They moved to Wilkinsburg, ten miles on the other side of Pittsburgh, to a rented room. He made $135 a month, or $31.15 a week, or $6.23 a day. When my mother spent more than $2 a day on the household, he was afraid they wouldn't make it. After that, they rented two rooms in another house, still sharing a bathroom. When the first baby was born in 1926, they took an apartment over a tailor shop. His salary was up to $175 a month, so they bought furniture on the installment plan. His career was going well, he was getting ahead in the world, and after five years of being in love, they finally had a place (and a bathroom) of their own.

But it was too far away. For my father. Every Sunday, both when Helen was pregnant and after the baby arrived, DeWitt insisted they take the three-hour trolley ride down from Pittsburgh to see his parents. After a year they were both sick and tired of doing that, so he took a job with Koppers Company. He was still in cost accounting, which he felt was beneath him, but the office was in downtown Pittsburgh, within commuting distance from Beaver Falls. That same year, he moved his wife and baby back to his hometown, six blocks away from his parents. No getting around it, he was a guy who had difficulty letting go.

My father nurtured two fantasies—that I know of. One was to be a cowboy; the other was to be a chess master. I never thought to ask him how he balanced these two opposites in his well-balanced mind.

In regard to cowboys, all he could do was read about them. It was easier no doubt to entertain his love of chess. On his business trips to New York City, he hung out at the chess clubs every chance he could. His triumph came when he beat the former U.S. Master; on occasion he played several opponents blindfolded.

But chess and reading were the only things he liked about traveling. When he was away, he called home every night to ask Mother what he should eat the next day. He had alternating constipation and searing diarrhea; most of the time he could swallow solids but not liquids. In his daily letters he called her "honey lover" and talked of missing their gin rummy games, talking to her, the children.

Meanwhile, Father's career in accounting was progressing. Here is part of a letter from one of his business trips to my mother relating a conversation he had with his boss:

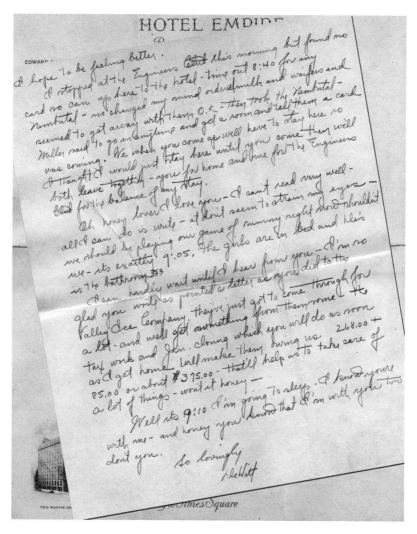

Its 8:00 and I'm in bed. Intend to write to you until 9:00, at which time I will go to ~~bed~~ sleep. Oh lover I just can't get along <u>any</u>place but home. . . . I talked some to Miller today—he brought up the subject. He told me I had been working too hard considering the kind of work I'm doing—said a fellow can do detail work until all hours of the night with the result that one just gets tired—but he reminded me that for the last five years I've been doing advanced work and have been taking it too hard. . . .

At some time my father decided that if he was going to be an important man, he should be a well-educated man. So he set about to read Will Durant's One Hundred Best Books for an Education. And like the good accountant he was, he made a list and checked them off as he finished them, one by one. Aristotle. Spinoza. Kant. Moby Dick. Books were important to my father. They were a way to get ahead.

And he was a good accountant. He was well liked, knew how to get along with people, was capable. He took a job—by this time it was a position—with a large accounting firm and quickly became one of their top men. It meant traveling more than ever, sometimes for two or three weeks at a stretch, but he was building his stable of clients, men who trusted and depended on him, as well as his own reputation. I'm told that when Bendix developed their washing machine—the one that had it all over the washing machine by Westinghouse because the Bendix didn't have to be cemented to the floor—Father went to South Bend and set up their entire bookkeeping system.

But for a man of some physical strength—his exploits on the ice wagon; a catcher in baseball good enough to be considered for the semipros—he had telling weaknesses. And they surfaced whenever he was away from his wife. On extended trips, he had my mother visit him to help get him settled, help him decide what to eat. Eventually when the company wouldn't make him a partner, he quit to start his own firm. That was what he wanted anyway, what he had been working toward all along. He wanted the prestige, the accomplishment, the acknowledgement. And though he still commuted to his office in Pittsburgh every day, he didn't call that traveling. He called that being at home.

Their first car was a red two-door Chevy that they bought in 1933 from the local dealer, Zigs Sahli. Or rather, Mother bought it: Father was out of town on business at the time. Zigs showed Mother how to drive it so she could meet Father at the train station when he got back. She spent a lot of her life picking up Father from the train.

She also spent a lot of her life buying things. Every time there was an important *purchase to be made, Mother made it by herself because Father was always out of town. She sometimes wondered if he planned it that way. His feeling was that the house was her business, that he had business of his own to look after. She traded in cars, bought furniture, selected furnishings. When they decided after renting for fifteen years that they should buy a house, they looked around Beaver Falls together to see what was available. But she was the one who signed the papers for the big brick house on College Hill and bargained the price down to $7,000—he was away in South Bend. Then a few days later she drove herself to the hospital one afternoon to have her fourth baby.*

Father's many business trips—and his related dependency on her, the fact that he got sick whenever he was away from her, away from home—and later his growing business life in Pittsburgh, a separate world thirty miles away, cashed in on her strengths. And she was a strong woman, no doubt about that. Though that didn't mean she necessarily liked it. At the end of the tape recording I made of our conversation about their life at this time, Mother says wistfully, "Father was a good man, he always gave us everything we wanted. But he was gone all the time, all . . ."

Before we go further and things get more complicated, I want to consider the photos of my mother and father, Helen and DeWitt, because a couple of things strike me. In the early photos of my mother, there is a certain confidence, an assuredness

of her abilities, that continues through her photographs later in life. Maybe it was living with, and surviving, the guilt of her mother's death; maybe it was the fact that, even though it may have been because she was the least attractive of the two, she was her father's favorite. No matter. She stands here in this photograph, feet apart, braced and open for what the world holds. Her sister, on the other hand, cozies up to a nearby post.

This at a time when not a whole lot was expected of a woman, especially not in the farmlands of Iowa, and especially not of daughters of a minister. At the time this photo was taken in 1911, women's suffrage would not come about across the nation until the following decade. In their favor, both girls were able to go to college because of their father's religious affiliation. And I think both girls caught that there was something in the wind, that women could in fact have wants. Alfleda got to where she wanted to go by using her charms if not her body, traveling the world and eventually marrying an Army doctor who became head of the heart department at Walter Reed Hospital and consultant to several presidents.

Helen's desires for herself were just as strong and as far-reaching, though she was left to pursue them through her intelligence and strength of will. In that regard, she shared the strength of character of her preacher-father, as well as something of the physical strength and moral wherewithal of that self-assured Scotsman. As a doctor attending my mother at the end of her life put it, "She's a strong piece of protoplasm."

My father, as I study the photographs, is a different matter. In his childhood pictures—there aren't many, and none taken outside the setups of a studio—there is a certain diffidence, a deference and accommodation, among his fine-boned features and delicate manner. I think it surprising in the child of a prominent doctor and citizen of his town. Something seems to be amiss.

In his teens, he seems to have made a concerted effort to toughen up—there was certainly incentive enough: he saw what happened to his baby brother, Stew, whom his mother dressed as a girl until he was eight—which led to his work on the ice wagon and his exploits on the baseball diamond. And for a while, it apparently worked. The photos of the college dandy; the young husband hoisting his bride; the young upstart accountant—there is a new strength and assuredness in his photos of this time. But it doesn't last. The diffidence returns; the deference and easy charm begin to take him over. It is almost as if he shot his wad, used up his resources and reserves, and turned tail back to the safety of accommodation. The stomach and other health problems that started when he was without his love came on stronger

after he attained it. By his mid-thirties, he was hooked on Nembutal and other drugs for life; his many pill bottles lined the dining room mantel. To his credit, he soldiered on with what he had, but he found he wasn't as strong as he liked to think he was. It was undoubtedly easier to turn to someone else's strength. And, human nature being what it is, ultimately turn against that someone for that very reason.

The Stories

Part Three

Moneybags

My father was a careful man. Careful and precise. He pushed his chair back from the dining room table, smiling, after the Sunday dinner. When he crossed his legs, he crossed them in proper fashion, keeping them close together; the toe of his shoe from his dangling leg touched the floor like a dancer *en pointe.*

"I'll tell you what. Today, let's count the money!" He smiled to his children.

He was a delicately featured man, slight and small boned, though close to six feet tall. He always reminded me, then as now, of Fred Astaire, though I think he would have preferred it to be Gary Cooper in *High Noon.* His sport clothes, the clothes he wore at home and on vacations—the only times he didn't wear a business suit—were color coordinated, before the time you could buy them that way in sets. Cream-colored shirts; light tan slacks; light tan shoes; and a bolo tie with his monogrammed initials. He only had to look down his shirtfront to know who he was.

Mother nodded. She patted her hand once and smoothed a wrinkle from the tablecloth, patted and smoothed.

"We could do that."

"The drawer's getting so heavy I can hardly pull it out."

My sisters and I were excited. Father looked from face to face, Barbara and Shirley on one side of the table, me on the other, raising his eyebrows to each of us in turn as if to say, *Would you like to? Would you?*

"Where would be a good place to do it?" Mother said, always practical.

"Right here on the table," Father said, good at details.

"Is there very much?" we asked, always curious.

"Wait and see," Father said, always mysterious.

My sisters and I looked at each other from across the table's centerpiece, a ceramic branch bearing glass balls, flanked by two candles. Barbara was the oldest, Father's pet, the love of the family. She was the only one in the family with black hair; her turned-down nose and large glasses made her look like a friendly owl. Shirley, in her early years in high school, still resembled Ingrid Bergman in her role as Joan of Arc, wistful and soft, only with more hair. I was the baby of the family at nine years old.

"We'll have to clear the table," Barbara said, already getting up. She stacked plates and silverware and headed for the kitchen.

"What do you want me to do?" Shirley asked Father.

Father didn't know. He looked at Mother. "Help Babsie, I guess."

Shirley got up and followed Barbara. My parents looked at each other, sitting at opposite ends of the table, across the expanse of table. They smiled to each other, but only with the corners of their mouths. Father folded his hands and looked at the patterns in the white lace tablecloth. Mother turned a spoon slowly end over end against her bare arm, making a small dent in herself, sliding her fingers each time the length of the shaft, then got up and followed her daughters into the kitchen.

I ran back and forth through the downstairs, slapping an imaginary horse over sage-covered prairies, through canyons, up arroyos. Father took his usual position in the blue overstuffed chair in the corner of the dining room, sitting at his card table as he added a few more precise figures between the lines of his large yellow balance sheets. He looked up, distant and remote, to watch me ride by.

Sundays were always a special day, the only day for certain that Father would be home from his office in Pittsburgh. Even then, of course, it was expected that he would set up his card table and spend most of the day working. But there were times, on Sundays, when we all got in the car, my parents in the front seat, my sisters and me in back, and took long drives through the towns of Western Pennsylvania and Ohio, stopping somewhere along the way for frozen custards or Cokes. The best trips were to Idora amusement park in Youngstown. I would spend all my money within the first half hour at the shooting gallery, aiming the chained ".22" at the parade of silver-flocked soldiers and rabbits, and have to be content the rest of the day to watch my sisters screaming through the turns of the Octopus and Wild Mouse. But at the end of the day, Father would relent and treat us all to the Dodge 'Ems. We jumped in the little cars and chased him around the slippery arena, the trolleys sparking overhead on the electric ceiling, while Mother stood audience behind the wooden fence, smiling benignly.

On the way home, Shirley would start to sing:

One elephant went out to play
Out on a spider's web one day.
He thought it such enormous fun,
He called for another elephant to come.
Two elephants went out to play,
Out on a spider's web one day . . .

Barbara and I would join in, and the counting sometimes reached the hundreds. Or we kept quiet and listened to the static-filled radio, usually the Pirates game in the summer, or if we were late getting back, Jack Benny and Bob Hope in the evenings. Or watched the other cars, the other families. Being the youngest, and being spoiled, I always got to sit by the window, usually on the right side behind Mother. I don't remember much of the particulars of these trips, but I still carry with me the smells of my sisters in the hot afternoons, and the feel of their skirts and crinolines, and sometimes their legs, against me.

I rode through the high chaparral, through mesquite, sagebrush, tumbling tumbleweeds. Barbara came in from the kitchen with a dishrag to brush the crumbs from the table. Father at his card table extended his arm to her and she folded into it.

"Babsie. How's my girl?"

"We're all done in the kitchen. Can I get you something?"

He looked lovingly into her face, his lips pursed in a slight smile, his blue eyes mischievous. The same look I'd see him use with waitresses, salesgirls. "Well, I could use a little cup of coffee. . . ."

"Sure, Father." She bounced away, back to the kitchen.

He looked at me and smiled. "Ditty-Witty."

I rode along a ridge, down into a ravine.

Mother and Shirley came from the kitchen.

"Well, I just don't think it's right, that's all," Mother said.

"But Kitty and Mary are going."

Mother stopped abruptly at the dining room table; Shirley followed so closely that she almost ran into her and had to back away. Mother looked drawn and tired. "I just don't think it's right."

Shirley looked like she might cry. I rode by, scouting the plains, and took a swat at her skirt.

"Oh, leave me alone!"

"What's the matter, what's the matter?" Father beamed from his card table.

"You can ask your father," Mother said wearily.

"Whatever you want, you can't have it," he grinned. His standard reply.

Shirley tried to keep looking hurt, but she had to smile when she looked at Father.

"That a girl." Father motioned for her to come over to his table. He reached in his back pocket and gave her a dollar from his wallet. "That's for the smile."

She tightened her mouth even further to show her pleasure. He presented his forehead and she kissed it. Mother looked wistfully from across the room.

I pulled up my horse, dismounted, and held out my hand.

"I'll smile, too."

He laughed and handed me a quarter from his pocket.

"Why just a quarter?"

"Because your smile is smaller. Wait till you grow up."

I was still rich.

"You better get in here, Babs," Mother said over her shoulder, leaning on the back of a straight chair.

Barbara came in with Father's cup of coffee.

"What did I miss?

"Father's handing out money again."

Barbara put the coffee on the card table in front of him and curtsied. "I'm sorry, kind sir, but I cannot accept your gifts and favors."

He laughed and hugged her, low around her hips. The coffee splashed over the edge of the cup into the saucer as he reached for her.

"Now then, let's get ready for the big money."

He was a happy man sitting there at his card table, drinking his coffee, watching his daughters scurry around to clear the dining room table of the centerpiece and tablecloth. Mother spread newspapers over the surface of the old scarred table. When the table was ready, Gabriel the cat jumped up and took a position in the center, thinking all the preparation was for him. Mother rubbed his head fondly.

Father lifted his card table away from his chair.

"All right, then. I'll go get the drawer."

I followed him upstairs, watching from the doorway of my parents' bedroom as he went to the dresser and pulled out the top drawer. He laid it on the bed and carefully took out the pairs of his long white silk stockings, each rolled tight as a fist, handkerchiefs, garters, matchbooks from restaurants in Pittsburgh, timetables for the P&LE. There were several folded slips of paper. He studied each one and put them in his wallet. As he did so, he noticed me in the doorway.

"Did you come up to help your poor old father?"

I nodded shyly, still afraid to go inside.

He smiled. "It's pretty heavy. I'll tell you what, why don't you bring the coin wrappers. That'll be a big help." He nodded to the top of the dresser, where there were several stacks of red and green papers held together with rubber bands. I ran over and gathered them up and followed him back downstairs.

"Here we go!" he announced, raising the drawer high so he could see where he was going. My mother and sisters lifted their eyes as we approached.

"Somebody grab the cat."

Mother lifted Gabriel from the table and cuddled him, rubbing his ears. He folded into her hand. Father placed the drawer in the center of the table and we stared at it for several moments, unable to believe our eyes. The bottom of the drawer was thick with pennies, dimes, quarters; one side of the drawer was almost half full. I had never seen so much money in my life.

"How much is there?"

"That's what we're going to find out," Father said, touching my nose.

"I'll get some paper to keep track," Barbara said.

"That's my girl."

"What can I do?" Shirley said.

"Well, I guess we can start counting."

We took handfuls of the coins and sorted them out according to denominations, then counted them in stacks of ten. There were special stacks for Indian Head pennies and Liberty quarters. Among the found treasures were Canadian coins with strange inscriptions, trolley tokens from Pittsburgh with a three-pronged star cut in the center, a few silver dollars that Father called cartwheels. The table was covered with money.

Mother and Barbara wrapped the stacks in the correct wrappers, folding the ends and tapping them on the table to make them tight. The afternoon grew to dusk. Mother turned on the chandelier over the table and brought a floor lamp to stand beside Father. We listened on the radio to mystery programs and the NBC Symphony Orchestra. My hands carried an acrid, metallic smell.

Finally it was counted and rolled.

"Well, what's the total?" Father asked Barbara.

She was still figuring. She looked up and laughed at being slow, and continued adding. She drew a final line, made a final dot.

"You won't believe this."

"Not unless you tell us what it is," Mother said.

Mother started to lean over to read the tally, but Barbara protected it against her breasts. She took it around the table to Father and stood beside him while he read it.

"One hundred eighty-seven dollars and eighteen cents!"

We hoorayed, hollered, clapped. I felt part of something warm and big.

"What are we going to do with it?" I asked.

"We?" Father said. "What do you mean 'we'?"

"Well, I . . ."

"I'm the man with the money around here."

"Moneybags," Shirley said.

Barbara knew what I meant. "He means what are we going to do with it now."

"Oh, probably put it in the bank. Or give it to your mother."

She nodded once in assent. "I know a couple of things we could do with it."

"Your mother never has any trouble spending my money."

"That's because I spend it on you and the family."

"Sometimes I wonder if she's hiding it away somewhere."

"Why would Mother do that?" I said.

"That's what I ask myself sometimes," he said to me like a fellow conspirator.

I looked at him, from Father to Mother and back again. Father was still smiling, but Mother looked suddenly tired.

"I guess I'll start supper," she said, getting up slowly from the table. Her mouth was small and downturned.

"Now, Helen, don't be upset."

"I'm not upset."

"Don't spoil our nice day."

"I'm not spoiling anything."

"We had a nice time here today."

"Yes."

"It was something we could all do together."

"That's right."

"And I didn't have to get tired out driving someplace."

"I didn't know you didn't like to drive."

"I like to drive, you know that."

"Well, that's what I thought. But the way you said it, it sounded like you didn't."

Father looked around the table at us, his hands open in supplication, but he was still smiling. "You kids know how much I like to drive, don't you?"

We nodded, looking at each other, wondering what was going on.

"There, you see? The kids know it. You're making something out of nothing."

"I guess I'll go get supper."

"Helen?"

She had made it to the doorway to the kitchen before his voice turned her around.

"What?"

Father looked around at us. He laughed a little.

"Don't you know I like to drive us places?"

"Yes."

"Then why did you say I didn't?"

She sighed and looked at him. Her one leg was slightly in front of the other, and she put her hand on it, resting her weight. "I didn't know I did."

"Well. Okay." Father rested his elbows on the arms of his chair and folded his hands. He looked at the rolls of money. I looked at the money, at my sisters. They were sitting with their heads bowed, as though listening to the blessing before a meal. Father looked pleased.

"One hundred eighty . . . What was it again?"

Barbara looked up at him. The tablet was in front of Shirley but Shirley kept her head bowed. Barbara reached over and picked it up.

"One hundred eighty-seven dollars and eighteen cents."

"One hundred eighty-seven dollars and eighteen cents," Father said. "That's really something, isn't it?

"Wow!" I said.

"Your old dad's not such a bad guy after all, is he?"

The girls murmured approval. They looked at him shyly.

"Hey, what's the matter here?" Father said. "Why's everybody so glum? Cheer up!"

Chamber Music

1953

"Isn't this nice?"

Father stretched out on the chaise lounge on the front lawn, trailing his hands in the grass like a floater on a raft. It was dusk, a summer evening. The sky above the valley was wistful, delicate shades of pink and blue. The traffic was slow on the hill from downtown.

"It's very nice," Mother said.

"Where are the girls?"

"Inside."

"They should be out here. They should be enjoying this. This is why I work so hard, so we can have nice things like this."

"They'll be out in a little bit."

Mother sat on the steps below the front door, her hand wrapped around the end of a clothesline. On the other end of the clothesline, twenty feet away, Mike, the small black kitten, crouched through the grass stalking bugs. Gabriel, the older, neutered male, sat at the far end of the other side of the yard, on his own, keeping an eye on the Munteans' dog across the street.

I sat on the lower set of steps, below Mother and nearest the sidewalk. Father looked over benevolently at us, smiled dreamily, and closed his eyes. I watched the cars coming up the hill on Route 18 slowly making the corner.

"I do want my lions, though," Mother said.

"We'll get you your lions," Father said.

"It's what I've always wanted in front of my house."

Father's smile became a little tighter and his eyes fluttered slightly, but he didn't say anything. We had spent every Sunday for the last couple of months driving around the towns of Western Pennsylvania, and even over into Ohio, looking for houses with stone lions out front. (What we were actually looking for were *cement* lions, but my mother had them in her mind as stone lions and stone lions they were.) In our travels we found a number of stone lions, but as yet we hadn't found anyone who, when my father knocked on their door to inquire, wanted to sell them. We knew of every house with stone lions in a radius of seventy-five miles. And the circle was getting bigger.

I was born at the start of World War II and grew up hearing about the conflict, though of course it wasn't real to me; it was only pictures in *Life* magazine of casualties on foreign battlefields and air raids on distant cities and maps with huge arrows sweeping over places called Europe and the Pacific theater. What was real to me were all the nifty new things we got as soon as the war was over. The postwar years brought a steady stream of changes to the house; rooms divided and remodeled; a washing machine instead of a wringer; a clothes drier instead of a mangle; an unheard-of luxury called a dishwasher. A new car every other year was a given. Now it was time to give an overhaul to the outside of the house. Mother had already enclosed the backyard with a new rustic fence, and staked out wagon wheels that her father sent Railway Express whenever he found them in Kansas and Nebraska. My favorite, though, was the round planter in the middle of the front lawn, tiered like a wedding cake and topped off with a large silver globe called a gazing ball. The ball had the effect of a fisheye lens; you could look in it and see yourself and the world around you, the houses and the trees and the traffic on the street, slipping around the curved surface. The only problem was that Mother had to take it in each night to keep it from vandals.

Mike, the kitten, crawled over my left arm and onto my lap, straddling my thighs momentarily to look at the world, then kept on going, stepping off to sniff the railing, then around behind me toward Father, then across my lap again. The line had run out of slack, gently tying my arms; the kitten looked at me, bewildered. When the Munteans' dog across the street barked, Mike panicked and tried to run and pulled the bonds tighter, the kitten wide-eyed as though I was trying to pull her to her doom. We laughed.

"Unwind her," Mother said. "The dog scares her."

"She's not the smartest cat in the world," I said, all knowing at thirteen years of age, ducking out of the line. The kitten still was unaware she was free.

"Cat's aren't known for their logic."

"Don't make fun of my cat," Father said. One rainy night a few months earlier, as my father arrived at the train station from his office in Pittsburgh, the black kitten had run through the crowd of commuters and sat on my father's shoe; after he shook himself free, the kitten followed him through the station and outside, where my mother was waiting in the car, hopping up onto his lap before he could close the door, soaking the lap of his Hart Schaffner Marx suit. My father looked at my mother and said, "Well, it looks like we have another cat." Now he rubbed his fingers together to attract her attention. The kitten was interested but wasn't sure the line would reach. Trixie, the dog across the street, trotted up and down the sidewalk in front of its house, its long nails ticking on the pavement. Gabriel watched it intently from the corner of our yard, calculating distances. Trixie had attempted to cross the street and enter our yard only once; after a brief skirmish Gabriel rode it back across the street, clawing for its eyes. The dog seemed to remember.

From inside the house came the sound of the piano, the slow center movement of Bach's Concerto no. 5 in F Minor. The introspective melody was muted by the depths of the house and the sounds of the evening. Father looked at Mother and smiled, then looked away again toward the street. My sister Shirley stood behind the screen door.

"It's nice out."

"All through?" Mother turned to look at her.

"Come on out," Father said. "You girls should be out here with your poor old father. Isn't Barbara coming out?"

"She's playing the piano."

Shirley let herself out through the screen door, carefully keeping the black Pekingese inside the sunporch. As Shirley sat down beside Mother, a small black face appeared above the bottom edge of the screen, a bit of red tongue sticking out between the lips. Nanki Poo whined momentarily, but Mother told him everything would be okay and the dog was quiet again. We sat without talking for a while, listening to the piano and the trucks on the hill and the cry of the first nighthawk.

"Is Barbara okay?" Father said, turning to us again.

Shirley shrugged. "I guess so."

"Her breath was tightening up a little, but I don't think it's anything to worry about," Mother said.

"I hope not," Father said.

"She's okay," Shirley said.

Father looked at the house as though he thought it might answer him. "Did she say anything about her date?"

Nobody spoke for a while. I turned around. Mother was winding and unwinding the clothesline around her fist, her mouth drawn together like the pull-strings of a purse. "I told her she shouldn't see him again."

"I thought he was funny," I said.

"Yes, well, you didn't help matters any," Shirley said.

"What'd I do?"

"You laughed at him." Shirley tried to look mad at me, but our eyes met and we both giggled.

Mother didn't say anything. She frowned the way she always did when she wanted us to know she didn't like what she was about to say.

"No, I felt I had to tell her. It just wasn't right, he was pawing all over her, trying to kiss her. Maybe they do things differently in his country, but I told her she was too nice a girl to be treated that way. Foreign students sometimes get funny ideas about girls when they come over here. I just didn't think it was right."

Father nodded agreement. Barbara was twenty-five, and it was the only time I ever knew her to have a date. His name was Saud, he was brown-skinned with a beaked nose, an exchange student at Geneva College a block away. She seemed happy to be with him though, and I felt bad because I didn't like him. When Barbara got back after her date, I heard my parents talking to her late into the night.

We nodded and smiled and mouthed hellos to a man walking up the street, in a brown plaid shirt and baggy brown pants and brown suspenders, a brown wool hat with a crushed brim, a mill hand from the looks of him; Father lifted his hand from the grass like a blessing. Each night we saw the man come up the hill from the direction of Locust Street and return a short time later from the drugstore with a newspaper under his arm. None of us knew his name or exactly where he lived.

"She's a pretty girl," Father said, after the man made his return trip. "She's a very pretty girl."

"And intelligent."

"Of course."

"She's doing a great job down at the office. All the fellows just love her."

"She's very capable."

"I don't know what the trouble is." Father shook his head.

Barbara had moved on to Chopin. She faltered, then stopped, playing a troublesome figure over a couple of times, then attempted the passage again, this time making it through without trouble. Father extended his index finger and beat time in the air like a metronome. Nanki Poo whimpered from the door.

Mother half turned. "Hush!"

The small black head, excited at the attention, bobbed up and down. Mother turned back to us. Shirley got up and followed the clothesline to free the kitten from where it had wound itself around the base of an umbrella tree. The kitten continued on across the lawn, toward Father's beating finger.

"I was wondering if dancing lessons would help," Mother said.

"For Barbara?" Shirley sneered.

"For both of you."

Shirley brightened considerably.

"There's an Arthur Murray studio up in Pittsburgh," Mother said. "You girls could take the train late in the afternoon, and afterward meet Father at his office to come home together."

"Really?" Shirley said.

"Do you think Barbara would like that?" Father said.

"I'd like it," Shirley said. "I think she would."

"What about me?" I said.

"You don't need dancing lessons," Mother said.

I wondered what was so special about dancing lessons anyway. Mike had made it across the yard and was sitting on Father's stomach. Father looked proudly to his wife and daughter, to make sure they noticed. It was starting to get dark. The sun was beyond the rim of the valley but the sky still carried the afterglow. Across the other side of the yard, Gabriel kept his vigil on Trixie. I crawled across the lawn on my hands and knees toward him.

"You'll get grass stain!" Mother said.

I kept on going.

"Please! Honey lover! Your pants!"

I lifted my feet higher off the ground, as if that would solve the problem, but it seemed to satisfy her—at least she didn't say anything more. Gabriel watched me approach. When I was a few feet away from him, he got up and walked nonchalantly into an opening under the rosebushes. I followed him as far as I could. He sat inside a vault of thorn-covered branches, just out of reach, regarding me without malice.

"You're not going to get him unless he wants you to," Mother said.

"I know."

"Leave him alone," Shirley said.

"I'm not hurting him," I scratched the grass to tell him I wanted to rub his stomach. To show he understood, he rolled over and scratched his back in the dirt. But he still wouldn't come within reach.

"I'll get him later," Shirley said.

I gave up and walked over to the steps.

"What I'd really like is a Coke," Father said.

"I'll get it!" I said, and leapt between Mother and Shirley into the house. I scared Nanki halfway across the sunporch. I could tell Shirley was mad because I was going to get it for Father.

The inside of the house was dark, solemn from the trace of daylight left in the windows. Barbara had returned to her favorite, the Bach. I went into the living room and stood beside the piano, watching her hands. In the dark room the keys of the baby grand piano seemed to glow. Barbara looked up and smiled and missed a note.

"Why don't you come outside?"

She smiled again, wistfully, then stopped in mid-phrase. "Oh, I don't know. I guess I just don't feel like it."

She knew I recognized the slight whistle that had come to her breath. She shook her head so her hair bounced slightly and started to play again, from the beginning.

I sat down beside her on the bench. She moved over a little, beating the crinolines beneath her skirt into submission away from me. She was just an average player, I suppose; she only wanted to play the same pieces over and over and had quit her lessons when the teacher made her nervous. But I loved to hear her play and sat beside her for hours sometimes. Sometimes, I sat under the piano, watching her foot on the pedals, close enough to her leg to smell the smell of her skin.

"Why did you come in? Isn't it nice out?"

"It's okay. I came in to get Father a Coke. I guess I better go get it."

She seemed a little disappointed. I didn't get up right away. She played a little while, then stopped, picking out a few phrases with one hand while she studied her fingers.

"Did Father say anything about me?" she said finally.

"I don't know."

She hunted around for notes.

"I mean about my date."

"Oh. Yeah. A little."

"Did he say anything about him?"

"No. Yes. He said he hoped you had a nice time."

She changed her search into a lighter key, picking up the rhythm a bit. We jogged our shoulders in time; then she stopped again.

"You laughed at him. Was he funny-looking?"

"No, I don't think so. I just, you know . . ."

"You don't have to explain," she said and pushed air in my direction. She began to play a slow theme from *Slaughter on Tenth Avenue*. On cue, I rose from the bench and did overdramatic sweeps and pirouettes around the dark living room. I exited the room and headed for the kitchen and Father's Coke. When I came back through the house, Barbara was working again on the Chopin.

Father looked at the Coke as if it were a surprise.

Mother was saying, ". . . and the tests show she's allergic to animal hair and dust, but that can't be so. She's always slept with one or other of the dogs, and she never had trouble before."

"I know," Father said. "I've even wondered if I could move the business to Arizona, but I just couldn't. I wouldn't have any clients there."

"And how do we know that would do any good?"

"Are we moving to Arizona?" I said.

"No. This doesn't concern you."

Father shook his head, looking perplexed. Then his face brightened, too much. The piano had stopped; Barbara was standing at the screen behind Mother and Shirley.

"Come on out and join us, Babsie," Father said, extending his arm.

"Maybe you'd better not if you're fogging up," Mother said.

"I'm all right."

Barbara stood in the darkness of the house, a dim figure behind the screen, looking out at the evening. She held Nanki against her breasts, under his forelegs, his body dangling down. She rubbed his white tummy; he stuck out his tongue and kissed her. She ruffled his head and laughed.

"If you're not feeling well, why don't you go to bed?" Mother said.

"I'm fine." She waited a moment. "But I think I will go up to bed."

"That's my girl," Father said.

Evening was close to night, the sky blue-black above the shadows of the house and the trees. Most of the passing cars had turned on their lights. As I watched, the streetlights changed from empty globes to a pale mother-of-pearl. I stood midway along the length of clothesline that Mother held in her hand, shaking a curl of the line at the kitten in the grass behind Father. Mike watched the curl approaching, fascinated at the movement stretching toward her in the darkness, but always surprised at the resulting jerk in her collar.

"And you don't have to worry," Barbara said. "I don't want to go to Arizona."

"We're not worried," Father said with a half laugh.

"We want to do everything for you that we can," Mother said.

Barbara smiled. "I couldn't leave here. This is my home."

She looked at the street, at the hills. Then she roughhoused the dog's belly and set him down on the floor, out of sight. "Good night." She disappeared back into the house with the good nights trailing after her.

I waited until I saw her bedroom light go on, and the light in the bathroom above the sunporch.

"I guess I'll go find Gabriel," I said and walked around the far side of the house.

"I'll get him later," Shirley said, but I didn't acknowledge her. I prayed the back door was unlatched and it was. I slipped inside and through the dark house. In the rectangle of the screen door, Mother's head was a dim silhouette. I eased up the steps to the second floor.

The water was running in the bathroom, the light shining under the closed door. I leaned against the doorframe and tried to see in through the crack, but Barbara was too close to the sink. I backed away and made some noise in the hall so she'd know I was around. I went into her room and waited.

Her bedroom was actually on the third floor, but since she'd been having her attacks she was sleeping in the front bedroom on this floor, closer to Mother and the bathrooms if she had trouble during the night. Gradually the room was becoming more her own than the one upstairs. The shelves above the closet were filling up with her collection of stuffed and carved Pekingese dogs; her old moleskin shirt, the one she always wore when she was sick, hung on the back of the chair, the collar permanently curled from sweat, the sleeves rolled up to the elbows to be out of the way. Beside the bed was the small folding table where she kept her Green Mountain Asthma Cure.

She wasn't coming. And I knew I shouldn't be there. Sometimes I'd lie beside her in bed when she was sick, or she'd talk to me dressed only in her panties and bra. If Mother knew I was there now she'd be furious. I left the room and went next door to my room, throwing myself on the bed; I lay in the darkness wondering what was wrong with me. I heard Barbara come out of the bathroom and go into her room; the dim light in the hallway wavered as she passed in front of her bedside lamp. Then the light wavered again as she left her room and came and stood in the doorway to mine. It was the first time I had ever seen her naked without having to peek through a keyhole or a crack. The first time I had ever seen any woman naked.

"I thought I heard you," she whispered.

"Yes, I'm here."

"Why didn't you stay outside?"

"I don't know."

I looked at her tiny breasts, her broad hips. In the darkness of the upstairs she looked ghostly. She was trying to be at ease, resting her hand against the doorframe; it occurred to me that she was posing. But she could no longer breathe through her nose, only through her open mouth, the air whistling at the back of her throat between phrases.

"Did you come in . . . because I was here?"

"I guess so. Yes."

She smiled. Or tried to. "I'm glad."

"Me, too."

Downstairs, the front screen door slammed. There were sounds of voices, and the lawn furniture being brought in for the night.

"You better get downstairs," she whispered.

I nodded.

"I think I'm going to be up tonight," she said, referring to the trouble she was having breathing. She would sit for hours on the edge of the bed, hunched over the folding table and the ashtray with the little mound of burning powder, the Asthma Cure, inhaling the smoke. The embers of the mound would glow, like the line of a forest fire rimming a distant mountain. Smoke would hang in the room in a solid cloud, growing down from the ceiling, filling the room and then traveling down the hall, extending to each room in turn along the corridor, eventually descending down the stairs and fogging the downstairs as well, a cloud of smoke inside like the cloud of smoke outside from the mills that lowered over the town each time it was going to rain. The house would smell of the smoke for days, and she carried the smell like charcoal on her, on her clothes and in her hair. A dark smell, something burnt. "Why don't you come back . . . and sit with me later? After everyone's asleep?"

"Okay."

She put her finger to her lips and tiptoed back to her room. I got up from the bed and went slowly downstairs.

"What are you doing in here?" Mother said. "I thought you were looking for Gabriel."

"I had to go to the bathroom."

"Is Babs in bed?"

"I guess."

"Poor dear."

"I'll go out with Shirley."

"All right. But then you get ready for bed. Father and I are going for a ride. Good night, dear."

I passed Father on the front steps, carrying in the cushion for his chaise lounge. I walked out across the lawn, the grass beginning to feel damp with dew. At the corner of the block, hundreds of insects circled around the streetlight, beating against the globe, but the glow of the light didn't reach me. I could hear the Munteans across the street talking in low voices as they sat in the darkness on their front steps. From the backyard I could hear Shirley calling Gabriel. I stood in the shadows as Mother and Father left the house, got in the car, and drove away into the night. Behind me the dark house loomed against the dark sky. I sat on the edge of the terrace where I could see Barbara's windows on the second floor, waiting as the dampness seeped through my clothes, waiting until her light went out and her window went black.

Mary Rutkowski

There were two record shops in Beaver Falls when I was growing up. But there was only one Mary Rutkowski.

Mary Rutkowski graduated several years ahead of me in high school, but I always associate her with that time of my life. I used to walk downtown every day after school, and sometimes at lunchtimes, to visit the record shop where she worked, to browse through the bins of modern jazz and big band swing, but also for the chance to see her walk up and down the aisles. In many respects, Mary Rutkowski was directly responsible for me owning the largest collection of jazz records in all of Beaver Valley. I can still hear the sharp report of her high-heeled shoes as she strolled across the linoleum floor of the shop, and still see the tilt of her head as she walked past me, smiling her little smile across the rows of records.

She was a blond-haired, sturdy girl, who made the most of a casual resemblance to Marilyn Monroe. Thinking back on her now, she didn't look at all like Marilyn Monroe, but it wasn't for lack of trying. Mary Rutkowski wore her hair in the same fluffy style as the famous calendar pictures and covered her broad Middle-European face with makeup thick enough to crack. Her lips were too pouty and too red, and her eyelashes were long enough to swat flies. But somehow it didn't seem to matter. She'd swing down the aisle on her high heels, or cradle her breasts as she leaned over the cash register, and I'd walk out with another half dozen records.

Maybe it was her thighs. She had been a majorette, the head majorette as I recall, and I had a particular weakness for the tiny white pleated skirts with the flash of orange and black satin panties underneath, the white tasseled boots cut to mid-calf, and the soft teenage thighs all plump and shiny on the chilly fall evenings of football season. Because she was several years ahead of me, I actually had never seen her thighs in the uniform, but I could imagine. At the record store her skirts were tight and long, and those full, peasant thighs seemed ready to burst the seams. They were the same thighs that drove Saul, the owner of the store, to distraction.

"Sweet Jesus!" he'd say under his breath as she squeezed past him behind the counter or squatted down to unpack a carton. "Sweet mothering Jesus!"

"I don't think He can help you," I offered.

"Nobody could help me with that. Nobody would have to. Jesus!"

"Have you tried?"

He brushed away the suggestion with his hand. "I never mess around with the help. Bad business. If only she was a customer."

I was unconvinced. I figured he didn't mess around with her because she went with a six-foot-three policeman named Charlie. I heard she had been seen in a patrol car parked after midnight at Brady's Run. Saul was a little man in his early forties, shaped like an ellipse. His hair had retreated some time ago toward the back of his head. His face was always heavy with worry, even when he talked about Mary Rutkowski.

He did know a lot about jazz, however, and directed me toward groups that I wouldn't have found on my own until much later—Charlie Parker, Dizzy Gillespie, Thelonious Monk. Mary Rutkowski may have been the reason why I kept going back to that particular record shop, and kept going back often, but she wasn't the reason why I was interested in jazz in the first place. One Sunday morning quite by chance I happened to see Dave Brubeck on a religious program called *Look Up and Live*. I never quite figured out why Brubeck was on a religious program, but he was, and it introduced me to an entire field of music and my listening habits were never the same. Saul realized he had a good paying customer on his hands and spent a lot of time talking music to me until I got to know him fairly well.

It took me longer to get to know Mary Rutkowski, mainly because every time she spoke to me I blushed. One day after I'd been going into the shop for almost a year, Saul wasn't there.

"Where is he?"

"He's up in Pittsburgh. Buying, I guess. At least that's where he said he was going."

My face must have shown my disappointment.

"Did you want to talk to him about something?"

"No. Nothing special."

"What's the matter? Don't you like to talk to me?"

"Oh, sure!" She was flirting with me, and I loved it. "Maybe he's got a girl up there."

Mary thought the idea was hilarious. "Him? Oh, he thinks about girls a lot, but he's not the type to do anything about it. Actually, I think he's looking around for a location for another store, but don't tell him I said that. Mr. Big Time wants to open another store in a shopping mall."

Her breasts were stirring around inside her red imitation angora sweater. She loved it when I got flustered.

"You live in that big house up on College Hill, don't you?"

"Yeah. How'd you know that?"

"I heard Saul talking about it. He tells his friends about you."

"Why would he do that?"

She leaned close enough that I could smell her face powder. "I'll tell you if you promise not to tell him I told you."

"Okay."

"He's got the idea that he can get you to get your father to invest some money in his new store. You know what I mean?"

I didn't, to be perfectly honest. Or rather, that close to Mary Rutkowski, I didn't care. She smelled sweet and sticky. It was wonderful.

We talked often after that day, and I was flattered that she was friendly to me.

"Did you see we got the new Clifford Brown?"

From her position behind the counter, she directed me down the aisle with her finger, telling me when to stop, then motioned me back to her with the same finger. She slit the seal with her ruby-red nail to play it for me. Actually it was a safe bet on her part because she knew I'd buy the record regardless, but it gave me the excuse to stand beside her at the counter to listen.

"Did Saul say anything to you about your father yet?"

I shook my head. She shrugged.

"He will. Saul says your father has a lot of money."

"I guess."

She smiled. "I'd like to meet him."

I was puzzled. She batted her eyes.

"He sounds like an interesting man."

"He's an accountant."

"That's okay. Maybe I could get him interested in jazz, too." She tossed back her head and laughed. Saul stuck his head out of the back room to see what was so funny.

I was very naïve. I thought she was serious about talking to my father about music; I was about to tell her what kind of music he already liked when a customer came in and she went to help them. The fact was my father even had a phonograph of his own, or one that he used all the time—an old portable of mine that he had set up in the dining room. He had fallen in love with the music from some of the current Broadway shows, and he bought and played the soundtrack albums to pep himself up. For a while he favored Gwen Verdon singing "Steam Heat," then it was Eddie Foy Jr. with "Think of the Time I Save." The family listened to "There once was a man who loved a woman, she was the one he gave his kingdom for. . ." until we were sick of it.

The old portable was good enough for his show tunes. But when he purchased an expensive set of talking records about taxes that came in its own leather slipcase, Father decided he needed a better outfit. I thought there was only one man to ask for advice.

"What, your father wants to buy a hi-fi?" Saul's hands were sweating. "Tell you what. Why don't you bring him into the shop sometime? Let me talk to him, get to know him. I can get him a real good deal on anything he wants. I'll give him the personal touch."

Standing behind him at the register, Mary Rutkowski rolled her eyes.

I explained that my father's office was in Pittsburgh and that he was hardly ever around during the day. Saul was disappointed.

"Well, I can get him a good deal on something. Just try to bring him around, okay?"

Mary Rutkowski snapped her gum and grinned like she sat on a wet spot.

A week later, Saul told me he had picked up a phonograph my father would like, a small table model in a wood cabinet with a dependable turntable. He said he'd keep it in the back until Father had a chance to come down and take a look at it—"No hurry, no hurry." I thanked him and told Father about it that evening, but Father never mentioned it again so I figured he wasn't interested. Weeks, months, passed; it was almost Christmas before Father brought up the subject of the phonograph again.

"They had one down at the store for you, but I don't know if it's still there or not. You didn't say anything about it."

"Why don't you call your friend down there and find out," Father said, finishing his coffee. "We need a little music around here for the holidays."

I called the store and spoke to Mary. She said Saul was out at a party and that she was going crazy with all the customers. "We've still got your hi-fi set if you want it. Saul wouldn't think of selling it to anybody else. I got to go."

Father rubbed his hands together. "Good, good. We can pick out a couple of Christmas albums while we're at it." He stood up from the table and sang his latest anthem from *Damn Yankees*, "A man doesn't know what he has until he loses it. . . ."

I thought of Mary Rutkowski and groaned. I could see Father making a fool out of himself in front of her, talking to her about his silly show tunes. My only hope was that he wouldn't come inside with me.

We drove downtown without talking; I was unaccustomed to going places alone with him, and under the best of circumstances we rarely had anything to say to each other. It was raining, after snowing earlier, and the streets had turned to slush. The Christmas decorations sagged on the wires across Seventh Avenue, heavy with ice; the town's one Salvation Army Santa Claus, huddled in the doorway of Murphy's Five & Ten, had given up ringing his bell. Luck seemed to be with me. The stores were crowded and there weren't any parking places close to the record store. It was Father's idea that I run in and pick up the phonograph while he circled the block.

Mary Rutkowski had given up trying to wait on all the people in the store. In response to the last-minute rush, she had slowed down to a crawl. She leaned against the cash register with bored, sleepy eyes.

"Did Saul get back?"

"You might call it that. He's smashed."

"What about the phonograph?"

"They're both in the back room. Why don't you go on back? Is that all, ma'am?"

I threaded my way through the customers flipping through the record bins and looked through the curtains at the rear of the store. Saul wasn't there. I started back toward the counter when I noticed the side door was ajar. I thought I heard crying. I opened it far enough to stick in my head. Saul was sitting on the landing of the stairs to the basement, under the light of a single bare bulb. A bottle of Old Crow sat between his feet, almost empty. He held his face in his hands to brace his sobs. He looked at me over his shoulder but didn't appear to recognize me.

"It was supposed to be a party, you know? You're supposed to have a little fun at Christmastime, you know?"

"I . . . I came down to pick up the phonograph. If you'll tell me where . . ."

"I don't know why people always have to spoil other people's fun. It was a Christmas party, you know? People always do crazy things at Christmas parties. . . ."

I started to ask him about the set again, but it was hopeless. I stepped back into the store and looked up toward Mary Rutkowski. She was leaning across the counter talking to my father. I was ashamed of him; I thought he looked silly. His dark blue topcoat without a suit underneath hung on him loose and shabby, and his tall-crowned hat, the rancher's Stetson of which he was so proud, seemed to perch clownish on his head. Saul came up the steps behind me, his face puffy and damp.

"You want your phonograph, right?"

I nodded, totally ruined. Mary Rutkowski was leading Father toward us, a big smile on her face, the bounce once more in her step. I was sure she was laughing at Father, laughing at me.

"I told you I'd get you a good set, and I got you a good set. Real good. You just bring it back if your dad doesn't like it. Old Saul's good on his word. Mary, what does this guy want, can't you see I'm busy?"

"You dumb—" She left it unfinished and smiled knowingly at Father as if they shared a joke. "Saul, this is his father."

It took a couple of seconds to sink in.

"His father. Your father. You mean you're—" Saul patted his own chest and belly a couple of times as if to make sure he was still there. Then he giggled. "Well, I'm very pleased to meet you. You know how it is with us businessmen. That time of year. We all have to blow out once in a while, right? I'll bet you've had some doozies in your time, right? Mary, get the phonograph, will you, take it up front."

Mary Rutkowski looked toward the cash register, at the several people waiting to pay, then shrugged and headed for the storeroom.

"I'll help you," Father said.

"He's sick." She smiled.

Father nodded and followed her down the aisle. They came back in a couple of minutes chatting to each other, Father carrying the packing case. I went over and took it from him. Saul was leaning against a bin of polka records, running his hand back and forth over the top of his shiny head as if trying to polish it. Father and I followed Mary to the front of the store, Saul trailing a little way behind as he tried to think.

"Thanks for all your help," Father said to Mary Rutkowski once she was behind the counter. "You're very kind. Will you accept a check?"

"I think I can trust you."

They smiled to each other and Mary handed him a pen. By the time my father signed it, Saul had somewhat collected himself.

"You know, it's a real privilege, uh, to meet you. Everybody knows you in this town. I mean, knows who you are, even though I never met you before, I mean, here I am now. . . . What I mean is, there's a couple of things I'd like to talk to you about sometime. You know, business things. Businessman to businessman, ha ha."

Father turned and regarded him for a few long seconds, then tore the check from the book and handed it to Mary.

"I can't imagine a thing in the world that you and I would have to discuss," Father said to Saul, but looking at Mary.

"I can't imagine it, either," Mary Rutkowski said. She and Father seemed to have some understanding between them, knowledge that was somehow beyond me. A different world. Father nodded to her.

"My dear, I hope you have a very nice Christmas. It's been a pleasure to meet you."

Mary Rutkowski colored and muttered something in return.

I followed him out the door, carrying the box to the car. As we pulled away, Mary Rutkowski was ringing up the next sale while Saul stood in the doorway of the shop staring after the car. I rode in silence beside my father through the wet, dirty streets, back to our house on the hill.

First Love, First Death

1955

The old man who was known as Uncle Hugh—he wasn't actually my uncle, he must have been my father's uncle—drooped in a wicker chair in his backyard, a plaid robe around his shoulders, a blanket wrapped around his legs. The screen door slammed and his daughter, Betty Jean, came out of the house carrying a tray with glasses of lemonade. A slight breeze had come up during the afternoon, stirring the branches of the maples overhead and the rose-bushes climbing the trellis. Betty Jean put the tray down in front of us and smiled to her father, going over to tuck him in a little tighter. He patted her arm. From her invalid's room on the second floor, Aunt Elda peered down at us through the rusty window screen.

"I'm a lucky man to have a daughter like this," Uncle Hugh said. "Without her, I would've been dead a long time ago."

"Hush, Dad."

"It's the truth."

"That's silly talk about dying. You're too stubborn to do anything you don't want to do."

"You see, DeWitt? Always pepping me up."

Betty Jean straightened the pillows behind his back and kissed the top of his head. She was in her early forties and, though not attractive, had all the healthiness and apparent stamina of a Scottish farm girl. My father, always aware of and attentive to the women around him, picked up her sweater from where it had fallen under the chair and handed it to her. She smiled when their eyes met.

"Don't ever get old, DeWitt," Uncle Hugh said between coughs. "It's not what it's cracked up to be."

"I don't know if I'd mind, if I had an attractive young woman like Betty Jean taking care of me."

The woman blushed. "You men are all alike. What about your own girls? You can't tell me they'd neglect you."

Father smiled at her and walked behind the swing where my sisters and Colleen, my teenage girlfriend, were sitting. He put his hand on Colleen's shoulder.

"What about it, Colleen? Would you take care of an old man like me?"

"Oh sure," the girl giggled. Father seemed thoughtful, sad. He looked at my sisters and smiled benevolently, patted each of their heads.

Mother closed the door to the car, parked in the gravel drive, and came across the yard winding the film in her camera. She stopped once, checking the exposure number in the window, and rejoined us.

"Good, let's take one more, just to make sure."

"You've taken enough pictures, Helen," Father said, at first impatient, then catching himself and turning on his businessman's smile. "Everyone's tired."

"I just want to make sure." Mother pretended to fuss and Father gave up. "I think we should have one more of the Snodgrass girls."

My sisters smiled uneasily. Barbara was starting to wheeze again from her asthma, and Shirley was anxious to get home and call her boyfriend from college. Before any of us noticed, Betty Jean had taken the empty tray and disappeared into the house.

"Where'd she go?" Mother said.

Uncle Hugh laughed. "She never stays around if there's a camera. She's afraid you'll steal her soul. She'll come out again as soon as you're finished."

"That's not true, Dad," Betty Jean said from the kitchen window.

"Then why don't you come out and have your picture taken?"

"I've got a few things to do in her. You go ahead."

We laughed. Undaunted, Mother proceeded to organize the girls on the swing. It was Barbara's idea to include the dog, a border collie that she had fallen in love with the moment we arrived, just as she loved all animals. It was Father's idea to include Colleen.

For years an enlargement of that photograph sat on a bookcase in my father's office in Pittsburgh. After he died, the photograph was moved to the family home, to the wall in the upstairs hallway where it remained for as long as there was any family left, a reminder of a day that needed no reminder. The photograph always seemed a bit irrelevant because it included the image of my girlfriend from my early high school days, my first girlfriend, long gone out of my life. But the photograph stayed because it was the last one ever taken of Barbara.

In the photograph, the three girls sit forever on the metal swing in the backyard of a little town in northwest Pennsylvania, in front of a clump of evergreens. Shirley is in the center, Colleen to the right, Barbara to the left. The dog sits on Shirley's lap, in the middle of the little grouping. All three girls are touching the dog, reaching toward it, but only Colleen is looking at the camera, straight into it, as if questioning the viewer. My sisters both look at the dog. The dog, on the other hand, is looking off to the side, bewildered perhaps by the sudden show of attention and, I suspect, looking for Betty Jean.

The girls are all dressed in the style appropriate for late spring in the mid-1950s—cloth jackets with wide lapels and large shoulder pads. Their hair is long, touching their shoulders at the back of the neck, and bobbed, though Shirley's is held back from her face with a broad ribbon. She looks uneasily at the dog, as if apprehensive of what it might do. Though her face will later flesh out with bearing six children, here her features still carry the attractiveness that we all said reminded us of Ingrid Bergman. Barbara's face is small and heart-shaped. She is wearing a sailor's outfit with a large bow under her chin. She looks tenderly at the dog, lovingly; almost expectant. But her lips are slightly parted, her mouth partially open; she is having trouble breathing, and her eyes are tired.

"I think we better be going," Father said.

The girls relaxed. The dog jumped free, only to circle around behind the swing and come up between Barbara's legs. Father came over and stood beside her, putting his hand on her shoulder.

"There's no need to rush off," Uncle Hugh said. "We don't see you for years at a time."

As predicted, Betty Jean appeared from the back of the house as Mother put her camera in its case. "You just got here."

"I know, but we better be getting back." He nodded toward Barbara. Everyone understood.

Barbara smiled apologetically between the increasingly difficult breaths. Father helped her up and walked with his arm around her to the car. Aunt Elda changed windows in her upstairs sickroom to watch us go. Betty Jean stood in the gravel drive, waving, until we were out of sight.

Barbara sat in the front seat, propped up between Father and Mother. I sat in the back, between Colleen and Shirley. No one spoke for a long time, each with their own thoughts as we watched the rich Pennsylvania farmlands rolling south.

"Now then, I guess we better get on home." Father seemed surprisingly cheerful.

"What about the picnic?" I asked.

"I thought we were going to stop," Mother said. "I made a lunch."

"I know, but Babsie's not feeling good." His voice was close to baby talk as he patted her knee.

"I'll be okay," Barbara said.

"We don't want to do anything that might hurt our Babsie."

It wasn't true. I didn't care at all about Babsie. I wanted to stop at Pymatuning Lake for the picnic so I could be alone with Colleen. After months of dating, with the frantic first kisses on her front porch, we had started the week-by-week progression of feeling each other up. So far we had graduated from tentative hands inside her bra to groping inside each other's underpants. I was desperate to continue my explorations.

"I don't think we should stop if Barbara's not feeling well," Shirley said.

"You just want to get home to call Rusty," I said.

She glared at me and started to say something, then kept quiet.

"How are you feeling, dear?" Mother said.

"I'll be okay," Barbara said. "Must be . . . all this fresh air. I'm not . . . used to it." She tried unsuccessfully to laugh.

"We only want what's best for Babsie."

Father looked proud of himself. Barbara looked broken. Mother looked worried. I didn't care. I sat in the back seat with a lump in my pants, aching to touch Colleen's skin. Shirley kept her eyes out the window.

Pymatuning was an unlovely lake, backed up unnaturally behind a dam and crowded with noisy groups celebrating the Fourth of July a day early. We bumped around the narrow trails for almost an hour looking for an empty table; we finally settled on sitting in the car, dividing the ham salad sandwiches and deviled eggs from the hamper. The ice cubes in the gallon thermos jug had melted, so the milk was cold but watery. After we ate, we sat with the doors open watching another family's softball game across the field. Shirley unrolled the edge of her Dixie cup with her teeth.

As it got dark, Colleen and I took a walk along the water's edge, away from the car. The water was flat, unmoving; it was black against the lighter sky, and seemed to stretch away forever. The evening was smoky from campfires, and there was the smell of gunpowder. Explosions, sparklers, dotted the groves of trees. Dark figures moved among the parked cars.

I tried to kiss her.

"No, don't, they'll see us."

"So what?"

"We can't."

She ran away, back toward the car. I loped after her, pouting, hurt. She ran back to me and took my hand and pulled me along the trail to the car. Mother was washing out the thermos and silverware under a pump. Shirley sat in the car. Father and Barbara stood on a grassy knoll, his arm around her, watching the last trace of daylight disappear from the sky across the water. Colleen ran up to them.

"This is wonderful!" she bubbled. "I've never seen anything like this. Thank you for bringing me along."

"I'm glad you like it, my dear," Father said, not pleased at being interrupted. He squeezed Barbara a little tighter, but she moved away, back toward the car, her hand on her chest to help her breathe. Father looked at Colleen, smiled, and put his arm around her instead.

We rode in darkness back to Beaver Falls, listening to the radio and my sister wheeze. Barbara kept a wad of Kleenex stuffed in her mouth as a kind of filter because she could no longer breathe through her nose. She rested her head on Mother's shoulder. Shirley leaned her head on the window and tried to sleep. I watched her for miles while I worked my fingers underneath the sweater on Colleen's lap, up her skirt to the dampness of her panties.

We had forgotten to leave any lights on in the house. In the darkness the two dogs—a mongrel puppy and a Pekingese—barked noisily behind the glass doors between the sunporch and the den. I opened the door, and there was a frantic scurrying around our legs, even after Mother turned on the hall light.

"Don't jump! Don't jump!" Father kept repeating, kneeing one after the other of the leaping dogs. The dogs didn't begin to settle down until Barbara knelt and gathered each of the wiggling animals into her arms.

Colleen went upstairs to the bathroom and the family spread throughout the house. I went upstairs on the pretense of getting a sweater and ambushed Colleen on her way back down. In the dark hallway I grabbed her breast with one hand and her crotch with the other, forcing her against the doorjamb of my room. She giggled and slipped away, skipping down the stairs. I followed a few minutes later. While Father got ready to drive Colleen home, I wandered out into the kitchen, still flushed with my boldness. Barbara was leaning on the back of the kitchen stool, watching the dogs eat their supper, while she fought for her breath. She looked at me over the tops of her tear-shaped glasses and tried to smile. And I hated her. I hated her always being sick, always having something wrong with her, spoiling the family's fun. I wished she'd go up to bed and get out of everyone's way. I wished she'd go away.

Father drove Colleen and me to her family's house in the lower end of town. He parked directly in front of her porch, and there was nothing to do but say good night without even a kiss. She ran through the leafy shadows of the streetlight, up the walk and into the small frame house. We rode in silence through the streets of Beaver Falls, my balls aching, back to College Hill. At close to eleven o'clock, every light was still on in the house. Barbara was in her bedroom, hunched over the small burning mound of Green Mountain Asthma Cure, breathing the smoke that slowly cast a haze through the upstairs of the house. Shirley's boyfriend had arrived, and they left for his parents' home in Erie.

It was a little after five o'clock in the morning when something called me from sleep and I heard something heavy fall in Barbara's room. I ran next door. She was lying on the floor between the bed and her nightstand, her arms and legs working awkwardly to right herself. I reached for her, and she reached for me. She saw me but she couldn't speak.

"Do you want Mother? Do you want me to get Mother?"

I think she nodded. I woke my parents but Barbara had lost consciousness by the time we returned. We struggled to get her back into bed. I lifted her shoulders and scooted backward across the sheet, dragging her, her head flopping against my knees. While Father and I watched, Mother sat on the edge of the bed rubbing the back of Barbara's neck, saying, "I think she's getting warmer, I think she's getting warm again." Finally she called the doctor.

"Maybe you should come over, she doesn't look too good . . ." she said on the phone.

Mother returned to rubbing my sister's neck, cooing to her, while we waited for the doctor. Dr. Boyd was casual when he came to the house almost a half hour later—I remember watching him get out of his car parked across the street, stretch, study the sky with the first rays of sunlight over the valley's hills, before getting his bag from the back seat—until he came upstairs and took one look at the girl, then worked frantically putting injections into her arm. But she was dead. He turned, bewildered, to Father, his boyhood friend, and Mother, unable to understand why they hadn't told him on the phone how serious it was. Father stood in the hallway, still dressed only in his undershirt and shorts, moaning softly in little breaths, looking at me. Mother repeated to no one in particular, "But her neck was getting warmer where I rubbed it. I thought I could feel it getting warmer."

Within the hour, the men from J. Orville Scott Funeral Home came to take her away. They put my sister in a large velvet bag and carried her through the house. For once the dogs behind the glass doors to the den stood perfectly silent. I only began to realize Barbara was gone when I wanted to tell her what all had happened that morning, and she wasn't there.

Ever Seen a Purple Cow

"Blood," Mother says, offering the red liquid to the light. She stands framed in the doorway to the kitchen.

"Blood doesn't usually fizzle," I say.

She lowers the glass and looks at it. "That's true," she smiles, coming into the room and taking a seat at the dining room table. "But you never know. Actually, it's cranberry juice. Or cranapple. I can't remember. Whichever, it's very good." She takes a swallow to show me.

I recognize where this is going—it seems like a kind of game, her endless attempts to fix me something to eat or get me something to drink; I try to believe it's not just to annoy me, or worse, control me; I try to believe that it's only an attempt to get some attention, to be useful the only way she knows how—but I signal I don't want to play and keep my attention on my camera.

In the luminous world of the viewfinder, what I'm focused on at the moment is a purple cow. As I frame the image, my mind is reciting in a singsong:

> *I never saw a purple cow,*
> *I never hope to see one;*
> *But I can tell you anyhow,*
> *I'd rather see than be one.*

In truth, it's probably a bull—Ferdinand, more than likely, because of the flower sticking out of its mouth. The small figure covered in purple felt sits on the mantel, pop-eyed, a contented, friendly silly smirk on its face. It is one of those small figures with its neck hinged and balanced so the head will bob up and down as it rides on the back ledge of a car for the amusement of passersby. What it is doing on the mantel in my mother's dining room, heaven only knows. Whatever, it has been sitting there for so long that there is a delicate network of cobwebs between its snout and its hooves.

There are other items across the mantel besides the purple cow. Or bull, as the case may be. A large glass vase with an arrangement of synthetic flowers; a studio portrait of my father, taken a few years before he died; a portrait of my mother that I took a few years earlier while photographing the house; a study of her hands that I did at the same time (I'm amazed that she not only displays the photos I took of her, she had them framed as well); a totem pole made of empty spools of thread, the faces drawn with crayons; a stylized figure of the stalking black panther; a studio portrait of my sister Barbara before she died—the parade seems endless. I'm not sure where to begin; the possibilities of arrangements seem endless. I sigh and tilt the camera slightly upward on the tripod, setting the edge of the mantel as the baseline. Within the limits of the frame on the ground glass, the march of knickknacks appears to make a little more sense. But not much.

"Do you want this?" I take my eye away from the viewfinder and turn around. Mother sits at the dining room table flipping through an old *Esquire* magazine with a picture of Truman Capote on the cover. She holds it up for me to see.

"No, thanks. I have a subscription."

Mother looks at me and smiles, not hearing a word I say, or if she does, pretending that she doesn't. I repeat it again, louder. She smiles and nods, informed.

I put my eye back to the viewfinder of the Rollei. There seems to be some relation of this line of figures and photographs on the mantel, but I don't yet see what it is. I try moving the tripod forward but bump into a chair. That isn't going to work. I replace the normal 80mm lens with the 150mm. Now the head of the purple cow fills the frame. That isn't it, either.

"Do you want one of these?"

Now Mother is looking through a picture calendar of the historic attractions of Beaver County.

"I don't think I have much use for it."

"It's pretty interesting."

"Hmm." I raise the tripod, trying for a new angle.

"This is the county where you were born and raised."

"You're telling me."

"Hmm, hmm, hmm."

I look back at her. "What's 'Hmm, hmm, hmm' supposed to mean?"

"Oh, just 'Hmm, hmm, hmm.'" She feigns interest in a drawing of a log cabin. Then she looks at me and smiles.

I go back to the little world inside the magic box. There is something interesting going on between a picture of my dead sister, the black panther, and what appears to be an Easter bunny made out of a shoebox. But the Easter bunny is looking the wrong direction, sending the viewers' interest outside of the frame rather than tightening the composition. And what's the Easter bunny doing in the image anyway?

"Do you see much of Carol?"

My estranged wife. I wondered when the subject would come up. There are snapshots of her all over the house. I don't know if they are always here, or trotted out on the occasion of my visit. The thing is, Mother doesn't even like Carol, never did. I don't look up from the camera.

"Yeah, her apartment's just a couple of blocks away from mine. We're still very good friends."

"That's nice."

"There's no reason why we shouldn't be."

"No reason at all."

"We started out as friends, and we parted as friends."

She doesn't say anything. Tucked in a rear corner of the mantel is a tall glass cylinder, five or six inches in diameter, into which my mother has placed a pewter-like statue of a Viking, complete with spear, shield, and helmet with horns. Why? More than likely simply because she could, she discovered that the statue would fit, and why not? It's an interesting combination of confinement and silliness and rage, as if the poor guy is trapped inside a time capsule. But the glass is colored so the image is a bit murky, and in the foreground there's a black giraffe with a knobby neck that can be wrenched into different positions blocking the Viking's face. The only way to get around the giraffe is to move it, and that offends the integrity of the image, the sense that this is the world as the photographer found it. I lift away from the camera, stretch, yawn, rub my shoulders, look out the window. Then I put my eye back to the little world of the viewfinder. I have a black giraffe and a purple cow. It's a start.

"Do you need a pair of pliers?"

"Why would I need a pair of pliers?"

"I don't know. I thought you just might."

I look over at her. She has laid six pairs of pliers on the edge of the table: three pairs of regular pliers, one of which is covered with rust; a pair of needle-nose pliers; a pair of monkey grips; a pair of locking pliers—as well as a device for opening wide-mouthed bottles. Where did they all come from?

"I have these," she says, folding her hands proudly across her tummy. "And I should have a couple more somewhere in the basement."

"If I ever need a pair of pliers, I guarantee you'll be the first person I ask."

She nods, happy.

A slight shift of the camera, and the image is in front of me on the ground glass, an ensemble of elements at the curve of the mantel. Interesting that I didn't see it before. There is a desk calendar in the shape of a flattened globe of the earth with the date fifteen frozen in time—no way to tell which month; a small stylized caricature of a child wearing a pirate's hat; the Viking enraged in his glass cylinder; the tall black giraffe with its knobby neck drawing the eye back into the composition; of course, the anomaly of the purple cow or maybe Ferdinand the Bull; and anchoring the right-hand side of the image, looking back at the other elements, a photograph of me in a hard hat during the time I was a construction inspector on high-rise buildings in San Francisco.

Little wonder I didn't see the composition before, now that I think about it. What does the juxtaposition of these elements in the image say about that young man in the photograph? More to the point, what does it say about the feelings toward that young man of the woman, my mother, who put these knickknacks in this arrangement? But no matter, there is something deeply gratifying, almost a kind of elation, when these possible elements of a composition click into place within the frame, are locked into time as a new entity.

"Money, business, and sex. Those are the three things that are most liable to ruin a marriage. Also, just plain sleeping arrangements, if you can believe it. One person likes it warm and the other one likes it cold."

Mother is looking through another magazine. I can't tell if her words of wisdom come from there or from her own experience. I consider throwing a pair of pliers at her, on general principle. Instead, I take out my light meter and pan over the scene.

"What's one and a half times forty-five seconds?"

Mother hunts around on the table for some scratch paper and a pen, and begins to figure out the exposure. I check the composition one last time.

"A minute, seven and a half—make it eight seconds."

I nod, decide to make it a minute twenty, and wait until the second hand on my watch comes around to twelve. I press the cable release and nothing happens. I mutter an oath to the Virgin of Silver Halides, advance the film to where it was supposed to be, and wait for the second hand again.

"Is it going now?" Mother whispers.

"Not yet. In a few more seconds."

The second hand hits twelve. I open the shutter for the time exposure.

"Now?"

"Even as we speak."

She shrugs down into her shoulders, accenting her efforts to be quiet. It is a little ritual we have worked out over the years of my photographing in the house. I take a chair and we sit silent in the morning like witnesses to a sacred rite. When the exposure is finished, I crank the shutter and advance the film for a second shot, just in case. She begins to whistle a song under her breath, tapping her hand in time on the table.

"Shh." I put a finger to my lips.

"Shh!" She puts a matching finger to her lips, and shrinks again into her shoulders.

As I close the shutter and wind the film, she whispers, "Is it okay to move now?"

"Yes, it's okay."

She nods but doesn't move.

I lower the tripod to a more reasonable height and pan slowly around the room. Faces of movie stars on the covers of magazines lie in piles along the baseboard; parts of hunting dogs are crumpled in the design of a blanket on the overstuffed chair, a floating head here, a pair of legs upside down there. Mother thumps the table twice to announce action and gets up and goes out to the sunporch, her legs stiff from sitting even for a few minutes. She returns carrying a new Polaroid camera and a package of film. She spreads the paraphernalia around her place at the table and sits studying the camera. When she notices that I'm watching her, she points the camera at me.

"Look at the birdie. Say cheese."

"Muenster. Brie. Baby Gouda."

The camera goes click without effect.

"You forgot your flash."

"Oh." She wobbles back to the sunporch and returns with a flash bar. As she sits at the table poking at the camera in various places trying to open it, I focus on a pair of her shoes on the floor. With the long lens, the spectator pumps fill the picture frame, a study of angles and curves in black-and-white leather. But by themselves the shoes seem uninteresting, either visually or psychologically, telling nothing of themselves or of their owner.

Mother taps the table to get my attention. She has spread half a dozen of her snapshots beside me. (Where did the pliers go? I have no idea. They are nowhere in sight, gone.) Pictures of my sister's children helping their grandmother around the house. A young girl pulling an old dress out of a box with an expression of amusement and delight; two young girls standing on either side of a stepladder, one of them doing a slight curtsy, while the feet of a third child appear on the rungs; the backside of a boy crawling under a chair. The pictures are off-balance and out of focus and washed out. But what interests me is the casual way they show the incongruity of the clutter around the figures. A pair of brand-new candles titling at crazy angles from the heat of the furnace; a mound of old rags with the orange eyes of a cat shining from the middle; the vacuum cleaner sitting upright in a dining room chair. I look back at the shoes, and replace the long lens with the wide angle. With the broader field of view, a third shoe has mysteriously appeared on the ground glass, pointing back at the other two. Now the image is starting to work. I must have smiled.

"There are a lot of messes for you to photograph around here, aren't there?"

She isn't looking at me. She is looking inside the back of her camera as she puts the film in place.

"I'm not photographing the messes, as you call them. I'm interested in the different tones and textures."

She smiles to herself as if she knows better. She's right, of course. She knows what I'm doing, knows the condition of the house and what it must look like to an outsider. Yet every time I ask her, she never objects to me photographing here, even encourages it. I suspect she's up to something, and I'm not going to let her distract me. I check the composition of the shoes once more in the viewfinder and take the reading with the light meter.

"I'm also interested in the way people live," I say, conceding a little. "The way that the things people collect around them reflect their lives."

"What are you going to call the photographs you take here? Your Mother's House?"

"I was thinking of Godzilla Meets the Clutter Monster."

A poor attempt at humor to defuse the situation. Mother tries to look martyred and long-suffering but somehow it doesn't quite come off. For a moment I feel a kind of empowerment, the superiority of when you think you see through another's motives, thinking I see through her attempt to work the same old games on me—the games my brother had made me aware of—the same tricks I thought she used on me when I was younger to try to control and manipulate me, the techniques she used when I was growing up to win our mother-son skirmishes, just like De said. But there's a more disturbing thought too, one for which I have no telling insights, no pat solutions: suppose it's something else entirely. Suppose her lack of conviction is because she no longer believes in the games, either. Suppose she no longer wishes to play them, either. I have no pat way to deal with that, or its implications. I push such thoughts aside and go ahead with the preparations to take the photograph.

"You wouldn't tell me the truth anyway."

Alarms go off in my psyche. *Zeros at twelve o'clock! Bandits in the sun!* "That's not a nice thing to say to your child." I wonder why I said "child."

"I know you don't tell me the truth about a lot of things. You never have. And I don't think it's fair."

"Fair?" I try to laugh. *Shields up! Phasers on stun!*

"That's right. Fair."

"Mother, I've never lied to you." I know I did right there. *Dive! Dive!*

"Oh, I suppose you think you're protecting me. I know you and your brother keep secrets from me, you always have."

I'm afraid she's referring to my brother's S. S. Gardons poems and the others we tried to keep from her, the descriptions of her as an emotional monster who sucked the life out of her family so she could tend the husks, who kept the house in perpetual chaos so she could reign supreme. No matter that my own understanding of her and the house has changed over the years, I feel that I'm a coconspirator in my brother's condemnations of her, his deceptions. To say nothing of my own.

"Mother, I—" The flash goes off in my face. She grins as she lowers the camera, her eyes twinkling. The mechanism inside the camera whirrs, and the undeveloped print pops out the front as if it sticks out its tongue at me.

"I hope it's a good one," Mother says, holding the print by the corner and waving it in the air. "Aren't these cameras wonderful?"

What happened to her sad-eyed martyrdom of a minute ago? Her incriminations? Now she's as merry as a troll. I have to get out of here, the situation with her is getting out of hand, my head is reeling. I guess at the exposure and reciprocity and release the shutter. When it's done, I collapse the legs of the tripod like gathering the legs of a three-legged stork, sling my accessories bag over my shoulder and head for the stairs, to the safety of my attic room. Mother is studying her picture; she heads me off at the doorway holding up the Polaroid for me to see.

"What do you think?" she says.

The photograph is as off-center and cockeyed as her others; the background is underexposed and fades off into black, while the figure in the foreground is washed out in the flash; the image of the man is jerky as if caught in the act of sinking into himself, or into oblivion, like in a Francis Bacon painting. But the features are still visible—the mouth slightly parted in protest or surprise, the eyes behind the glasses just beginning to close—and it's undeniably me. A disappointing me. I would like to see someone who is sure of himself, strong and capable, a person to be reckoned with, but there's something tentative about this fellow, something that seems, if not lost, at least undiscovered.

Pop! Pop! Pop! For a split second I think, *It's a gun!* I am thinking, *Good God, she's shooting at me!* I wheel around. Mother holds some plastic packing material in her hands, a crinkled transparent sheet with cells of air that she's snapping between her fingers. Then she drops it on the hardwood floor in front of her and begins walking on it, a kind of dance with small shuffling steps. The cells pop like firecrackers thrown under the feet of a Chinese dragon dancer. She looks at me, delighted.

"Isn't it wonderful? They sent it with the medicine for the cat. I'm going to have to see where I can get some more."

She continues her little dance until all the cells are broken. Then she kicks it out of the way and sighs, exhausted though grinning. She rests her weight against the back of an antique carved chair, the back as high and ornate as a throne, her hip cocked in my direction.

"You know, my young son, from the expression on your face right now, you'd think I was having fun just to make you feel bad."

I wonder if it's true. Or am I simply lost on an old battlefield, trying to dig up old corpses that are better left at rest. I look at the figure in the Polaroid as if in a pocket mirror, but this shaky young man in the image has no answers.

"Here, I'll throw it away," Mother says, reaching for it. "Maybe later we can try another."

"No, I think I'll keep it," I say, tucking it away in my shirt. Aware that it may be all I have to go on.

Album III
A Family Is a Funny Thing

They say the firstborn in a family, and particularly a firstborn son, is the most likely to succeed, will be the most intelligent and goal-oriented of its siblings, because of the attention received from the parents, the self-confidence instilled from the unwavering devotion of the mother. Being the last-born, I never liked to think about that theory too much.

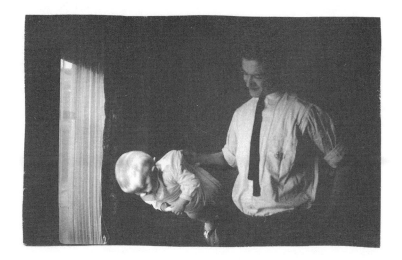

But there's no question that my parents were able to spend a lot of time with my brother. Mother had little else to do at the time, what with a small apartment and her husband working in Pittsburgh. And Father, because he was treading water with his career, devoted his evenings to playing with De. My brother would wait for him every night, standing at the window or in his walker on the porch, shouting "Big De! Big De!" as Father came up the street from the train station.

Two stories stick in my mind. Once De started to roll off the couch. Father was too far away across the room to stop the baby, but he leapt and got his hands under De before he struck the floor. The baby cooed as if he thought it was just another game.

The other story concerns De when he was a little older, able to walk. Father would grab him by the knees and hold him stiff-legged in the air. The baby would wave his arms joyfully over his head, almost touching the ceiling, as Father carried him triumphant from room to room to my mother's applause.

For Helen and DeWitt, 1928 was a special year. They returned to Beaver Falls after living a year on the other side of Pittsburgh, in Wilkinsburg. It was the year DeWitt got out of cost accounting and got a position with a respected CPA firm. And it was the year their daughter Barbara Helen was born.

They lived on Eighth Avenue at the time, a block behind the main street in town, in the house of a man named Ad Davidson—on the first floor, with Ad upstairs on the second. It was a solid, sturdy house, though, and almost as good as living by themselves. DeWitt was busier than he had ever been—still commuting to Pittsburgh every day—and he started taking business trips. But the children were the center of his life. Especially now that they had a little girl. His Babsie.

The following photograph was taken by their mother. I've wondered at times who would be in the center if the photo was taken by their father.

Regardless, the little girl knew how to get to her older brother. It was easy: all she had to do was to tell him he was wrong. About anything. She'd take a side on something that she knew wasn't right and insist on arguing about it with him. It never failed to work. It never failed to drive him nuts.

There was a radio program in the mornings where a man sang the praises of Lava soap. Barbara would sit in her rocking chair, her knees tucked under her on the seat, leaning over as far as she dared and singing along as loud as she could. Only she'd turn the lyrics around.

De's nickname for her at the time was Tadpole. "No, Taddy, it's 'Takes the dirt and leaves the skin.'"

"De," she'd growl, "it's 'Takes the skin and leaves the dirt.'"

Then she'd rock back and forth, laughing herself silly as she watched him squirm. It seems there were a number of things about her that could turn him inside out.

De and Barbara had a private world of their own. They played together, slept together, were inseparable; you never saw one without the other. De was apparently never jealous of the attention his father gave to Barbara. Probably because he idolized her just as much. Something they shared. And, besides, he still had the attention of his mother.

The two children were the darlings of the neighborhood. As they got older, they would sit together on the curb in front of the house, singing at the top of their lungs, "Yes, Jesus loves me! Yes, Jesus loves me! The Bible tells me so!" John Garrett from around the corner would come by and said more than once, "God loves 'em, you know he loves 'em."

There was no question that the two children loved each other, too. Though later De didn't seem quite so sure. He recounted in an interview how he once tried to lure his little sister to lean out an attic window to see him in the window below, the idea being that maybe she'd lean so far that she'd fall out. He said he was grateful that somebody happened along and put a stop to it. Amazing, the vagaries of the human heart.

Shirley sort of got lost in the shuffle, both with her parents and with her older brother and sister. De thought she was cute, all right; when he first saw her, he said

her name should be Sugar, not Shirley. And Barbara would mother her when Mother wasn't around. But De and Barbara were a closed society, a world unto themselves. It was a good thing Shirley had her imaginary friend, Bobey-Dobey.

Bobey-Dobey was the ideal friend for a lonely little girl. Bobey-Dobey always wanted to go everywhere and do everything that Shirley did. When things went wrong, Bobey-Dobey took the blame. When Shirley left the house, she could leave Bobey-Dobey in charge of her dolls and nobody would touch them. She sometimes insisted that they set a place at the dinner table for Bobey-Dobey. When the big people turned out the lights at night and went away, Bobey-Dobey stayed with Shirley in the dark and sang the same lullabies that Mother did.

Shirley and Bobey-Dobey formed a closed society of their own that lasted until she was in her teens. When I was five or six, I asked Shirley one day if Bobey-Dobey would go outside and play with me. Shirley said Bobey-Dobey didn't want to.

When Shirley was three or four, she was also in love with the man next door. Not

the boy; the man. She would sit on the front lawn for hours and watch him practice his golf swing, wondering why she couldn't see the ball go. They would discuss it at length, her and Bobey-Dobey.

In school, De was a tough act for his sisters to follow. Most of the teachers knew Father, and his father—at least, knew the family. And De lived up to everyone's expectations. He was intelligent and quick; an outstanding student, the kind who pleases teachers. The girls weren't up to his level at all. When it came to school, De was the center of attention, the star.

Barbara and Shirley tried to follow his lead. But he increasingly pulled away from them, particularly if any of his friends were around, almost as if he were ashamed of his sisters. Mother said she thought it was because the other boys teased him about the girls, made fun of them. Or rather, made fun of him on account of them. I suspect it was because he was older, and a boy; an adolescent boy with a lot of adolescent boy things on his mind. Aware, on some level of his mind, that he was having urges and feelings that he wasn't supposed to have.

It is easy to think that I was a mistake. And there's certainly a good chance of that. After all, there was quite an age spread between me and my nearest sibling, Shirley—seven years. And there's no question I disrupted things in the household. The family patterns were firmly established by the time I came along, and no one except my mother was ready for another baby. My arrival seems to have been particularly disturbing to my brother, completely unhinging his known world. Mother told me that up to this time, De got along with the tough kids from families of mill hands by being a class clown, most notably in high school by wearing the tiger mascot suit and sitting on the goalpost crossbar during football games. But my birth gave physical evidence that his mother and father were intimate—worse, in the viewpoint of teen-age boys: his father was screwing his mother—and the kids were merciless in teasing him about it. Not being tough himself, high-strung and nervous by nature—as he *said about himself in an interview later in life, he had always been afraid of hitting someone, drawing back subconsciously at the last second from the physical act, pulling his punches as it were, not from fear of hurting the other person but leaving himself open to be hurt all the more—he ended up coming home in tears. To find me, this little bundle of joy—I'm told I was always the most pleasant of babies, very self-contained, unlike the other three; at the youngest age able to entertain myself for hours—happy and gurgling and cradled in his mother's arms. Who wouldn't resent a younger brother like that?*

I'm told my brother never wanted to touch me, avoided me like a disease. Wanted as little to do with me as possible. In a videotaped interview later in his life, he described one of his few memories of me as a baby:

I know I made one blunder at one point, I knew that if I had, if he was in the baby buggy—and I was rolling him back and forth and he was crying and fussing and carrying on a little bit—if I tipped him a little bit, ah . . . he would stop crying and laugh, he would find that funny. And so, even though my mother had told me not to do that, I, I would do that. And one day he slipped and slid out of there onto the floor. And I thought, Jesus, I, I may have damaged him, he could have hurt his head and, you know, I don't know that fontanel was still . . . was closed at that point completely. And I, I get to wondering, was I trying to get rid of him? Like apparently in some ways I was trying to get rid of my sister at one point . . .

The girls were unexceptional. They were not particularly intelligent. They were not particularly pretty. Each showed some talent when they were younger—Barbara in music; Shirley in drawing—but it didn't last, for whatever reasons, beyond high school. They were pleasant. Average. Common. No one, I think, ever turned around to get a second look at either of them after they walked by. No one, I think, would have given much to be with either of them. They were ordinary, like most people.

Except, apparently, to the males in my family. Speaking just for me, I thought my sisters the most attractive things on the face of the earth. I spent a lot of time growing up trying to see my sisters naked. Early mornings as they got ready for school or work, I would creep up the stairs to catch a glimpse of them in their bedrooms through the balustrades of the railing on the third floor. Or I would man the keyhole in my room to see them go up and down the stairs in their bras and panties. I particularly lucked out one morning when, quite by accident, one of my sisters opened the bathroom door and I saw my brother's future wife reflected in a mirror as she stepped from the tub—O Blond Transcendence!

I don't know what dreams Barbara and Shirley had, the way they hoped their lives would turn out. But whatever dreams they had, again like most people, I don't think they got them.

De married the Queen of the May. He met Lila before he went into the service, when he started at Geneva, and she lived with us a couple of winters while he was gone because she hated the dorms. When he came back, they got married and stayed a year at the house while they both finished at Geneva, where she was May Queen. But then De transferred to the University of Iowa for graduate work and they moved away.

For a while he wanted to be a timpanist, but there were only half a dozen jobs available in the country, and they were taken for the most part for the next fifty years. For a while he wanted to be a cellist, but the middle twenties was a little late to start. For a while he wanted to be a choral director, but I don't know what happened to that. For a while he wanted to be a playwright, but at the University of Iowa workshops they told him his stuff was lousy. At someone's suggestion, as a last resort, he tried poetry.

Meanwhile, Lila looked on bewildered. They had a daughter—Cynthia;

Cindy—but the marriage was slipping. He turned out to be a good poet, better than good. But he discovered things about himself in writing that were not always easy to live with. Such as that he no longer considered his wife a queen. He also determined that he wasn't all that crazy about his family, either.

It was a house of fencing foils and tennis rackets; symphonies on the radio and phonograph; stacks of sheet music, kettledrums in the living room and a cello in the corner; a baby grand piano on the sunporch; marionette theaters and maquettes for stage productions. Because I grew up mainly around my sisters, I always assumed that they were interested in these things. And in most cases they were—the kettledrums, not so much—but it was generally De who introduced them to the house.

Both girls were at home now, waiting, though for different reasons. Barbara tried going away from home for one year, to attend Thiel College up in Greenville, all of sixty miles away, but she missed home so badly that she was sick all the time. The

Sunday visits of the family every week only seemed to make matters worse. I can still see her standing on the edge of the campus, underneath a tree bare in winter, waving to us until we were out of sight. After that year, she stayed at home, to go to Geneva a block from the house and then to work for Father, and never left home again.

Shirley was a little luckier. She made it through all four years at Thiel and met the guy she eventually married. Rusty was a carefree, self-contented fellow who drove a Chevy panel truck with a sofa in the back and planned to be a swimming and/or driving instructor. First, though, he had to go to the Army for a couple of years, so Shirley filled the time with some postgraduate business courses at Geneva, doing some part-time work for Father, and filling a hope chest with towels.

It started as bronchitis, the year Barbara went to Thiel. Through the years after she came back home, first to finish college at Geneva, then to begin working for her father's firm, it developed into asthma. They knew she had "nerves," as the saying was in those days. They knew that she was shy and retiring. But they kept hoping that it was something else. They took her to specialists in Pittsburgh who covered her back with test patches. The results showed that she was allergic to the dust that filled the world she lived in, the smog from the mills, the hair of the animals she

loved. It was agreed that the doctors must have gotten the patches mixed. The nerve specialist down the valley told them that she should get away from home, take an apartment closer to her job, or move out of the area all together. But that was the catch, of course. Everyone agreed that she was too weak to do anything like that.

Father opened a branch office in Ambridge, closer to Beaver Falls, just for her. Every day Barbara rode the bus there, an hour and a half each way. Father was always pleased to visit and walk in and see her sitting there, but Barbara felt she had been shunted away from the main office in Pittsburgh, wondered why he wanted to get rid of her. Barbara told him that she wanted to become a certified public accountant, but father only smiled. Barbara told him that she wanted to buy a car with her own money, but father laughed and said she didn't need it. Evidently, Barbara didn't argue with him.

I remember her favorite joke came from a Martin and Lewis comedy. After some particularly crazy business, Dean asked his partner, "Are you for real?" Jerry answered, "No, I'm just make-believe."

When Barbara came home from the office in Ambridge, she often brought gifts for the family as if she had been away a long time. For her, I suppose, it was.

Father finally had the realization that she needed to get away for a while. She was missing so many days of work because of her asthma attacks, he hoped a good long rest would set her right. She was to go away for a long trip, two months, stopping in Iowa City to see De, then on out west to Arizona. It was to be her flight from the nest, a chance for a blowout. Shirley had completed her business courses at Geneva and was to start taking over the Ambridge office the following week.

The next-to-the-last time Barbara came home from the office, a Thursday, she brought a brand-new dress for Cindy—De's firstborn, who had spent the summer with us and was going to travel back home to Iowa with Barbara. On Friday, Barbara brought home a big Mexican straw hat for me (how or why she found a sombrero in Ambridge, Pennsylvania, I'll never know). "You see," Mother told me later to help ease my worried mind, "the last person Barbara thought of was you." Somehow that didn't make me feel any better, ease the feeling that I had failed Barbara in some way. Failed to love her enough. As if that might have kept her alive.

There is a psychological theory that sometimes it is necessary for a family to try to drive one of the children insane, or close to it, in order to reaffirm the sanity of the other members. There is a theory that it is sometimes necessary for a family to destroy one of its children, as a sacrifice to strengthen the bonds between the living. In Barbara's case, the doctor's report reads "coronary occlusion." An idle little clot of blood that got hung up in an opening. I once asked Dr. Boyd if it was possible for a person to just die if they didn't have anything to live for. He looked at me like a doctor and walked me to the door. "Forget about things like that. Whatever happened is over now."

But no one in the family ever forgot, each in their own way. Here's my mother close to the end of her life, from a tape recording I made at the time I photographed the house:

Well, I think she had a sort of frustration. She couldn't see that her life ahead was anything but going to have as many frustrations as it had had. Father was no help. He couldn't see the need for help. She was his little girl, and he wanted her always near him. And if she'd have gotten married he'd a been a perfect pest. And . . . he just wasn't any help at all. Now, if she could have gone back to Thiel the second year, and that's what I wanted her to do even though she was having some bronchial trouble . . . and all . . . But he persuaded her to stay home, he said, "Aw, it would be so nice to have you here and all." She didn't always accept that, she didn't always like it. She didn't like to be favored more than the rest of the children, she resented that very much. But she didn't accomplish anything with it. . . . He really wanted her to stay home and be his little girl forever.

The Stories

Part Four

Everybody Loves a Wedding

1956

The living room was full of ferns. There were ferns in front of the fireplace, ferns in front of the bookcases, ferns along the mantel. Some of the ferns were sitting on the floor; others were placed in metal stands of varying heights and spaced around the room. The ferns crept up the walls in a green leafy mass, and the room carried the smell of dark, damp soil.

My older brother, De, sat in an armchair on one side of the doorway, reading a *Saturday Evening Post*; Reverend Stewart, known to my parents as Arch, sat in an armchair on the other side of the doorway. A deliveryman stood in the center of the doorway, holding another fern.

"Where do you want me to put this?"

The man looked at my brother. De looked at the deliveryman, at the plant, and shrank back into his magazine, shaking his head violently. Reverend Stewart made a gesture in the direction of the mountain of ferns.

"Somewhere, I guess, anywhere . . ."

"Sure are a lot of ferns."

The man sat the plant near the windows, keeping a wary eye as if he were afraid something might be hiding among all that foliage. Or that the foliage itself might reach out and grab him, pull him in, absorb him. He backed away carefully.

"There certainly are," Reverend Stewart said.

The deliveryman jumped. "What?"

"A lot of ferns."

"Oh. Yeah."

He looked at De for confirmation, but my brother only shifted deeper into the chair. The deliveryman marveled at the ferns a few more seconds, then left. There had been a steady stream of deliverymen for a day and a half in preparation for the wedding. My job was to make sure the dogs, Buff the terrier and Sam the Pekingese, were shut in the den so they wouldn't run out while the front door was open. I watched the latest deliveryman go down the steps and climb in a green panel truck marked Reader's Florists before releasing the two yapping dogs. While Buff and Sam ran through the downstairs to see what had been added to the forest of ferns, I went up to the second floor.

Shirley was in the front bedroom with Mother and Jan. Shirley raised her arm to show me the tear in the gown.

"Well, that's too bad! Too bad! The gown is torn, the wedding's off!" Shirley laughed gaily.

Mother looked at the tear. "Now, hold still a minute. Let's have a look to see how bad it is."

"Oh, it's bad, all right. Bad, bad. It's too bad for the wedding."

Jan, my sister-in-law, held the two sides of the tear together.

"Now, don't worry. That won't be hard to fix at all."

"I knew it wasn't bad," Mother said, then realized her voice was sharper than she meant it to be. "I was just wondering if there is some way to fix it without having to take off the entire dress."

"No, no, can't do that," Shirley said. "Can't take off the entire dress just for that. I guess I'm stuck with it."

Mother was tired. She had ordered the white brocade from New York, along with the same material in blue for the maid of honor, and had made the gowns herself. That the maid of honor was the bride's sister-in-law, not the bride's sister, was too much on everyone's mind. Mother had worked through the night for weeks, completing the gowns, preparing the house. And now that the wedding was almost here, she seemed grateful for Jan's help.

"I'm sure I can sew it the way it is," Jan said. "If you want me to."

"Please," Mother said.

Jan gathered the material together and started to work. Shirley giggled and turned away.

"That tickles!"

Jan grinned at her. "You wouldn't be a little nervous, would you?"

"Who me? Who me?" She laughed and held her arms like the Statue of Liberty, only to snap them down again to her sides as soon as Jan touched her. "I'm afraid you'll stick me."

Father appeared in the doorway, trying to decipher what was going on.

"You don't have to worry," Jan said. "I learned a lot about making last-minute repairs when I did costuming for the theater."

Shirley laughed hysterically. "Did you hear that, Father? She's used to working with costumes. This is a costume, all right, all right."

Jan snipped off the end of the thread. "There."

"You look beautiful," Father said, sad though smiling.

For a moment, the three of them looked at Shirley in silence. I thought Father might cry. Then he drifted away, down the hall. Shirley was uncomfortable but smiling desperately.

"Well, now we'll see if I can go to the bathroom in all this." She rustled out of the room and down the hall, closing the bathroom door behind her. Mother and Jan stood quietly for a while.

"It's hitting Father very hard," Mother said finally, gathering up the needle and thread and scissors. "He can't help wishing it was Barbara. You know, he always said he got this house because of the stairway, so he could walk down it to give his daughters away. And his favorite is gone. It was wrong for him to make Barbara his favorite, but it happened."

"It wasn't fair to Shirley," Jan said.

"I know, I know." Mother wandered out of the room. Jan looked at me and shook her head, and followed her.

Downstairs, the dogs were still trotting back and forth between the rooms, the buff terrier in the lead, with Sam the Pekingese tagging along behind, painting heavily and not just from the exercise, waiting for the other to stop.

"I don't know," Reverend Stewart was saying, "I find modern poetry very hard to understand. It doesn't seem to tell me anything."

"Anything worthwhile requires a certain amount of work," De looked at him mischievously, as if he knew a secret his opponent didn't, smoothing the bottom fringe of his mustache with his finger.

"But is it worthwhile?"

In the dining room, the leaves had been added to the table, and the surface covered with a long white tablecloth for the buffet lunch after the service. Mrs. Stewart, a small gray-haired woman, sat in a straight chair next to where she was told the coffeepot would be, ready to serve. In the kitchen two black women from the caterers, dressed in nurses' whites, were going through the cupboards, sniggling to each other. When they noticed me, they nudged each other and were quiet.

The doorbell rang. By the time I got the dogs into the den, Father and I got to the front door at the same time. Mr. Scott from the funeral home was standing on the front steps.

"I brought the folding chairs, DeWitt," he said in hushed tones. "Where would you like us to put them?"

Behind us the two dogs barked and scratched frantically at the door to the den; Buff's head sprang up occasionally in one of the glass panels as if he were on a trampoline. Father looked around helplessly. Mr. Scott understood and held the screen door open, directing the two men in black gabardine to stack the chairs beside the piano on the sunporch. He was a slight, distinguished man my father's age, with silver hair and pinstripes running the length of his tailored black suit. I had not seen him since my sister's funeral, a year earlier. Prior to that, I had never seen him before in my life.

"I'm leaving you a dozen. Are you sure that's enough?"

"Oh, I think so. We can never thank you enough, Orville. . . ."

Mr. Scott waved him into silence. "DeWitt."

The old friends looked at each other. Something had fallen out of Father; he slumped a little.

"Would you come in for some coffee?"

"No, no, I'm afraid I can't. We have a service in a few hours, you understand." He looked around apologetically. They were unloading the chairs from the back of the hearse. "We really have to be getting back. Business, unfortunately, is good."

Father nodded. Mr. Scott watched his associates for a moment.

"There is one thing, DeWitt. . . ."

"Certainly, Orville, anything. . . ."

Mr. Scott eased past Father and looked in the door from the sunporch to the main part of the house. De and Reverend Stewart stopped their conversation to look at this figure in the hallway dressed in black. Mr. Scott put them instantly at ease with a wave of his hand, made a quick tour of the living room, and returned to the sunporch. He shook his head with admiration.

"Thank you, DeWitt. I heard down at the home that Reader's was doing the room all in ferns. I just had to see it." He drew close to Father. "They do such fine work. So professional. I've considered suggesting something of the sort for my clients, but I wasn't sure how the effect would work. You know how it is, sometimes the best-laid plans . . ."

They nodded knowingly to each other and shook hands. I watched while the hearse pulled away and headed back downtown. Father and I studied the stack of folding chairs. *J. Orville Scott* was stenciled on the back of each one.

"I guess you could start setting them up."

"Where do they go?"

Father didn't hear me. He was looking at the books in the case near the door. Then he wandered into the house, through the hall and upstairs. I decided to distribute the chairs through the rooms.

"But I've always thought that poetry should give the truest insight into a man's soul," Reverend Stewart said. He was a tall, thin man, well over six foot three, with a firm though pleasant face. His long legs spilled out of the overstuffed chair. He was the director of missions for the United Presbyterian Church, and an old friend of my mother's from her college days. He and his wife were the only people who had ever come to dinner at our house, and that only happened once.

De was studying him. "Maybe so. But it can also tell you a great deal about the body, too."

"But that's exactly what I mean. Is that a good thing?"

"If body and soul are irreparably joined, at least here on earth as Christian dogma dictates, can there be a difference?" De's eyes twinkled; he thought he had him.

Reverend Stewart bowed from where he was sitting. "Very good, very good." Like he was commenting on a well-played ball in tennis.

"De!" Jan's voice called from upstairs. He motioned an *Excuse me* to Reverend Stewart and went to the foot of the stairs. Jan was squatting down at the top of the stairs, as if to be closer to him. She was wearing her blue brocade gown and veil. She cocked her head affectionately.

"Do you like it?"

"I can't really see it."

She stood up and twirled around a couple of times. All I could see from where I stood were her ankles and her blue high-heeled shoes, making a small circle. She had been a dancer once, and still moved like one. When she squatted down again, I moved so I could see her face. She looked pleased with herself about something. That seemed to bother De.

"Isn't it fun?" she stage-whispered.

"It's bizarre."

"She made these dresses herself!" Her eyes grew large. The more enthusiastic and appreciative she became, the more pain showed on my brother's face.

"Are you doing okay?"

"Oh. Well." He stuck his hands in his pockets and looked around helplessly. "How are you?"

She smiled warmly. "I just wanted to show you the gown and say hello."

"Oh."

She smiled again, though she looked puzzled by his mood. Then she disappeared beyond the balustrade on the second floor. De stood there for a while, staring up to where she had been, at the stained-glass window at the top of the stairs, the castle on the distant slope of a valley. Then he shuffled back into the living room, a new spring to his step, as if he had a new purpose in life. He raised a finger to get the reverend's attention.

> When as in silk my Julia goes,
> Then, then (me thinks) how sweetly flows
> That liquefaction of her clothes.

"Herrick. Not bad for a clergyman, huh?"

Reverend Stewart pulled a face and added:

> Next, when I cast mine eyes and see
> That brave Vibration each way free;
> O how that glittering taketh me!

De whooped and pounded his leg. "Oh no, oh no, oh no!"

Buff trotted into the room, wondering what all the commotion was about. Sam the Pekingese came along behind him, the tip of his tongue sticking out. When the Peke was reasonably sure that his companion was going to stand still for a moment, he hopped up on his back and started working his hindquarters. Buff snapped at him and trotted off toward the dining room, Sam in pursuit.

I looked up the stairs. Mother was coming down backward on her hands and knees, unrolling a large bolt of white cloth over the stair runner and pinning it in place. Father stood at the top, watching her descend.

"Mother! What are you doing?" De leapt out of his chair and ran up the stairs to meet her.

"I just wanted to cover this so Shirley's gown wouldn't drag and get dirty."

"You can't do that!"

"Who says I can't?"

"I mean you shouldn't. You shouldn't have to do that. There's other things for you to do. You should get yourself ready for the service."

She was halfway down the steps at this point. De tried to reach around her to take the bolt of cloth away, but she cuffed him playfully on the wrist. De was startled.

"You can't tell her a thing," Reverend Stewart said, watching the proceedings from his chair near the doorway to the living room. "I learned that a long time ago. Her husband learned it, too. Right, DeWitt?" he called upstairs.

Father stared dumbly from the top of the stairs, looking at something far away. Reverend Stewart looked at Mother affectionately as she knelt at the foot of the stairs. Then he looked at me.

"One time, your mother there decided she wanted to ride back with us from a school play. Remember, Helen?"

Mother had made the corner at the bottom of the stairs and was working her way across the hall and into the living room, presenting Arch Stewart and her youngest son with her backside in her off-white A-line skirt as she scuttled along. As she passed, she looked up at the man and smiled at him or the memory or both. Buff and Sam followed her, trailing along the white cloth, wondering what Mother was doing down at their level.

"There was a fellow named Bryce and me and Helen. She made up her mind that she was going to come with us in the car, and nothing could stop her."

"And I heard about it afterward," Mother said.

The Reverend looked surprised. "From who? The school?"

"My father. He gave me the dickens for doing that."

We watched Mother crawl across the living room floor. Sam was now trying to mount Buff as they followed along.

"This is insane," De hissed to no one in particular and went out through the sunporch to stand on the front steps. I was sixteen; this was my family; I didn't know what he was talking about.

Reverend Stewart was sitting sideways in the overstuffed chair; he had pulled his left leg up and rested it against the inside of the chubby arm of the chair. Mother had turned around and was now pushing the remains of the bolt of cloth toward the fireplace in the living room where the service would take place. Reverend Stewart peered over his knee as he studied Mother's bottom wiggling across the floor.

"I didn't know you got into trouble for that, Helen."

"There are a couple of things you don't know about me, Arch. Oh yes, Dad gave me the dickens. My sister, Flee, was always out riding around with some fellow and Dad never said a word, but I did it once and, well . . ."

"I'm sorry to hear that."

Mother finished unrolling the bolt and got to her feet. She was as gay as a schoolgirl again. "You needn't be. I'm actually very proud of it. It was a very cold night and I had to ride in the middle. We had a delightful time. And when Dad asked me about it, I told him, 'Well, at least one of them had to drive.'"

Reverend Stewart burst out laughing, his large roar shattering the quiet of the house.

Mother smoothed her dress coyly. "Now, if somebody would keep an eye on the dogs so they don't get into trouble, I'll go get ready."

"I'll be glad to, Helen." As Mother left the room, Reverend Stewart raised his hand and for the briefest moment their fingertips touched as she passed.

Buff was sniffing at the ferns. Sam sat nearby, his hind legs folded to one side beneath him. He was still panting. He looked over at the Reverend's leg stretched out from the chair, at the large shoe resting on its heel.

"Hello, puppy," Reverend Stewart said.

Sam looked at him, looked at Buff. He got up, sniffed the shoe a couple of times, and mounted the Reverend's ankle. Reverend Stewart quickly snapped his leg back, but Sam held on.

"Oh dear," Mother said, starting up the stairs. "I guess we better put them down in the cellar."

Reverend Stewart finally kicked his leg free. Sam seemed satisfied and waddled off. Reverend Stewart looked disconsolately at his sock. Mother came back downstairs and she and I each grabbed a dog and ran them through the house, pushing them through the cellar door. As I closed it, Buff looked at me as if he were condemned. Sam looked at Buff, panting.

In the kitchen, the two black women tried to fill the large coffee urn with water from the tap, but it wouldn't fit under the faucet. They began to giggle. They tried to fill it with individual cups of water but collapsed with laughter.

"What we need is a bucket," the one said loudly.

"Or a hose." She had to lean on her friend for support.

"Well, it is a wedding," said the first, and they both nearly fell over.

Mother looked perplexed. In the dining room, Mrs. Stewart was still sitting at her place at the end of the table, still waiting to serve.

"Can I get you something?" Mother said.

"I'm afraid we don't have anything to give you yet," the woman said, a born missionary. "But we should have something pretty soon."

Mother walked into the hallway and spoke loud enough for everyone to hear.

"I think we should have a dress rehearsal, to see how everything works."

Shirley and Jan leaned over the railing on the second floor.

"Isn't that bad luck?" Shirley said. "For everyone to see me in my gown?"

"Everybody's seen you in it anyway."

"You're right!" Shirley exploded in laughter. "Maybe we better call the whole thing off!"

Father looked at her benignly. Reverend Stewart came out of the living room, still favoring his raped ankle.

"I think that would be a fine idea, Helen."

Reverend Stewart put his arm around her shoulders. For a second I thought she might rest her head on his chest, but she didn't.

"Okay then, let's just try coming down the steps."

Father seemed to come alive. "We'll need some music."

Reverend Stewart, Mother, and I started to hum the wedding march. Mrs. Stewart joined in from the dining room; the caterer ladies peered in from the kitchen, stifling their giggles. Father and Shirley started slowly down the stairs, at first getting their timing mixed up so they were bobbing up and down on different steps. Then they found the rhythm. Shirley beamed at Father; Father patted her hand on his arm. Jan followed behind looking stately.

Halfway down, Shirley and Father started rocking back and forth against each other like a high school cheering section, bumping in time to the music. By the time they got to the bottom of the steps, Shirley was flouncing her gown left and right and Father was giving little kick steps like a cakewalk. De came in the front door and stood dumbfounded.

Reverend Stewart ran ahead so that he'd be waiting for them in front of the fireplace. When everyone was in position, Father bowed, Shirley curtsied, and everyone except De applauded. Jan went over and kissed De on the lips. He did not look happy.

"As long as we've gone this far," Shirley said, "it's too bad we just can't go ahead and have the wedding now."

"There's the little matter of a groom," Reverend Stewart said.

Shirley laughed. "Oh, he doesn't count."

"I'm not so sure he'd feel that way about it."

"He'd go along with anything, if I said it."

Father grasped Shirley's shoulders in his two hands.

"Now, before I forget it, I want to make sure that you'll call me tonight, wherever you stop."

Shirley smiled and started to say something, but De broke in.

"Did you just tell her to call you on her honeymoon?" His face was flushed, his eyes enraged.

Father smiled. "Well, yes. I think that . . ."

"Shirley, if you let him do that to you, I'll never speak to you again!"

"But De, I don't see . . ." Shirley was confused.

Jan said something quietly to her husband. He moved her aside.

"No, I won't be quiet. And don't you talk to me that way, this is none of your business. I mean it, Shirley. Don't let him do that to you. If you call him tonight, I mean it, I'll never speak to you again."

Shirley looked from De to Father. De started toward them, but Jan stepped into his path. He drew up into himself.

"I was just teasing the girl," Father said.

"You were?" Shirley said, obviously hurt. "I would have."

De glared at them across his wife. Then he turned and ran upstairs, Jan following.

Father smiled wanly to all of us around the room. He opened his hands, as if the answer were revealed there. "The boy's upset."

"It's understandable," Reverend Stewart said.

"He's upset!" Shirley laughed. "Why should he be upset? I'm the one who's getting married."

"You look lovely, dear," Mother said, trying to calm her. She got her started toward the stairs.

Out the curved window in the living room I watched a car turn the corner and pull up in front of the house; a load of plump, overdressed women climbed out, looking up at our house, pulling at their skirts and adjusting their hats.

"I think the guests are starting to arrive," I announced.

In the cellar the dogs were barking incessantly. From the kitchen, one of caterer ladies hooted, "They're wedding bells, not wedding balls!" Mother started up the stairs to get ready, but Father let out a groan and his legs buckled. Reverend Stewart grabbed him around the shoulders and steadied him.

"I know, DeWitt, I know. It's hard to lose a daughter."

"Oh, I did, I did." We followed his line of vision to the photograph of my sister Barbara, his favorite, dead one year, sitting among the ferns on the mantel.

Mother came back down the steps and took his hand, leading him.

"Come, dear. We have to get ready."

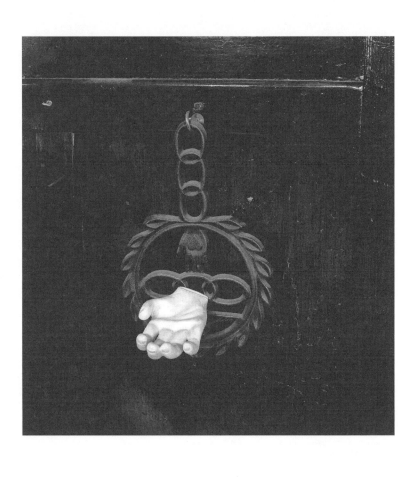

Car Car

You have to be careful what you ask for, you just might get it.

1958

My father never said that I could have a car of my own. It was just that he never said I couldn't.

When I learned to drive at sixteen, I never even thought about having a car of my own. I didn't need it. I had full access to the family car, a four-door Ninety-Eight Oldsmobile, less than a year old. That, and the family credit cards. In the evenings, as soon as Mother returned from picking up Father at the train station, I took over the car, driving up and down the main street of town until midnight; on weekends, I drove the same route all day long. During summer vacation, Mother had to ask me when she could have it to go to the grocery store. Why did I need a car of my own?

Then one day my friend Gus noticed a '31 Model A Ford coupe for sale down at Locke's Service Station, at the foot of College Hill.

"You'll love it," Gus said, stroking his Viking-like beard. "I know you, you'll have to have it."

"I don't need it."

"You'll see."

He was right. One look and I had to have it. The car was close to its original condition, except that the black paint had been replaced with two-tone brown. The owner, a guy who worked part-time at Locke's and full-time at the Armstrong Cork Works across the street, found it in a barn in Enon Valley and used it as his work car. He'd take $100 for it. I dreamt of magnetos and spoke wheels, rumble seats and spring-metal bumpers.

"But why do you need a car?" Father said over the tops of his bifocals. He was sitting at his card table in the dining room, working on someone else's taxes. It was the season for taxes, which meant he didn't have time for resistance.

"So I won't take the family car so much. You always say I take the car too much."

"I don't care if you take the car, but your mother needs it."

"This way I'll have a car of my own. Please, Father?"

"I'm a businessman. And a businessman always wants to know what he'll get in return for the money he invests."

"I won't ask you for a more expensive car."

It was not the type of logic that put my father's mind at ease when he thought of grooming me to take over his accounting firm. He did, however, understand blackmail. He smiled, crossed his legs, and wrote me a check. I met Gus at the back door.

"Just like that?"

"Just like that."

"Doesn't it ever bother you? I mean to get things so easily?"

"No," I said, and meant it. "It's the only way Father and I both feel good. Let's go buy a car."

We climbed in Gus' MG TD and sprinted down the hill. The guy at the service station explained about the spark advance and the hand throttle, and the gymnastics involved to start the engine with the various pedals and levers. I putt-putted my way back up the hill and parked the car proudly in the backyard. The neighbors gathered around.

"It's a real antique."

"We used to have one just like it. Best car we ever had."

"Rumble seat almost closed on us. Could still be in there, ha ha."

Father came out the back door, nodded, smiled, and went back to his work. Gus and I sat idling in the noisy cab, among the smells of gasoline and motor oil and smoldering insulation, talking about all the things we could do with a car like this. Then we turned it off and took my family's Olds out to Wampum to get a pizza.

The Model A lasted several months, its life limited to occasional sorties around the block for curious friends. Meanwhile, I kept up my hours cruising Seventh Avenue in the Olds. The last time I drove the Model A, I inadvertently reenacted a scene from a Mack Sennett comedy when the car stalled as I tried to back it up the steep driveway into the backyard. For a moment I confused the spark with the hand throttle, and Dickie Blackwood and I shot in reverse up the drive and across the yard, through my nieces' sandbox and the garbage cans and my mother's prize rustic fence before we fought it out of gear. After that, I let the car sit where it was.

It sat so long, in fact, the battery went dead. When I called AAA to get a quick charge, the serviceman told me it was the second old car he worked on that afternoon. The first one belonged to an old lady a few blocks from my house, a '39 Ford sedan. She used to drive it to the A&P, and once to California, and then let it sit in her garage for the last couple of years. The man thought I could probably get it for a couple of hundred. I dreamt of chrome headers and Lake pipes, candy-apple paint jobs and custom Naugahyde interiors.

I waited until Father was watching *Gunsmoke*. His happiest time of all.

"But you don't drive the car you've got."

"That's because it isn't safe."

"Why is this other one safer?"

"Because it's newer. Please, Father?"

"Is it a good investment?"

"I really want it."

I had to wait for the next commercial break, but he wrote out the check for $200. Gus was sitting on the lawn. He shook his head, amazed.

"That's quite a racket."

"It's not a racket."

"It'll do until a racket comes along. Let's go get your car."

The sedan turned out better than we'd hoped. There were only thirty-two thousand miles on it; a new battery, an oil change, and it was ready to go. We assumed the car was black, but when I got it home and started working on it with rubbing compound, it turned out to be a rich emerald green. Gus, Twig, Irish, Sonny, and Cobe worked three days to install the new headers and glass-pack mufflers; Killer and Bork painted the wheel rims red and mounted the four new white sidewall tires—paid for with my parents' credit card, of course. I forget who sawed off the floor-mounted gearshift lever ankle high. My job was to snap the flipper-disc hubcaps into place. For weeks the backyard was full of cars, guys working on my car, guys working on their own.

As I walked through the house one Saturday afternoon, wearing my white coveralls, which had yet to see a speck of grease, Father was standing at the back window in the dining room, drinking his coffee. He was watching Cobe-A-Dobe and Bo-Dally trying to hoist an engine from a '56 Chevy hardtop with a winch slung from a tree limb.

"It looks like a used-car lot," he said without rancor.

"They're not all mine."

"It's nice to see your friends working together."

"There's not too many places where they can work on their cars."

Cobe and Bo stopped to look at the bent tree.

"What we really need," I continued, "is a garage to work in. Someplace with a level floor, and good strong beams to hoist from."

"Well, we've talked sometimes about putting a new garage out there in the back corner. I guess we could make it a two-car garage."

"I was wondering if we could make it three? That way we'd have a lot of room, and Gus would have a place to keep his MG in the winter. Please, Father?"

In a couple of weeks, a bulldozer leveled my mother's sunflower patch; concrete mixers poured the ground slab; masons erected scaffolds for the block walls. When it was complete, the garage was bigger and stronger than some of the houses on the block. Gus had his MG parked inside and the engine half stripped down by the time the roof went on. The day after overhead doors were installed and painted, we posed the cars in front of the garage for photographs—Gus' MG without the engine; the Model A without a battery; and the '39 sedan with a broken fuel line. Then we pushed the three cars inside and took the Olds down to Jerry's in West Bridgewater for hamburgers. I dreamt of chrome-finished socket wrenches, timing lights, hydraulic lifts.

Gus rebuilt his engine, repaired my fuel line. I polished the sedan once a week. We rolled open the overhead doors; we closed the doors. We revved our engines until the Funkhausers across the alley complained. We had the best garage, the best place to work on cars in town. And there never seemed to be anything to do.

"What is it this time?" Father said across his roast beef.

"A '32 coupe. Chopped and channeled."

Father had no idea what that meant. "You already have two cars."

"I'm going to sell the Model A."

"Who'd buy a piece of junk like that? It never runs."

"Rusty."

Father didn't say anything. He had only recently decided to take my brother-in-law into his accounting firm.

"He won't give you as much as you paid for it."

"Actually, he gave me fifty dollars more."

"Rusty?"

I nodded. Father didn't know whether to laugh or cry. Beside his chair at the dining room table, Sam the Pekingese sat upright like a furry log. Father carved small pieces of roast beef and dropped them to him. Sam snapped them up in midair with a noisy sucking sound. Each time the dog made the noise, Father looked at him curiously.

"Where is this car?"

"Jamestown."

"Oh, up near Sharon."

"No. Jamestown, New York." I started to explain that Mimms knew a guy who had a friend who heard about . . . Father shook his head, waved his hands.

"How much?"

The next morning, with a check for $700 tucked in the pocket of my jeans, Gus and I took his father's Chevy and headed north, past Erie and into New York State. We found our prize in a small lakefront community, sitting in a patch of tall grass behind a garage that catered to summer people. The coupe had been lowered over the frame, and a section taken out of the cab supports to lower the roof. The original engine had been replaced by a '48 flathead Merc. Someone had painted the car baby blue. We rigged up a tow bar and headed back home, watching our reflection pass in the store windows of the towns along the way, thinking that we must look like a racing team. I dreamt of Isky cams and Moon discs, checkered flags and racing slicks. We almost made it home, too.

It was dusk, on a detour outside of New Castle, less than fifteen miles from Beaver Falls, when the motorcycle fender over the right front wheel of the coupe snapped a brace and wrapped itself around the tire. At first it didn't seem too serious and we worked by the glow of the Chevy's taillights, finally removing the fender altogether. Except that in the process we drained the battery dead in the Chevy. We tried pushing the Chevy with the '32 to get it started—me in the '32, Gus in the Chevy; the towed pushing the towee as it were—but the Chevy wouldn't turn over and we ended up pushing the car for nearly two miles without headlights along a dark windy road until we almost ended up in a ditch.

There seemed nothing left to do except disconnect the '32 altogether and take it to go for help. Without mufflers, fenders, license plates, windshield, hood, or headlights. Gus climbed in beside me and I peeled rubber down the road. There was nothing open in Wampum at that hour, so I flew through the little town, figuring they wouldn't see us. I figured wrong. We stopped at Shine's Pizza to call Locke's Service Station for his road service truck, ate a couple slices of pizza (our traditional, with pepperoni and anchovies), and walked back outside to find every police car in the area waiting for us. The charges ranged from reckless driving to being a public nuisance, with a host of vehicle citations in between. I distinguished myself in handling the situation by breaking down in tears. John Locke appeared with his service truck, and because the police all knew him, they let me off with warnings, threats, and general disgust. (It didn't hurt when Locke told them who my family was: "You know, that big orange-brick house on College Hill with the lions and round windows.") By the time we got the car home and in the garage, I was too mortified to ever drive it and sold it to a couple of guys from White Township. I heard they ran it once and the engine put a rod through the block.

But the '39 was running well, and when I got tired of cruising Seventh Avenue in the family Olds, I'd alternate with the old sedan for variety. Rumor had it that there was a full-blown Corvette engine under the hood, fostered no doubt by the throaty growl of the exhaust headers, and I did nothing to dispel the rumor. Whenever someone pulled up beside me at a stoplight and revved their engine in challenge, I'd respond with a couple of meaningful *vroom-vroooms*. Then as they charged off frantically down the street, I tooled along slowly and went home and got the Olds. Thus are reputations made.

Made so well, in fact, that when Bob Cory from the local Oldsmobile dealer came to the house to sell Father his new car for the year, he asked that I be present. Father was as puzzled as I was.

"You see, DeWitt, the boy here is quite well-known as a driver around this area."

Neither one of us knew whether that was good or bad.

"Oh, it's good, I assure you. People, particularly young people around here who know cars, know your son. That's why I have something special for you."

Bob Cory had a deal. He could get a luxury interior package from Oldsmobile by special order. Gray-on-gray brocade seat upholstery and headliner; custom black leather dashboard and door panels; carpets half an inch thick. At the same time, Oldsmobile was offering something new that year called a high-performance package. There were a lot of technical terms that he didn't want to bore Father with, but he wanted to have one in the valley, one that he could refer to: "You know, like the Snodgrasses have." Bob Cory said he'd let us have them both for the price of the interior package alone. Father shrugged and said, "Sure, okay, Bob, if you say so."

The result was a fire-engine-red four-door Ninety-Eight hardtop sedan, as luxurious inside as a Victorian bordello, that could burn the wheels off anything on the street. I dreamt of the Indianapolis 500, super stock racers, busty girls awarding trophies.

"How'd you talk your way into this one, Snots?" Gus said, circling the car as if it were a caged tiger.

"You wouldn't believe it, Gus. I didn't say a word."

"You're right. I don't believe it."

The high-performance package included a high-lift camshaft, oversized pistons, balanced crankshaft. For starters. The principal feature was three twin-barrel carburetors on progressive linkage. That meant that for normal driving it only used one of the carburetors, but when the accelerator was floored, the other two kicked in. The result was a car that could cruise along at eighty miles an hour and still burn rubber when you floored it. A feature I was demonstrating to some friends one day out on Highway 51, heading toward Ohio, when an old '51 Chevy tried to pass us.

"Look at that crazy bastard!" Gus yelled against the rush of air from the open windows. The Chevy was rattling and shaking; the driver looked over at us wild-eyed, frantically trying to reach something under his dashboard as he fought against the shimmy.

We laughed and hollered and waved. I floored it again, the tail dipped down, and with a chirp of rubber the big red car leapt forward and climbed to somewhere over a hundred with a great sucking sound under the hood. I eased off again when the road narrowed from four lanes to two a few miles from the border, and the old Chevy caught up with us and tried to pass again. The driver was still trying to reach whatever it was under his dash.

"I think he's got to keep goosing it with his finger," Gus said.

I toodled my fingers to the man. The man waved back and finally got a hold on what he was reaching for. The siren.

The local constable was near hysterics as he recited the charges against me, claiming he was going to lock up every rich lawyer's son from Aliquippa that came roaring through his district. Fortunately I was in better control of myself this time; I told him I was actually a rich accountant's son from Beaver Falls. He was unimpressed. The fine was close to $100, and Father probably would have made me pay it out of my allowance, except a friend in town heard about the incident, an older guy who worked as a mechanic and respected the Olds because it had sucked up his four-barrel Chevy, and he had a favor coming from a state trooper who knew the justice of the peace who knew . . .

"I think it's time you settled down," Father said as I drove him home from the train station one night. "You're going to get in trouble."

"I know. I'm getting too old for squirreling around."

"Squirreling?"

"You know, hot rods."

"Well, I'm certainly relieved to hear you say that!"

"Yeah. That's kid stuff. I'm selling the '39."

Father settled back in his seat, folding his hands on his briefcase. "If you're serious about that, your mother and I would consider getting you something sensible to drive. We know you should have a car of your own."

"I promise to really take care of it this time."

"And no hot rods or junkers."

"It'll be more expensive."

Father nodded. "I realize that. But it'd be worth it to have you driving something worthwhile."

It took Gus and me several weeks, but we finally came up with a car we considered worthwhile. A black Jaguar roadster.

Father just blinked.

"It's a used one. They just got it in at a dealer down at the lower end of town. It's beautiful."

"When I said worthwhile, I meant something like a Ford or Chevy."

"A Jaguar is one of the best cars in the world."

"It's also a sports car."

"A high-performance vehicle."

"A sports car."

"Please, Father?"

He sighed and rode down with us to take a look at it. I sat in it in the showroom, revving it up; Gus crawled underneath to examine the pan full of oil under the block.

"You have to expect a certain amount of overthrow with a high-speed engine like a Jag," the salesman said.

Father looked dubious, his checkbook in hand.

"Isn't it awfully loud?"

"It's a sports car, Father."

"That's what I thought." But he went ahead and wrote out a check for $1,800.

Actually, it *was* awfully loud. We should have suspected something, driving it home, when the red generator light came on and we took off the battery cover to find several wasp nests inside. It had apparently been sitting somewhere for a very, very long time. But it was black and it was a Jaguar and it was mine. The twin overhead cams chirred like monstrous sewing machines; the interior smelled of rich cracked leather. I dreamt of the Mille Miglia, Juan Manual Fangio, Monte Carlo.

There was no question that the car was the safest one I had owned so far. For the main reason that it only ran for a couple of hours. Total. On the other hand, it almost proved fatal to Gus. The next day we took it for a brief run in the hills back of Chippewa. Gus was following me in his MG, and coming back toward West Mayfield I performed the first and last four-wheel drift of my driving career. I watched in the rearview mirror as Gus also drifted the corner, except that he kept on going into a telephone pole. I made a U-turn up a dirt embankment and headed back, expecting to find his head through the windshield. Instead, through grace or luck or blind indifference, he was kicking the little car as it embraced the telephone pole like a lover, saying, "Why don't you handle like a Jag?"

We had the MG towed back to the garage, but neither it nor the Jaguar ever ran again. I found out later, after selling it to a Geneva student who patiently restored it, that someone along the line had left off the crankshaft pulleys. But my change of heart went beyond that. Something had changed for me when I saw Gus almost lose it on that corner.

"You're ready now for a sensible car?" Father asked.

"Yes."

"And you'll let us pick it out?"

"That's okay."

"We'll call it your mother's car, but you can drive it whenever you want."

"Whatever."

"My boy, I'm proud of you."

They picked out a red and cream '55 Chevy two-door hardtop, and I think my mother drove it twice—both times on occasions when I had a grudge match for the mighty red Olds. Then Father traded the Olds in on a Cadillac—not the black Cadillac that he wanted, because he was afraid people would think his accounting firm charged too much; it was white, but it was still a Cadillac—and the Chevy was mine.

And I was totally content. I didn't put flipper discs on it; I left the mufflers alone. The only bit of customizing I did was to replace the gearshift lever with a large yellow-handled screwdriver, but that was a necessity after my girl and I snapped off the lever late one night when we got too rambunctious while parked down at Brady's Run. Gus and I still hung out together, but not as often. We each had different interests now; we each had girls.

Maybe *content* is the wrong word. After high school, nothing made much sense to me. The world became a confusing and demanding place, clamoring for decisions about going to college or getting a job, earning your own way, preparing for the future. I didn't know which way to turn. The Chevy was the one thing that was sure in my life. I found my ambitions rose no higher than to keep on cruising up and down the streets of Beaver Falls, my girl curled at my side. And at night I dreamt about having a wife. A place of our own. Thighs.

Word Made Flesh

A little over a year after I attended my first Mass when I was a senior in high school, I was struck by the Sacred Heart of Jesus. Not just a mere touch, mind you; I was actually clapped on the head by a plaster statue. I undoubtedly shouldn't have, but at the time I tended to take such things personally.

I was working as a janitor at St. Joseph's Church in New Brighton, across the river from my hometown of Beaver Falls—to be honest I was really only the assistant janitor—and the pastor told me to remove the shrouds over the statues after the three-hour noontime service on Good Friday. At the time I wasn't Catholic so I wasn't too sure why the statues were covered in the first place, but I went around the sanctuary dutifully pulling off the purple velvet sacks, bobbing up and down with genuflections every time I passed the altar.

The problem was that I placed the stool I was using for a ladder too close to the statue of the Sacred Heart, and I didn't think about the outstretched hand beneath the folds of cloth. I raised up and took a crack on the head that sent me flying backward on the floor. From the few stragglers left in the church I heard some sniggles, but I didn't care, I stayed right there on the floor for several minutes, to make sure there wasn't something moving underneath that shroud. I hadn't been around Catholics very long, but the one thing I had learned so far was that they believed the impossible happened every day, and I wasn't taking any chances.

My interest in Catholicism hit me in much the same way as did the statue, and with about the same results. I was going with a girl who was both Catholic and Italian; her father and her eight uncles made it clear that my Scotch-Presbyterian soul didn't have much chance of being accepted into the family, much less salvation. But I thought I could at least show my good intentions by attending midnight Mass on Christmas Eve. The Mass left an impression on me, all right, but not necessarily the one intended. The church was crowded and I had to stand at the back through the long service, though I finally found what I thought was a good leaning place, resting my backside against the rim of what appeared to be a large marble birdbath. It turned out to be the font for holy water, and when the service was over and I walked outside I found the seat of my pants soaking wet.

The real surprise, however, was the fact that my father was upset because I went to the Mass. I was never aware of Father being too concerned about anything I did, one way or the other. And he certainly was not a religious man. I can remember him only once at a service at my family's traditional church, the First United Presbyterian Church of Beaver Falls; I was eight or so and Father stood beside me in a pew, a pained smile on his face, while the rest of us sang the closing anthem. On Sunday mornings he normally stayed home and worked on things from his office. But Father was a man of surprises.

We were sitting around the table on Christmas Day, after dinner. My sister Shirley and her husband were there, along with their daughter, Hope, and their newborn, Billy, and Father pushed his chair back to take his grandson on his knee. He nibbled at the baby's toes. The baby gurgled appreciatively.

"I wish someone would tell me," Father said, "why God made babies' feet so cute when they're small, and then lets them grow up big and ugly and smell bad."

The day had filled my brother-in-law, Rusty, with religious sentiment along with too much turkey. "Because of His infinite wisdom and goodness."

"Wisdom and goodness, huh?" Shirley said.

"Well, wouldn't people look pretty silly if their feet stayed that small all their lives?" Rusty jutted out his face at her, pretending to be childish.

"I don't think that's what Father meant," Shirley said, getting up to help Mother clear the table.

Father carefully held the baby's foot in his accountant's hand. "Spinoza would say everything endeavors to persevere in its own being. I guess the being of a baby's foot is to grow big and smell bad."

"Harrumph," Rusty said, thinking the conversation was meant for him. But it wasn't. Father turned to me.

"What would the Pope say about that?"

"The Pope?"

"Yes, the Pope. If you're going to Mass, you must've heard of the Pope."

"I only went once."

"The Pope tells Catholics what to think. I'd like to know why he thinks babies' feet grow up to be ugly, or why some babies are born crippled or deformed, or why some children get maimed or never have the advantages other children have. The advantages you've had, for instance. I'd like to know what he thinks about things like that."

His sudden bitterness surprised us all. Shirley froze, her hands full of plates; Rusty stared at his fork. Mother came in from the kitchen. Father's fine blue eyes were leveled on me. Then, faintly, the twinkle returned.

"But I guess the Pope doesn't care for babies' feet as much as he does their soles."

He minced at his own pun, to lighten things up again. But the conversation bothered me. Father never showed temper, beyond getting perturbed once in a while, and he was as careful with his words as he was with his moves on a chessboard or the figures he entered on his balance sheets. As soon as I could I left the house and went down to JoAnn's for a second meal, this time of wedding soup and roast beef, homemade raviolis and chicken.

The truth was that the Mass had made an impression on me—besides soaking the seat of my pants. I was impressed that people believed enough in what was going on during the service that they'd get down on their knees—in my church such a thing was unheard of. And of course there was the beauty of the ceremony itself, the incense, the colorful robes, the liturgy and the ringing bells. At the First United Presbyterian Church the only ceremonies were the Candlelight Service, where we all held tapers (there was always the problem of hot candle wax dripping on your hand or staining your clothes) and the Communion Service, where we passed around jiggers of grape juice and ate the stale flatbread that Mrs. Duff made in the church basement. I was even more impressed, maybe *flabbergasted* is the word, when JoAnn explained exactly why they were doing all that kneeling and praying.

We had stopped at St. Mary's to make a visit—as she called it—after shopping on a Monday night. As she knelt in the empty church, I got carried away with the beauty of it all and tried to kiss her. She crossed herself and sat back beside me.

"I'm sorry, I couldn't here, not in front of Him."

"Who?" I said, looking around. The church was still empty as far as I could tell.

"Him," she said, gazing at the altar.

"Oh, Him."

"He's really here, you know."

"You mean you can see Him?"

"Don't be silly."

"I didn't think so." I was afraid for a moment that I had a kook on my hands. Or worse.

"Nobody can see Him now. He's inside the tabernacle."

"You mean that little wafer?"

"That's the Host. That's Christ."

"You mean it's the symbol of Christ."

"No, I mean that's really Christ."

"It can't be really."

She smiled tolerantly. "But it is. That's what we believe. That's what the priest does during the Mass. He converts the bread into the body and blood of Christ. It's called transubstantiation. That's what we learn in catechism. . . ."

"Wait a minute. . . ."

"You shouldn't talk so loud."

"I have to get this straight. You believe that God is a biscuit?"

"You're trying to make fun of it. But that's the whole basis of Holy Mother Church. It's a miracle that happens every day."

I was having trouble getting my thoughts around what she was telling me. For one thing, if what she said was true, I couldn't understand why she took it all so calmly.

"Well, I've known about it all my life," she said when I asked her. She smiled at me beatifically, then gazed affectionately at the small marble house on the altar.

Somehow that didn't quite satisfy my troubled soul. It seemed to me that if you accepted that miracle as fact, there wasn't enough you could do in regard to honor and worship and praise.

So, of course, I took it upon myself to try to do it all. I started to go to Mass on Sunday, and when that didn't seem enough, I got a copy of the missal and went every morning to follow the saints' feast days, sitting in the back row along with half a dozen old women in babushkas and a few worried businessmen at the eight o'clock High Mass for the schoolchildren. I read books, probably too many books, and all the pamphlets in the racks in the entryway; I wore a filthy sweat-stained scapular under my undershirt until I broke out with ringworm; I hung a crucifix on the wall of my bedroom and prayed the rosary on the bare floor until my knees gave out. In Pittsburgh I bought a copy of the Divine Office and felt badly when I couldn't find time to pray seven hours a day like the cloistered monks. JoAnn was more than a little troubled.

"But you don't have to do all that."

"I don't see how you can get around it."

"You don't see anybody in my family doing all that stuff, do you? We don't do half, a quarter of what you're doing."

I had been meaning to talk to her about that. She took hold of my arms.

"Look, it's not your job to do all those things. It's the priest's job."

"I know."

She looked in my eyes, already frightened.

"Kiss me!"

My father, on the other hand, was more pragmatic about the prospects.

"If you're going to devote your life to the Church, doesn't that mean some kind of vow of poverty?"

"Of course."

"Then I was thinking maybe I should take away your allowance and the car. All for the good of your soul, of course."

He smiled. He had a point, I had to admit, so I decided it was time to start thinking about a job. When I heard they were looking for a janitor at St. Joseph's across the river in New Brighton, I took it immediately. It seemed a perfect act of humility, an opportunity to be around the peace and beauty of the church building—and it didn't interfere with my seeing JoAnn on her lunch breaks or in the evenings. I envisioned myself working there the rest of my life, maintaining a small, saintly existence in the shadow of the old brick structure, the lowly caretaker, taking care of the House of the Lord. When I told my father, he just shook his head and went back to work on other people's taxes.

The disappointment with the job was that most of my work was in the adjoining school, not in the church. Four hours every day, from three in the afternoon to seven in the evening, and all day Saturdays, I cleaned the classrooms and lavatories for grades one through six. In no time at all, I learned to hate little kids. I offered up to the poor souls in purgatory every wad of chewing gum and paper I fished out of the urinals, and said an Act of Contrition for every filthy word I washed off the walls—the girls were worse than the boys—and still wanted to drown some of the little bastards in my scrub bucket. The nuns haunted the long wooden corridors in black-robed silence; in the late afternoons, the voices of the children playing outside in the courtyard floated through the empty classrooms like forgotten memories of more carefree times. Rather than spiritual, the place often seemed downright spooky. There were nights when I locked the doors and ran.

But the job did give me the chance to know my first priest. There were two regular priests assigned to the parish—they all lived in the rectory on the other side of the courtyard from the church—but Father Fretter had suffered a nervous breakdown while serving a mission overseas and had been sent to this sleepy parish to recuperate. He said Mass every morning, but it was the first Mass, at five o'clock, so no one would see him if he started to freak out, and they tried their best to keep him out of the confessionals, unsure what he might say to the penitents. His principal activity was to sit at a back table in the cafeteria after school was done for the day, lay out his collection of awls and swivel knives, punches and stamping tools, and transform strips of leather into hand-tooled belts and wallets.

"You have the life, Brother Dustpan," he told me one day as I worked around him, collecting empty milk containers and sweeping up pieces of food. He was a smallish man, chubby and wall-eyed, his face crosshatched with the broken blood vessels from his particular problem. "Yes indeed, the life."

"I don't think I understand, Father."

He spoke between taps of his hammer. "Well, you have a decent . . . job.

You have nice . . . at least pleasant surroundings . . . and I assume . . . you have a girlfriend. . . ."

"Yes. . . ."

"It all sounds . . . idyllic." He liked the sound of the word so much that he stopped to hear it again. "Idyllic."

"I guess." I finished mopping up a pool of milk. "I've thought sometimes of becoming a priest."

He stopped to adjust his glasses in my direction.

"Well, not a priest. A monk."

"Why would you want to do a thing like that?"

"I've been reading about the Trappists."

"Thomas Merton?"

"That's right."

"*The Seven Storey Mountain.*"

"Have you read it?"

He took off his glasses to rub the bridge of his nose. His face looked naked.

"You're not Catholic, are you?"

"No. But I'm taking instructions. . . ."

He put on his glasses and started tapping again. "The thing is . . . not to take all this . . . stuff too seriously until . . . you understand more. Then . . . well . . ."

He didn't finish, and I didn't ask.

JoAnn continued to watch me uneasily. I made a pilgrimage to the Shrine of the Immaculate Conception over in Carey, Ohio, and did penance on my knees across a stone floor. JoAnn thought it might be nice if we figured out how much money we'd need for a down payment on a house. I spent a week with the Trappists at Gethsemani in Kentucky, getting up in the middle of the night at the sound of a clapper to hear them chant, and felt guilty became they gave me a bed to sleep on instead of a pallet. JoAnn made lists of saints' names for our children. I took to partial fasting, with total abstinence on Fridays and feast days. JoAnn sat in her short shorts on her front porch, reading *Cana Is Forever*, totally miserable.

Things got a little more serious when my uncle threw me out of his house for calling him a hypocrite. I didn't know my father's brother that well—the two families only saw each other briefly once a year at Christmas—but I stopped by on my way home from work one evening when he called and asked to see me. We sat across from each other in overstuffed chairs, in his cozy living room in his trim brick house across the street from the country club in Patterson Heights, gas logs burning cheerily in the fireplace, as he told me that I was hurting my chances in the business world if I became a Catholic. What I told him was that I disliked Protestants and Protestantism precisely because of that kind of phoniness and hypocrisy. His face turned the color of his red cashmere sweater and he told me to leave his house. Word of the confrontation had reached my own house by the time I got there.

"You shouldn't have said that to him, you know," Father said. He thought a moment. "What did he say when you told him that?"

"His mouth sort of dropped open and he sputtered a bit."

Father tried not to be amused. "He *is* your uncle."

"I know. But I believe what I said."

"You can't always say what you believe in this world. And continue to get along with people."

"I don't think that's right."

"Maybe so, but it's what you have to live with."

"I'm thinking of going to St. Vincent's in the fall."

I stood in the middle of the dining room; he sat at his card table, his hands folded on a client's large yellow balance sheet.

"I see. To become a priest?"

"Maybe. I don't know. There's a college there besides the monastery. I'll be able to make up my mind later."

"And who do you think is going to pay for it?"

"You will. Or if you won't, I'll find some way to pay for it myself."

Mother came in from the kitchen to listen, a small, plump, unhappy figure with a dishcloth.

"You have it all figured out," Father said.

"Yes."

"I'd be interested to know why you think I'll pay for something like that."

"Because you want me to go to school. Because you want to be able to tell your clients that your son's in college. Not that he's a janitor. And St. Vincent's is better than nothing."

I showed my triumph too soon.

He recrossed his legs beneath the table. The toe of his dangling shoe pointed down like a dancer's. "I would like to know what you're trying to prove by all this."

"I don't know what you mean."

"All this with the church. It seems like it's geared toward me in some way or other. Are you trying to show me something? Or is it just to shock me?"

"Why would I want to do that?"

"I thought maybe you could tell me. Chances are, though, you don't know why you're doing it, either. I guess in the long run it doesn't matter. Yes, I'll pay for you to go to St. Vincent's. But there is something you should know. For a while I was against you becoming a Catholic, if that's what you're going to do. I thought just like your uncle; I thought it would be bad for business. But I was wrong. I'll admit it. And I'll tell you the same thing I told him on the phone: I've found out it's just the opposite. It's a good thing for my business to have you a Catholic; it gives me something to talk about with my Catholic friends in Pittsburgh; they think better of me for it. I've actually gotten two new clients on account of it. I suppose the same will be true if you become a priest. It's liable to be even better. So you're not hurting me at all with these shenanigans. You go ahead with whatever it is you're doing, I don't care. But remember one thing, my young son: when it's all over, you're the only one who's going to have to live with it."

I didn't go down to see JoAnn that night. I didn't go to pick her up at lunchtime the next day. I needed time to think; suddenly things didn't seem so clear to me as they once did. I prayed for guidance, but the voices I heard still belonged to my father. When I went to work, it was all I could do to move the mop along the snaggy wood floors. I was sitting in an empty classroom at one of the tiny desks, the front legs lifted in the air, when Father Fretter stuck his head in the door.

"Brother Dustpan?" He was out of breath. "I'm sorry, your name is Dick, isn't it? There's a phone call for you, they said it was important."

I took it in the downstairs hallway. It was important; my sister had found her baby dead in his crib. I hung up the phone and walked slowly into the cafeteria. The room was dark except for the row of lights over the table where the priest was getting back to his leather. The man didn't look up from his slow tapping as I approached.

"Not bad news, I hope."

"Yes, it was."

"That's . . . too bad."

"My sister's baby just died."

"Oh. Oh." His eyes squinted a bit, but he didn't look up from his rows of indentations. "Had the baby . . . been sick?"

"No. She just put him down for a nap. When she went back a half hour later, he was dead."

I waited for him to say something, but he only kept tapping.

"I didn't know the baby that well. I don't think I even particularly liked him. But now he's dead. My sister is a good mother, a good woman. Why do things like that happen, Father?"

He picked up the strip of leather to look at it closer, then looked at me, but his eyes didn't appear to focus. He started to say something, then stopped. He gave a little shake of his head and went back to tapping the petals of a flower on the leather. I waited another minute, then went outside into the evening air, across the courtyard, and into the dark church to pray for us all.

Depth of Field

1959

The morning my brother's book arrived, Father was home from the office. He was recovering from one of his early operations. The progression of operations that started simply enough, my parents assured everyone and themselves, to correct a hernia, then to remove a lump from his forehead, to take out his prostate, to explore those spots on his lungs, to remove his lymph nodes, and ended with hacking off his limbs piece by piece—first his lower right leg, then most of his left arm, then the rest of his right leg, then part of his left leg—in sacrifice to the cancer that was determinedly taking over his body. But at this time he was still in good spirits and had set up his card table in the dining room to do some work from the office.

Mother unwrapped the package; the stack of books, *Heart's Needle*, with their red-and-white dust jackets sat on a corner of the dining room table. We each took a copy. Father turned it over in his hands, weighing it, then flipped through the pages.

"Well, it certainly isn't very thick."

"It's not supposed to be," Mother said. "They're poems."

Father thought about it. "The boy's done all right for himself, hasn't he? A book."

"Yes, indeed."

"You know, they'd make nice presents for some of my clients. I wonder if De could get me a discount."

"The least you can do is pay full price for them."

"I guess you're right."

I had never read much poetry, only what was required in school— *Hiawatha*, *The Merchant of Venice*, a few sonnets. I opened the book carefully but the binding still snapped. After reading a few lines, I wondered if my parents had any idea what my brother was talking about.

> . . . *it seems just like it seemed. His folks*
> *Pursue their lives like toy trains on a track.*
> *He can foresee each of his father's jokes*
> *Like words in some old movie that's come back.*

Father balanced the book in his hand until he noticed that I was watching him. He smiled. He carefully put the copy on the corner of his worktable, aligning it perfectly so that it was equidistant from the two sides, then put his bifocals on his nose, selected a pencil from the row of pencils he kept in front of him, and started to work again.

Mother was a quarter of the way through her copy. I couldn't tell from her expression what she thought of it. She put it down on her lap and thumped it with a knuckle.

"It's wonderful, isn't it?" she said.

Father looked up from his rows of figures. "It certainly is."

"We're very proud of him. Very proud indeed." Then she looked at me. "We're very proud of both our sons. We've got a great poet in the family, and someday you'll be a great photographer."

I closed my copy, then reopened it to the blurb inside the front cover:

Robert Lowell
says of
HEART'S NEEDLE

Except for Philip Larkin, Snodgrass is the best new poet in many years. He is *the* poet with content. He flowered in the most sterile of sterile places, a post war, cold war mid-western university's poetry workshop for graduate student poets. Most of the poems here have a shrill, authoritative

eloquence; a few, such as *The Operation* and *April Inventory*
are tremendous accomplishments. . . .

I looked up to find them both looking at me. I tossed the book on the stack
with the others and went upstairs to my room.

Morning sunlight filled my attic window. The windows were open but
the air was still. Outside came the sound of the traffic making the corner
on Route 18, the sound of the bells at the college library striking the quarter
hour. Students drifted down the hill toward their classes. I climbed up on
the table in the dormer, pulled my knees up under my chin as I looked out
the window, and tried to think what I was going to do with my life.

I was still undecided about college. I had been accepted next fall to
St. Vincent's, a college attached to a monastery in central Pennsylvania; I
had even announced my intentions to my family, but now I wasn't so sure.
The fall after I graduated from high school, I had tried Geneva, the college
a block away from our house, but quit after a few weeks. Geneva had a
lot to recommend it, but growing up playing cowboys and Indians on its
campus made it difficult to take it seriously. It was also affiliated with the
Reformed Presbyterian Church, in other words, Covenanters; and regular
Presbyterians are to Covenanters as a bicycle is to a particle accelerator. I
only lasted to the day the professor of the required religion class drew a large
crude circle on the blackboard, flecked it with chalk marks, turned to us,
and suggested that we think of the Supreme Being as a colossal free-form
tapioca pudding floating in the Void. I sputtered out loud, gathered up my
books, and left. It was as good an excuse as any, I suppose, and better than
most. After I dropped out, I was told that an English instructor who had
gone to school with my brother used me as an example in one of his lectures
as the type of person who would never amount to anything. I was beginning
to wonder if he was right.

I had tried to get into the University of Rochester to study photography,
but my grades weren't good enough, the penalty for not applying myself in
high school. My interest in photography started in the ninth grade when I
discovered I could find pictures of naked girls in photography magazines at
the drugstore. *Modern Photography. U.S. Camera. ART Photography.* Eventually,
to my credit, I turned the page and discovered the work of Ansel Adams,

Edward Weston, W. Eugene Smith. My mother tried to help this budding interest in camera work (at least it wasn't becoming a priest) by talking to the manager of the book department at Kaufmann's Department Store in Pittsburgh and presenting me at various times with books by Walker Evans, Henri Cartier-Bresson, Paul Strand. But too often my interest in photography amounted to thinking about taking pictures rather than actually taking them.

The fact was I was at a total loss as to what to do with myself. During the year since I graduated from high school, I had made several visits to my brother's, seeking clues and support as to how to build a life for myself, and he introduced me to a world very different from the one I knew in Beaver Falls, a world of art and good books and fine music, of university life and dinner parties with interesting people talking about interesting things. But how to make it happen? As soon as I returned from the visits, De's grand new world seemed further and further from me. I was frozen with possibilities, the knowledge that only I could make it happen. Left on my own, I only knew I wanted to be with my girl, and I found my life revolving around the times I delivered her to or picked her up after school or work. That, and praying and going to daily Mass, a result of my recent conversion to Catholicism. (I was aware that most of my prayers were for forgiveness for the things I was doing with my Italian girlfriend, the person who introduced me to Catholicism in the first place, but it didn't seem to slow either activity.)

My parents had stopped trying to persuade me one way or the other. I still had my car, my family's credit cards, and an allowance that was as much as some of my friends made in the mills. Between the times I saw JoAnn, I spent my days leafing through photography magazines, trying to read *The Sun Also Rises*, and arranging sentimental still lifes of Bibles and roses to photograph.

I climbed down from the window and took out my camera, a Japanese imitation of a Rollei twin-lens reflex. I carried it around the room, aiming it at one thing or another, trying to find something to photograph. I had seen Walker Evans' images of beds and chairs. I looked at my own bed and chair on the ground glass. It wasn't the same. I aimed the camera toward the window. The sunlight made a strong line across the wainscoting, and there was the contrast of the shadows on the woodwork and the white curtains and the day outside. But how to photograph it? Should the line of the curtains be in the center of the frame, or off to one side? And what about the sunlight on the wall? Was the sunlight the subject of the photograph, or the shadows? Or the wall itself? Disgusted, unsure, I snapped shut the viewing hood and put the camera away.

Downstairs, the phone rang. Mother called Father: "It's Ruth." His secretary from Pittsburgh called every day at this time; he would be on the phone the rest of the morning. I looked at my watch. There was most of a day to kill before JoAnn got out of school and I would meet her to drive her the two blocks to her job at City Market. I paced around my bedroom as if it were a cell; I rested my head against the window, staring down at the street. There had to be something I could do. I grabbed a stack of my latest prints and put them in an old Kodak box, gathered up my camera, and hurled myself down the stairs.

Mother was in the spare bedroom on the second floor, down on one knee looking into a chest of old clothes she had pulled from under the bed. When she heard me, she looked up and smiled sadly. Downstairs in the living room, Father was still on the telephone with Ruth, talking softly into the mouthpiece, holding the phone like a lover's hand. When he saw me, he said, "Hold on a minute," and put his hand over the mouthpiece; he smiled and waited until I was out the door. I got into my Chevy hardtop and drove downtown.

I cruised Seventh Avenue a couple of times, but all the guys I knew were either at work or away at college. It wasn't the time of year for short shorts; besides, the girls who might wear them were in school at this time of day. I cruised by the high school, hoping against hope that I might catch a glimpse of JoAnn through a window—or that she might catch a glimpse of me—but the orange-brick building with its Moorish towers was as unyielding as a cell block. I chirped rubber for the benefit of no one in particular and circled for another run through town.

I parked on 12th Street and went into the Brodhead Hotel. Greene's Studio of Photography was on the balcony above the lobby; inside the rippled glass door I found Polly on the phone. She waved hello and motioned for me to take a seat. I wiggled my nose at her to make her smile and went to the window.

The window looked out over the marquee on the side street. Across the street, on the opposite corner of the alley, I could see the windows of my uncle's office on the bottom floor of the Masonic Building. From this distance I couldn't read the gold lettering on the door, but I knew well enough what it said:

Snodgrass and Company
Certified Public Accountants
Bruce DeWitt Snodgrass
Stewart R. Snodgrass
Pittsburgh, Beaver Falls
Ambridge, Steubenville

Greene let me use his studio as if the place were my own, and I was aware the only reason he did so was because of my family's name. I walked in one morning, having never met the man before, and asked if he needed an assistant. When he found out my name, he asked the question I had heard around the town from the first time I entered a classroom or delivered a paper.

"Are you Stewart's or DeWitt's boy?"

"DeWitt's."

Greene nodded. "I don't know your father that well. He's up in Pittsburgh most of the time, isn't he?"

"Yes. His office is there. My uncle has the office here."

"Well, they're both fine men. Fine men."

After a fifteen-minute chat, he told me he didn't need an assistant, but he gave me a key to his studio, saying I could use the place day or night, whenever I wanted. He even fabricated a lens board for his enlarger so I could adapt his 4x5 outfit for my smaller negatives. I usually came in after dinner, the nights my girl had studying or something else she had to do, after Greene and Polly were gone.

Polly looked at me, smiled, and toodled her fingers. She was talking to someone about frames. I roamed around the reception room behind her. Her feet were locked around the braces of her swivel chair. She was somewhere in her thirties, with a long face and button eyes. She was a homely woman, at best, but her smile was hard to resist and there was a brightness about her that could take the shadows out of a room. She had gone to high school with my brother and spoke of him in reverential tones.

The studio wasn't the biggest in town, and it certainly wasn't the busiest, but Greene seemed content with his niche in the valley—an occasional wedding, a few steady commercial jobs, some portrait sittings here and there. Before Greene's I had worked for a time in the most prominent studio in town, Luskin's, but it didn't work out. I was there as an unpaid apprentice, which meant I spent most of my time spotting prints and retouching negatives of the faces of kids who had been behind me in high school, JoAnn's included, removing the blemishes and acne from their graduation portraits. Luskin was a short, energetic man in his sixties whose studio was on the first floor of a large house at the beginning (or end, depending on your point of view) of the main street; a grand curved stairway—good for pictures of wedding parties—led to his home on the second floor, which he shared with his equally short and energetic wife.

Luskin was thrilled and took it as a personal achievement that he had the son of a Snodgrass working for him, and made a point to tell customers. Looking back now, I realize he bore a certain resemblance to an aging Picasso; and there was no question that he considered himself an artiste with a camera. But I soon learned that what he liked best about taking portraits was taking portraits of girls and young women, specifically the opportunity to drape them with his collection of multicolored scarves and lengths of chiffon that he kept in a special metal chest behind the lights.

"It is the best part of being a photographer," he said to me one day, admiring the image he had taken of a particularly buxom young woman. "You'll see. All these young women come to you and offer themselves to you, all in the hopes that you'll make them pretty. You ask them to take off their blouses or their sweaters, and they take off their blouses or their sweaters, gladly because you asked them to. You get to see their favors before their husbands do. And if, while you're positioning a cloud of chiffon around their shoulders, your fingers just happen to brush against the tops of their firm young breasts, well, it can't be helped. You are the photographer; you are as trusted as a doctor. And I'll tell you what, when you brush against their breasts, they like it, every one of them."

With my daily routine of morning Mass and rosaries for special devotions, I knew I had to get out of there for the good of my soul—JoAnn was one of the young women he'd recently "draped"; if I found out he just happened to touch her breasts I was afraid I might kill him—as well as for my development as a photographer.

Beyond the reception room in Greene's Studio, which doubled as a gallery and mounting and spotting room, there was a small camera room with a portrait view camera mounted on a dolly along with half a dozen spotlights of various sizes and strengths. A latticework backdrop sat against the wall along with a garden setting that could be rolled into place; a couple of plaster columns could be added if elegance was required. The darkroom sat off to the side, through a curtained light trap. The enlarger was an ancient model on a wooden stand; the sink tended to leak on your shoes; the trays were stained black with use. But though the operation seemed a bit scattered and shabby, there was a good feeling about the place that I attributed in many ways to Polly.

She finished her conversation and tossed the phone good-naturedly on the hook.

"That man can talk forever! How are you, what have you been up to?"

"Not much." I liked her a lot but often found myself a little shy around her.

"You must be up to something. I noticed you were here in the darkroom the other night. Get some good stuff?"

"A couple things."

"Good, good. I suppose you're looking for the man of the house?"

"Is he around?"

"The gentleman went downstairs for a bite to eat. You'll find him in the coffee shop. You'd think he'd be nice enough to invite me along with him, wouldn't you? But he says somebody has to look after the store. You'd think he owned the place."

"I'll look after things if you want to go down."

"You're very sweet. But I guess I better stay here, though. You run along, tell him everything's under control."

With her unfailing cheerfulness and air of competence, she reminded me of my brother's wife—they were both tall and dark and angular, with the ability to make you feel special when they focused in on you. I don't think

I had a crush on her—okay, well, maybe a little—but I was disappointed every time she stood up and I saw her withered leg, her hobbling walk. It never seemed to bother her, though, and that made me feel all the worse. I went downstairs and across the lobby to the coffee shop. It was a long narrow room, with a counter along the side and wooden booths at the back, and glass cases with notions and cosmetics up front. White globes and fans the size of airplane propellers hung from the tall ceiling. The place always smelled of a mixture of perfume, coffee, and carbonated water.

The photographer was folded into one of the booths, considering the remains of a bacon, lettuce, and tomato sandwich. He was a tall, lanky man with graying hair and touches of gray in his mustache. He was my father's age and had something of my father's inherent air of distinction, but there the similarities ended. Whereas my father always reminded me of Fred Astaire or maybe Joseph Cotten in the movies, Greene made me think of a college professor in his mannerisms and ill-fitting tweed jacket; whereas my father smiled a lot but remained inscrutable, Greene was loose and friendly and seemed genuinely interested in people.

I arrived at the booth at the same time as the waitress with a pot of coffee. Greene looked from one to the other.

"Good grief! Everything happens at once!"

He drained his cup so she could fill it and I slid into the booth across from him.

"Diogenes Snodgrass, I presume," he said, pulling his dishes a little closer to him to give me more room.

I didn't get the reference.

"You don't know about Diogenes? Shame on you, you better go to college after all. Diogenes was a Greek philosopher who believed that social conventions should be ignored and pleasures should be avoided, that they were a distraction. It is said he walked through Athens in broad daylight carrying a lantern, looking for an honest man. You, on the other hand, go through Beaver Falls with a camera, looking for who knows what."

I laughed with him, but I wasn't sure what he was getting at. He picked up a carrot stick and began munching.

"Were you upstairs? How's Polly doing?"

"She said to tell you that everything's fine."

"It always is when she's around. If I could just get her to take the pictures as well, I wouldn't have to do anything at all."

Greene was a puzzle to me, and a bit of a problem. I didn't expect him to be a great photographer, but he wasn't even a good businessman. He preferred to take things easy, content with being neither particularly successful nor accomplished, and I didn't know what to make of it. It wasn't what I knew of businessmen from my father; and it wasn't what I knew of artists from my brother.

I think Greene knew I had mixed feelings about him, but it didn't seem to matter to him. He regarded me with a bemused expression on his face.

"Well, have you been working lately?"

"A little. Some portraits of my girl."

"Portraits, good. Is that what's in the box? Let's take a look at them."

He called the waitress over to clear the table and turned on the lamp over the little mirror on the side of the booth. He rubbed his hands together as though expecting a feast. There were half a dozen eight-by-ten prints, all of JoAnn, all taken during the same Sunday outing to Brady's Run Park. The poses were pretty much the same: JoAnn leaning against a tree, looking to the right, to the left, at the sky. In one, shadows played across her face; it was different but I didn't know if it was good. My favorite showed her looking straight at the camera, head tilted to one side, her smile open.

He looked at them all and nodded. "She's a beautiful girl."

I felt better. He shuffled through them again and picked out my favorite. "I like this one. At least it's the best of the bunch."

"What about the one with the shadows?"

"It's too confusing, too busy. All those dark spaces take away from the face. In a portrait it's pretty simple, you want to show what the person looks like. Sounds easy, but it turns out to be pretty hard. This one's better. For one thing, you're closer."

I was very proud. He looked at the picture a while longer.

"Too bad her head wasn't titled quite so much. The way it is now, it looks like it's about to fall off."

He was right, unfortunately; I didn't want to admit it to myself, but once he said it I had to agree. I felt a wave of depression. He must have sensed my disappointment but he barely acknowledged it.

"That's one of those things you learn with time. So, what are you going to work on today? Want to use the darkroom?"

"I think I'll just roam around town. See what I find."

"You ever notice those old men who sit out front of the library? Why don't you try some pictures of them?"

I hung around while he finished his coffee and bought a packet of mints for Polly. "Got to keep the little lady happy." Then I wandered back to my car and exchanged the box of prints for my camera. I walked up the block to the library and watched the old men from across the street. There were maybe a dozen of them sitting along the benches, talking among themselves or watching the people go by. I opened the hood of the camera; from this distance I could hardly see the men. I crossed the street and tried to appear casual, leaning against a parked car as I hid the camera in the crook of my arm. But one of the old men noticed me and stopped talking. For a few seconds our eyes met and I looked into his inquisitive face. Then I lowered my eyes and turned away, heading for the back streets.

I was no photographer. I didn't know what a photographer did, how or why. All I did most of the time was lie on my bed looking at photography magazines and thinking about being a photographer. I walked away from the main part of town, toward the factories and the railroad tracks and the valley's hills. Along the sidewalk, the roots of the old trees tried to force their way up through the bricks and concrete. On one dirty frame house, rows of Christmas lights still outlined the front porch; Frosty the Snowman hung upside down looking like a distress call. In the side yard of another house, sheets and blouses swayed along the clotheslines. A grotto with a plaster Virgin took up the front yard of a third house. Were these things to take pictures of? What about the houses themselves, the sagging steps, the imitation brick siding, a window open with the curtains billowing in the slight breeze. Were these things important? Were they the stuff of photographs? And if so, how did I select what to include? How did I arrange them in the frame? I didn't know.

I didn't want to think about it. I headed back to the studio. If they weren't busy today, Greene would want to talk, not about photography necessarily, just talk. He liked to sit on the radiator cover, in front of the window across from Polly's desk, as they discussed orders or he gave a running commentary on the people passing below. I'd sit on the stool across the room. We were like old friends or a little family, talking about one thing or another. At the prospect, I began to feel better already. I closed the camera in its case and slung it over my shoulder.

But when I got back to the studio, the door was locked and the *Back in a Few Minutes* sign was on the knob. I decided Polly must have won after all. I thought of going down to join them in the coffee shop but decided to wait for them in the studio. I unlocked the door and went in.

I sat on the radiator cover for a while, watching the sidewalk below; then I explored the shelves with the extra lenses and the units for the strobes. In the other room, I opened the shutter on the ancient view camera and tried to get used to seeing the world upside down, but my neck got stiff and I gave it up. I wondered what they had been working on in the darkroom and stepped into the light trap.

The print washer was going, the water bubbling softly like a stream; they must have left the radio on, there was the murmur of voices. I parted the curtain cautiously as my eyes got used to the dark. In the yellow glow of the safelights, Greene was standing with his back to me, his arms spread out to rest on either side of the sink, on either side of Polly. She was working at something, pulling prints out of the tray of developer and dropping them into the stop bath, then into the hypo, while Greene stood behind her, close enough to be against her, his chin almost touching her shoulder. As I watched, he said something in her ear and she laughed softly. He reached around her to make sure one of the prints was immersed in the tray; she turned her face to him and they kissed.

I slowly let the curtain fall back into place. I tiptoed through the studio and out the door, locking it behind me. I drove back through town and up College Hill to the big orange-brick house on the corner. The house was as dark as usual on a summer afternoon, the sun unable to penetrate the deep-set windows, the heavy drapes and Venetian blinds. My mother was asleep in the big red rocker, the copy of *Heart's Needle* open on her tummy, her head fallen to one side as if halfway lopped off, her mouth open as if taken by surprise. Beyond her chair, my father looked up from his ledger sheets on the card table and smiled his smile, rotating a single upraised finger as if in a silent *Whoop-de-do!* I went on to my room in the attic where I sat again in the dormer window, knees folded to my chin, watching the occasional traffic below, the trees on the hills of the valley's wall, the shadows lengthening through what remained of the afternoon. Safe.

Life Studies

1959

Sometime in the middle of the night, a drunk started banging on the side door downstairs, underneath my window.

"Let me in. Please let me in. I've lost my key. Please let me in. . . ."

The voice was sad, weepy. After a half hour of the calling, another man on the floor opened his window and told the drunk to shut up. For a while he was quiet. In the other rooms along the corridor I could hear snoring, men turning in their sleep, coughing. Someone flushed a toilet in the communal bathroom. Then the drunk started up again. I was afraid to go to the window to look at him.

The Y was in the neighboring town of New Brighton. I had been living there a week after telling my parents I was going on a trip to Ohio, but my money was running out and it looked as though I'd have to go back home. I lay in the metal frame bed and watched the growing light turn the cheap gauze curtains a pearly gray. Outside the main street of the mill town turned blue, then pink, then daylight, early summer, and the traffic increased with the change of shifts. When it was light enough, I dozed.

I woke to the sounds of the showers running in the communal bathroom, the sounds of men's voices echoing down the corridor from the gym. The heat had already taken over the room, a presence to be reckoned with; the curtains hung lifeless against the open window. I sat up in bed, braced on the folded pillow, and tried again to make my way through Robert Lowell's

Life Studies. I had found the book in my family's house; the same department store book buyer in Pittsburgh who kept my mother informed of my brother's literary activities suggested it to her, aware that Lowell said the book was influenced by the work of W. D. Snodgrass. De told me he worshipped Lowell, I felt it was almost a duty to learn about my brother's mentor and now rival, but I was having trouble getting through the poems, the references were beyond me. Who was Marie de' Medici, Ford Madox Ford; why should I care about them? The poems were at least readable when he talked about his family, but I still didn't get the same kind of significance, something to hold on to, life lessons, words to live by, when Lowell talked about his family—*"Anchors aweigh," Daddy boomed in his bathtub, / "Anchors aweigh"*—as when De talked about his. What did it mean when skunks came marching up the main street of a coastal village? I was clueless, hopelessly unaware. *I alone am Hell; / Nobody's here*—well, at least I understood that well enough.

I dressed and shaved and checked out. There was still time to see my girl before she went to work at the market. My car was parked in front of Bricker's, where I had been eating most of my meals. Through the door propped open with a chair came the smells of stale milk and disinfectant. The manager, scrubbing the floor in a paper hat, waved. He had gone to school with De and never seemed to tire of telling me stories about him—how they were rivals for the same girl, about De playing the kettledrums in the school orchestra, how De wore the Tiger mascot suit and sat on the crossbar of the goalposts twirling his tail to taunt the opposing teams. I waved and put my suitcase in the car and drove back across the bridge to Beaver Falls.

I avoided the main street, Seventh Avenue, for fear my mother might be out running some early morning errands, and took the back streets up through town, parking near the alley on 16th Street. I adjusted my rearview mirror so I could see along the old brick sidewalk, lumpy from tree roots, and stretched out across the seat with my back against the door to wait. A woman sweeping her front porch watched me suspiciously. In the side yard two boys with broom handles were having a shootout.

JoAnn came along the sidewalk on the other side of the street, crossing over when she saw the car.

"We can't stay here!" she whispered frantically in the window. "Daddy didn't go to work. I think he's suspicious."

"Come on, get in."

"I can't!"

"It's okay, you've got time."

"What if he sees us?"

"Come on, get in."

She hesitated, then opened the door and climbed in. I started the car and roared up the street. As I glanced down the alley I thought I saw a puff of exhaust from her father's car parked in the backyard.

"You're right, I think he's coming!"

She turned in the seat to look out the back window. I made the light on Seventh Avenue and turned up the main street before he could pull out of the alley. In a couple of blocks I turned off onto a side street. He hadn't seen us.

"Don't worry, we've lost him."

"But he'll be wondering why I'm not on my way to work. He'll want to know where I was."

"Take it easy."

I didn't want her to spoil the little time we had together. She was still turned on the seat, keeping watch for her father, her knees curled against my leg. I reached down and touched the olive skin, slipping my hand up under her skirt. She whimpered. I headed toward the last streets near the river and parked among the workers' cars near Moltrop Steel. I reached for her crotch as I kissed her but she moved away.

"What's the matter?"

"I have to get to work."

"We have a little time."

"But I'll get all sticky down there."

I worked my fingers around the elastic. "Did he say anything after I left last night?"

"A little. He was drunk when he got home from the Owls."

She was Italian, with brown hair curled along her shoulders, brown eyes, and light brown, olive skin. Her father, a barber in West Aliquippa, called me a cake-eater. Though he grinned when he said it, it was neither a joke nor a compliment.

"What did he say?"

"He wanted to know why you aren't living at home."

"What'd you tell him?"

"Nothing. I told him I didn't know." She looked away and closed her eyes as I brushed the soft mound between her legs with my fingertips. The material was already damp. I kept watch out the windows for passersby. From the old brick building of the plant came the ring of a load of steel being dropped.

"I guess I'll have to go back home today. I'm about out of money."

She sat for a while rubbing a spot on my arm.

"Why aren't you staying at your home?"

"I told you. I had to get away. It's deadly there."

"Daddy doesn't think it's natural."

"Your family's different than mine. Your way of life is different. That's why I love you, it."

She waited a moment. "He's afraid you're not going to go to college."

"What business is it of his?"

"He thinks you're going to stay here. In Beaver Falls. Because of me."

He was right, of course. I had been accepted to several schools—including the University of Pittsburgh for English—but I couldn't bear the thought of being away from her, not even thirty miles down the river.

"What do you think I should do?"

She looked at me. "I can't tell you what to do."

"Do you want me to go away?"

"Of course I don't want you to go away. But I know you have to."

I was desperate for her to tell me to stay. I was desperate for her to give me a sign, an indication of which way to go. To tell me she loved me. Or to tell me in such a way that I finally believed her. I tried to reach my other hand up under her blouse to her bra, but she resisted.

"I have to go. I'm going to be late for work."

I pulled away, feeling hurt. I started the car.

"You know I want to be with you," she said. "You know I want to be with you all the time. It's just that there are other things. . . ."

"There's always other things."

I drove slowly back up the hill toward the main part of town. She sat staring out the window, almost crying. I knew she'd be thinking about me while she was at work.

"Pick you up at lunch?" I said a block from the store.

"If you want to."

"One thirty?"

She nodded.

I touched her knee again, and this time she was more willing. I knew at lunch I'd get my fingers inside her. I pulled up in front of City Market and she leaned over and gave me a passionate kiss as though we'd be separated for years, before she ran inside. But the moment she was in the store, she seemed to forget about me after all. I watched through the large plate-glass windows as she walked to the produce department, laughing with the older men she worked with as she put on her apron, touching their arms. I squealed away from the curb, burning rubber through the intersection. In the rearview mirror I thought I saw her standing at the window, the smile gone from her face.

I headed up College Hill but went straight at Geneva, avoiding my house a block from the campus, and doubled back on 35th Street to the Gutherman's. I walked around the side of the small frame house. Mrs. Gutherman was frying eggs in the kitchen.

"Come on in, Schultzie," she called to me through the screen door. "Do you want some eggs, too?"

She was a tall cheerful woman with her hair pulled back into a bun, wearing a housedress and an old pair of Herman's slippers with white socks. I must have looked longingly at the skillet.

"All right," she laughed. "I'll add a couple more. Gus is in with Herman."

Gus was sitting at the dining room table drinking coffee with his father.

"God damn it, Schultz," Herman the German said. "Are you holding up my breakfast?"

"It'll only be a couple of minutes," his wife called.

Herman frowned. He was still dressed in his white uniform from the milk-processing plant, home from the midnight shift, waiting to go to bed.

"Take it easy, Herman," Gus said. "You'll get your food. There's a letter for you, Schultzie."

Herman pretended to grouse as he reached for my letter on the sideboard and handed it to me. The letter was addressed to Richard Schultz, c/o Gutherman. We all had nicknames on College Hill—Cobe-A-Dobe, Brownie, Bo-Dally. Gus's real name was something like Harold. His father was included as Herman the German because he worked nights and was often around during our adventures. My name was the logical progression from Snots to Snultz to Schultz.

"What are you up to now, Schultz?"

"Why do you want to know, Herman?" his son said.

I was staring at the envelope as if it were a prize. It was from my brother.

"Well, you've got to admit that it's a little strange, even for Schultz, that we get his mail for him under an assumed name when he lives a block away."

"Ah, there's your problem," Gus said. "You're trying to understand Schultz through the faculty of reason. Schultz doesn't run by reason."

"He'll run by eggs," Mrs. Gutherman said, distributing plates around the table.

"My eggs," Herman said.

Gus was my closest friend, though he was several years older and a student at Geneva. He was tall and blond, with a Nordic, rather horsey face, thin and bearded, and built like a long-distance runner.

"Schultz runs by powers that are beyond the comprehension of ordinary mortals. Like you, Herman."

Herman looked dubious. "That may be, but that still doesn't explain why we get mail for him."

"You see, Schultz is, you might say, running away from home."

"How can he be running away from home," Herman said between bites, "when he's sitting here eating my eggs?"

"It's just that he hasn't run very far."

Mrs. Gutherman came in with the toast. "Schultz, why would you want to do a thing like that?"

"What's so strange about Schultz wanting to get his mail?" Gus said.

"I don't mean that." She swatted at her son with a spatula. "I mean, why would he want to run away from home?"

"He hasn't," Herman said. "He's sitting right here."

Gus and Herman snickered. Mrs. Gutherman, always rather staid, looked confused.

"It's sort of hard to explain," I offered.

"Maybe you better not try," Mrs. Gutherman said. "We don't want to get involved with your family problems."

"What kind of problems could Schultz have?" Herman said. "Except figuring out how to be here for the next meal?"

"Mom's right," Gus said. "You don't want to know."

He looked at me and grinned. We had spent many hours over the last six months parked late at night near my house while I tried to explain the workings of my family, the dangers I thought my parents and their way of life represented to me, the way my thinking had changed since I visited my brother a year and a half earlier, a visit that had turned into a three-day psychoanalysis session when all my childhood grievances and terrors came spilling out. Gus listened but he didn't understand, or if he understood he didn't agree. But he never seemed to tire of it; I think he found it all fascinating. He'd listen to my hate-filled tirades against my family and say simply, "Well, Schultz, if that's what you think." I wondered sometimes if he was using the material for a psychology paper.

After breakfast Herman went to bed and Gus read a sports-car magazine. I went out on the back porch and read my letter:

Sunday Morning

Schultzie-lad,

First of all, let me apologize for taking so long to answer—everything is pretty frantic around here. We got sick just after Easter—we just seem to be getting over it now, some kind of bug—and everything's gotten out of hand. We got a cat but it caught distemper right away and died. We felt awful! The proofs for the English edition of Heart's Needle *have been lying around here for weeks, and I still haven't looked at them. Crazy! And there are applications for fellowships, talks, etc.*

It sounds to me as though you're really coming along there. You seem to have found out how to turn their techniques around and use them against themselves—sort of like emotional judo. Bonsai! Your story about selling your Jaguar is hilarious (the only way you could get a smile out of them is to complain about something!) and oh-so-true. I think you're probably right in suspecting an emotional trick, a Wabbit, in the business about selling the car. You've got to remember that the more dependent you are on them to buy you things like cars, the more you'll come to expect those things, the more you'll turn to their way of life, the less you'll have a life of your own. Remember, Wabbits multiply so fast and in so many directions at once, you can wear yourself out chasing them around in circles. And catching nothing. It doesn't really matter how they wear you out and wear you down, just so they incapacitate you in some way. And the results are the same, you are trapped. KILL THOSE WABBITS!

As for your lady-friend, I'm not surprised to hear that you're having troubles right now. How could it be otherwise? After all, when your life goes sour it's natural to ask your wife, husband, girlfriend, etc. to make up for it. "Please be good to me so I won't have to worry about the H-bomb, depressions, or my own murderous tendencies." And of course it scares the hell out of anybody to be asked to mean that much to anyone else. About as fast you can say to somebody "You're my whole world," they run as fast as they can go, in the opposite direction. And so would you. Because you know that you just aren't able to be a world; one can only be one's own struggling, difficult self.

I also suspect that you may not be finding her satisfying right now. You're going to have to ask yourself some of the most difficult questions of your life. For instance, does the girl have the toughness you're going to need? When you left here, you were filled with the excitement of making a new life for yourself, one of your own choosing—a career, college, etc. Now you're confused, in emotional chaos. I suspect that much of that confusion comes from the fact that your girlfriend is sitting around looking unhappy at your plans. It is the most destructive trick in the book, and the dirtiest. Remember that what you're fighting is to get away from a woman, our mother, who looked that, unhappy and displeased all the time. It's a technique that we're both terribly susceptible to. I had a pretty wife once—one that looked unhappy all the time. I ended up spending all my time wrapping around her ankles like a gelded cat so she might smile and approve of me. After seven years it still hadn't happened, and we were more dependent on each other than ever.

The sad and terrible truth is that there are many people in this world you can love, but very few you can live with. I have a feeling that you are ambitious, at least from what you've told us about yourself. And as appealing as her simple way of life is—the Italian family gatherings, the little house in the little town, the children and the nine-to-five workaday *world—it may not be the way you want to live. Only you can decide that, and I don't think you'll have the opportunity to make that kind of decision until you're far away from the Wabbits, the money, the easy way of life, the sad-looking ladies. What the world really boils down to is how well you're able to love, the kind of strengths you have, and the techniques you use with other people. You will have to have something to offer, really, to make your reaching out for other people anything more than a cry for help.*

We want you to remember that we're with you, all the way. If things get too bad, we'll even come down there and take you away. Keep pulling, old engine. You're on the right track.

> *Love,*
>
> *De*

P.S. I say this in all seriousness. What you are fighting for is your right to your own world. You are fighting for your life, for your very soul. Don't let anything stand in your way. You must will to win. There is no other way.

I sat for a long time on the back stoop, unable to reread the letter, unable to think. I was numb, exhausted. In the kitchen behind me, the water was running while Mrs. Gutherman did the dishes. Across the alley in the parking lot of the College Hill Apartments, children were chasing each other among the parked cars. A robin hopped across the grass, listening for the sounds of munching beneath its feet. Overhead the leaves of the maples and sycamores confused the sunlight.

Gus came out the screen door, in his bare feet and cut-off jeans, scratching his stomach. Through the backyards, a block away, I could see a glimpse of my family's orange-brick house, a part of the gabled roof, the encircling white fence and rosebushes. Gus leaned against the roof post, looking at the day.

"Well, Schultz, what're you going to do?"

Nightjar

1975

In my old room in the attic, I can hear my mother below on the second floor, bumping through the rooms, moving the piles of her children's never-to-be-worn-again clothes and the mementos of their childhood from one place to another. I'm sure the only reason she's working at this now is because I'm up here, that she wants to keep an eye on me. No, that's too harsh—but she is staying close to wherever I am, perhaps to see if she can get me something, perhaps just to be close to her youngest son on his visit home. Whichever, I'm worn out, weary of photographing the house, weary of dealing with her and the feelings of being a thirty-five-year-old child. I lie on the bed, on the familiar tufts and cornrows of the chenille spread, remembering all the times I lay here in high school to masturbate and absolutely, positively refusing to give in to the inclination to do so now, and fall into a brief, heavy sleep.

I'm a resistance fighter in the Spanish Civil War. I'm captured along with an old man and taken to the top of a high wall of a castle. We are dressed as workmen—baggy woolen pants, torn tweed sport coats, cloth caps. The view from the wall is beautiful, overlooking the roofs of the village to a perfect lake and the mountains beyond. But the Guardia Civil hands us automatic rifles and we are left to kill ourselves. I joke, wondering how we're supposed to manipulate the triggers while aiming at ourselves. The old man tries it and only succeeds in mutilating himself. In kindness, I fire a burst into his head, but he only smiles and walks toward me. I back away along the high wall, but he comes after me, his hands open, trying to explain. "Don't be afraid. It's a beautiful day. See? It's starting to snow. Forgive. Forget. There is only this moment: now. Look, the snow is falling!"

There is an explosion and I think they must be shelling us. But it is only a flatbed trailer truck bouncing in and out of a pothole on the street outside. I wake to find my room in darkness, the only light from the glow of the dormer window at dusk. The dream lingers on. I'm amazed at its message, amazed that I might feel that way, that I would give myself that message. But I think as well of the latest letter from my brother—or rather, my brother's wife, in letters she calls "Snot-O-Grams"; De no longer writes to me himself, having given me up as a lost cause. His young (my age), most recent wife already accepts my brother's viewpoint of the family, even down to the terminology we always used, when she discusses their impression of my work here to photograph the house: "We're all worried about you here, brother-man, we're all hoping that you haven't fallen into the clutches of the old trickster in her Wabbit Pit. Your work shows a great vision, Dick, it's just that it has nothing to do with reality."

I get up from the bed and go over to my camera case on the floor, take out the Rollei Single Lens Reflex and hold it for a moment, taking a kind of comfort from its presence as one might from a cat. In a way I envy my sister-in-law for her certainty as to who the monsters are; I remember when I was that sure. These days it seems my only certainty is the images I take, the truth of the images I find on the ground glass, yet I'm aware that these can change with the twist of a camera angle, a movement a few inches to the right or left. I put the camera back in its case and go to the window. Evening has settled in the valley though the sky is still an eggshell blue above the shadowed hills. Above the sounds of traffic on the hill comes the solitary, repetitive whistle of a nighthawk at work early in the dusk. I wonder again if coming home here is a mistake, if trying to photograph the house is a mistake, a subterfuge for darker, less honorable intentions, the old sorriness and guilt for wanting a life of my own making, an indication that I still prefer the comfort of losing rather than becoming an individual on my own. My thoughts are spinning, I can't think about such things anymore. My certain certainty at the moment is that I'm hungry. Full of renewed intention and determination, I leave my attic room and hurl myself, arms braced on the banisters, down the steps two at a time, the way I used to as a teenager, almost doing myself in when I hit the newel-post at the bottom.

Mother is in the kitchen, her back to me, futzing with something in the sink; either she didn't hear me come down the stairs (how could she not?) or is pretending she didn't. The cat, Merry Anne, is in the process of turning around in small circles on top of the stepstool, vying for space with a wet dish towel. She solves the problem by squatting with her haunches not quite touching the cloth, pretending to sit. She looks at me with long-suffering eyes. When Mother notices me she smiles and turns around, folding her arms on her little shelf of a belly, patting an elbow.

"When wouldst thou partake of something to eat? And if thou wouldst, what would thou wouldst?"

I glance at the cupboard beside my head. There is a stack of pre–World War II Jell-O boxes, two cans without labels, a monkey wrench, twelve cans of cat food, an unopened box of something called Space Food Sticks, and a glass turtle filled with a congealed tomato sauce–like substance. My eyes keep returning to the red mass in the bottom of the turtle's glass stomach.

"We have some scrambled eggs and some bacon. Or there's ham. Or I can go over to the store and get something else, if you can think of anything you'd like."

I look at the two skillets on the stove, at the bits of old meat stuck to the layers of grease. Mother awaits my answer with her arms outstretched in an inverted V, twisting her torso back and forth like the governor on an engine.

"I'm in a hurry, I want to develop some film as soon as it's dark enough. I'll just have an orange."

She gives me her look that says she doesn't believe me. I try to ignore her and go to the refrigerator. On the door are at least twenty small magnets, the type used to hold messages, arranged in a great sweeping arrow like a symbol in a war game. Except that there are no messages. I consider asking her about them but decide to leave well enough alone. On the stepstool, Merry Anne is tired of squatting and is trying to think of some way to move the cloth without getting her paw wet.

"There are some oranges in the vegetable bin," Mother says.

"I got some yesterday when I was out."

"I know. But I wish you'd try one of mine. They're very good."

Inside the refrigerator, the shelves are as cluttered as in the cupboards. I count eight containers of cottage cheese, six of half-and-half, two half gallons of milk, two quarts of skim milk, half a dozen bottles of Coke, a child's rubber ball, a musty collection of half-empty ketchup, mustard, and relish bottles, and an untold number of plastic containers full of suspicious-looking masses. One shelf has collapsed and is supported by a large jar of peanut butter. The smell is cold and overbearing.

I had looked at her oranges the day before, which was why I went down to the A&P to get my own. I take one of mine and close the refrigerator door. To show I'm not at all bothered by her sad-eyed look, I toss it jauntily in the air. Grateful to the gods above that I'm able to catch it.

"So, you're not even going to try one of mine," she says. We stand across from each other over a clutter of dirty dishes, the top of the cabinet she's painted blue and uses as a makeshift counter and room divider.

"How can you tell one orange from another? Maybe this is one of yours."

"Hmm, hmm, hmm." She smiles to herself, all knowing. I proceed with the ritual my friends in California follow when eating an orange; I bite off the end opposite the navel and then attempt to peel it with my fingers as a single piece. It never works.

Mother takes a carving knife from a drawer in the cabinet and waves it at me.

"This would help."

"That's cheating."

She smiles tolerantly.

I accomplish the unraveling in two sections; not too bad. I pop a section into my mouth, then wince. Sour.

Mother tries not to look too pleased. "You see, if that was one of my oranges it would be good."

I try another section but barely choke it down. Weary of sparring with her but unable to simply leave, I go back to the refrigerator and take one of hers from the fruit drawer. I should suspect something because of the orange's softness.

"That'll be a good one," she says as I take my place again across from her.

"Won't you feel terrible if it's not?"

"You'll see."

I flip the orange bottom side up and take a bite. Beneath the orange skin, the inside is a mass of black, moldy fibers. I spit the end across the room and make for the sink. As I rinse my mouth with water, Mother goes over and rummages through the vegetable bin.

"I don't know how that could have happened. Do you want to try this one?"

"I think I'll pass on the oranges for now."

Her backside and the open refrigerator door block the way back out of the room, so I lean against the counter, at the place where she stood before, to wait. She brings a couple of the oranges to the counter, to the place where I was previously, takes up the carving knife, and slices one of the oranges in two, showing me the halves.

"This one looks okay to me."

"I really don't want any oranges."

She slices the other orange in half, examines it, shows the halves to me, then goes back to the refrigerator, this time removing the entire vegetable drawer and bringing it back to the counter, pushing coffee cups and dirty plates out of the way to make room for it. One by one, she takes out each orange, slices it in half, and holds it up for me to see. The countertop is quickly covered with orange halves.

"That was the only one in the bunch," she says.

"I guess I just got lucky."

"You probably picked out the bad one on purpose, just to make me feel bad."

She smiles as she says it—is she trying to make a joke?—but her eyes are sad and rheumy. And I am a teenage boy again, hopelessly enmeshed in the same struggles with her that we were in twenty years earlier. Nothing has changed; I haven't changed. It's as if the intervening years never happened and I'm right back where I started. Worse, it seems a part of me never left. In my rage and despair, in the briefest of seconds, I see me grab the carving knife from her and plunge it into her chest, gut her from breastbone to navel, feel the weight of her collapse against me as her warm innards spill out over my hand and arm and the hideous look of surprise and terror on her face as I end it once and for all.

But it isn't her. She's not the problem—she's the difficulty to overcome, perhaps, but she can only be who she is: this is Helen Jessie (or maybe Jessie Helen) Murchie Snodgrass at the age of seventy-five, the sum total of her joys and sorrows of her lifetime. And I am her youngest son. If there is blame involved here, it's for my failure to learn how to deal with her, to come to terms with myself about who she is, not condemn her for who I wish she could be. But I know I'm no closer to achieving that now than I ever have been. I only know to break off the engagement, leave the field of battle, having learned over the years that neither victory nor surrender is possible. I give a little shake of my head and walk around her, pulling a face; there is nothing more I can say. I reach the vestibule to the dining room when I hear behind me, "I don't suppose you know what you want for dinner tomorrow, do you?"

I whirl around, ready to explode, but she's standing there laughing, then shuffles around the counter like a troll, ducking her head, pretending to be afraid I might throw something at her, chuckling gaily to herself. Merry Anne looks at me with neutral eyes from her perch on the stepstool as if to say, *What did you expect? Why did you come here?* I have to smile at the antics of the old woman, my mother, in spite of myself. But all I can do in response is turn and walk away, heading for the stairs and the safety of my attic room.

Album IV
Love and After

My father didn't have a history of success with his ventures. When he was a boy, for instance, he once built an airplane—not a model, a real one—and saw no reason why he couldn't fly. His father—Doc Snodgrass—happened to look out the window in time to see his oldest son come running down the hill, bedecked with wings, and end up in a pile of splinters at the bottom. Nor was my father particularly innovative. When he was a teenager working on the ice wagon, a horse stood on his foot. Father howled and punched and screamed at the animal to no avail, until a man came along and said, "Giddyap."

Nevertheless, his new accounting firm did well from the start. It should be noted that it was the early 1940s, the start of World War II, which was a good time for business generally, and particularly in the steel-making region of Pittsburgh. In a few years he brought his brother, Stew, into the firm, and Snodgrass & Company was born, with offices throughout the tristate area. It grew to be one of the largest—and *for a short time, the largest—independent accounting firms in the country. He was a respected member of the business community, a member of the prestigious Duquesne Club, the Pittsburgh Athletic Club (which had everything to do with Pittsburgh and not that much with athletics), and the family was listed in the Pittsburgh Blue Book. I've been told he had the reputation as the best CPA around.*

It was a family joke—though one he never quite enjoyed—that CPA meant "Can't Prove Anything."

While Father contributed to the war effort by making a killing with his business in Pittsburgh, Mother maintained the home front in Beaver Falls. She sold war bonds for the College Hill Woman's Club. She knit gloves and scarves for the refugees. (She also participated in a kind of black market ration stamp operation, securing for our family extra sugar and butter and meat out the back door of the local Clover Farm Store.) When the blackout sirens rang, she dutifully hung old Indian blankets over the windows. And twice a week she put on her white warden's helmet and rode the elevator to the roof of the General Brodhead Hotel—the tallest building in Beaver Falls, all of seven stories—to take her turn scanning the sky with binoculars for signs of German bombers. A silly venture if you think about it, but at least it shows the level of commitment.

Eventually, my mother became regent of the Beaver Valley Chapter of the Daughters of the American Revolution. She was also president of the College Hill Woman's Club, chairman of the board of education, and the teacher of her Sunday school class. A society woman, as it were, in the small-town world where she found herself. It shows, I think, the degree to which my mother was trying to make a world for herself. Because the house was no longer theirs together, hers and DeWitt's. Father's life and interests were centered now in Pittsburgh with his office. The house was hers. A place to which he came, increasingly, as a visitor only. Which in time became its own kind of war, where battlefront and home front were the same.

My father had certain words he lived by. Such as "There are no passenger trains on this line." That came from a family drive one Sunday outside of New Castle. As we waited in front of a clanging gate to cross the railroad tracks, I expressed the hope that maybe we'd see one the New York Central express passenger trains that

ran between New York and Chicago. Of course, no sooner had my father made his pronouncement than a string of NYC coaches roared passed. To his credit he could laugh at himself—or at least pretend to—and he would quote himself ever after, undoubtedly to stave off one of his children quoting it for him, any time he hazarded a statement of certainty.

Another favorite saying of Father's was "Who's coming down my steps in the morning, said the Old Troll?" That came from a children's book, Three Billy Goats Gruff, *and Father greeted each of us with the saying as we came down to breakfast, long after the time any of us were children. There also was the moral incantation from* The Little Engine That Could: *"I think I can . . . I think I can . . . I think I can . . . IthoughtIcould, IthoughtIcould, IthoughtIcould. . . ." Rolling up his sleeve and waving his forearm to show off what was left of his muscle, he often said, "When I was a boy, when I was a boy . . ." but he never finished it.*

His motto: I must be up and doing, with a will for any fate.

His inspiration: Every day in every way I must keep getting better and better.

His creed: Whatever it is, the answer is no; whatever it is you want, you can't have it; whatever it is you did, it's wrong.

My father had a pocket for everything, and everything had its pocket. He always carried two handkerchiefs in his pants, one on which to blow his nose in the right

front pocket, and a clean handkerchief for things like wiping his glasses neatly folded in his right rear pocket. He also carried change in the right front, a selection of carefully chosen denominations for any occasion that might arise. The left front pants pocket he reserved for items he wanted to keep clean, such as mints or chewing gum.

He didn't carry much in the pockets of his suit coats, so he wouldn't disturb the lines of the tailoring, though if he wasn't wearing a topcoat he'd carry his keys in the right-hand suit coat pocket. The inside vest pocket was reserved for important papers—his train tickets and schedules, and several blank sheets of paper folded lengthwise into quarters on which to note telephone numbers, addresses, memos to self. He also kept his glasses case in there for his bifocals.

In his shirt breast pocket would be a row of three mechanical pencils, all of the same type—though the type or brand might change—all with fine lead. There he also kept his cigarettes—Pall Malls; he went through two packs a day—and his lighter—a Zippo that he sometimes liked to click open and shut repeatedly when he was thinking. If he wasn't wearing a suit coat, he kept his glasses case there as well.

What made me think of all this is the memory of his bulging shirt pocket. But that isn't it, either. What I remember is that every time he bent over—from either forgetting it was there, or maybe hoping this time it wouldn't—all the stuff would tumble out. The thing is, it never stopped him from putting the stuff in there.

My mother could whistle. Oh boy, could she whistle! She could whistle and trill louder and higher that anyone I've ever heard, so piercing in fact that Gabriel the cat would come down from the third floor or from across the alley to see what was going on. Every time he showed up, even if she wasn't calling him, Mother rewarded him with a piece of raw beefsteak. Gabriel was one fat cat.

Like the dwarfs in "Snow White," Mother whistled while she worked—she said it showed that she was happy. She also sang. Sometimes lullabies, sometimes just wordless humming. If she sang an entire song, it was usually the same one:

> When I grow too old to dream,
> I'll have you to remember.
> When I grow too old to dream,
> I'll still have you in my heart.

If Father was trying to work at his card table, on the ledger sheets he'd brought home from the office, he'd ask her to stop—he said it hurt his ears. If she started to sing, he'd look at her quizzically, then wave his forefingers in the air like railroad semaphores and sing his own favorite song, the one he first heard the time the three of us went on a trip to New York City and saw Gwen Verdon in Damn Yankees: *"I got—fsssss—steam heat. . . ."*

While I was growing up, De as my big brother was more an idea than a presence, though I liked the idea of having a big brother. As noted it wasn't mutual. He had a strong aversion to me from the time I was born; I was a crawling reminder of his mother's sexuality. My earliest memory of my brother is the time the family took him to the airport in Pittsburgh on his way to shipping overseas with the Navy. I remember sitting on the tile floor of the terminal, surrounded by a forest of young men in uniform and their concerned families. My interest, however, was not in De's going away; I was busy playing with the plastic model of a B-17 Flying Fortress that I saw in the gift shop and wheedled my parents into buying for me. As I recall, I was glad when De finally got on the plane so we could go home and I could play some more with my new toy.

De was not a strong young man. He had tried working at the tube mill one summer but had to quit the first week because the noise of the grinding machinery and dropping loads of steel made him sick. He was frail, and his eyes were bad. Nevertheless, in World War II they drafted him into the Navy and he ended up on Saipan, in the South Pacific, armed with a typewriter before the island was secure.

Snipers' bullets occasionally singled out stragglers; there were spiders the size of seat cushions; and the holdouts from the Japanese army would sometimes come down from their caves and end up in the chow lines.

The fears on Saipan were real enough, but they apparently didn't stay with him; as soon as he was back in civilian life, they went away. What did stay with him was a lesson from basic training where he learned to gouge his fingers into an enemy's eyes and rip off the entire face mask. He learned he could do that. That was horrible. Possible. Lasting.

On summer evenings when I was growing up, Father organized softball games in our backyard, rounding up every kid in the neighborhood to come join us. My sisters played, of course, and Mother watched from the kitchen window as she did the dishes. But I was always made to be the star. Father saw to it that someone just

happened to muff my pop flies, that someone just happened to make a wild throw home while I was rounding third. Not that I'm complaining. It was just that I spent a long time of my life afterward trying to get those feelings back again.

When my brother came back from the Navy, he had a more down-to-earth, if not cynical, viewpoint of his younger brother. Before he left the South Pacific, he mailed home pins made from seashells for my sisters, and a large tin steam shovel for me. When I thanked him for it, he acted as if he was embarrassed and more or less disassociated himself from it; I learned later that mother told him to get it. He was a total stranger to me, but I was thrilled the afternoon he suggested we go out on the front lawn on a brisk, gray November day and toss a football around. I proved to be no good at it, but Joe Mulroy from across the alley joined us and De began throwing to him. "See, that's the way you do it," he said to me as Joe made another spectacular catch. "Why can't you do it like that?" I remember I eventually went back in the house and left them to their game.

The number of conversations I had with my father over the years—conversations of consequence, that is; more than just "Dickie, please stop playing your drums in the middle of the night!" or "But I just gave you $20"—can probably be counted

on two hands. Possibly even one. Nevertheless, he had an indelible effect on my life. One evening when I was in grade school, I came home crying after witnessing some of the neighborhood boys torture to death a baby bird that had fallen from its nest. He listened sympathetically, which surprised me, though I remember he said I'd find that there were a lot of bad people in the world and the sooner I realized it the better.

And there was the time a few years later the family or what was left of it went on a trip to Boston and Father took me on a late-night search for a piece of apple pie with "rattrap cheese," his favorite. As we sat in the hotel coffee shop looking out the plate-glass window at the stragglers on the dark street, he observed that the city poor are the poorest of all. All things considered, it wasn't very profound, I suppose, but it does show something of his concerns. That he considered himself a city person, that cities and not small towns were his world. And that he was probably concerned about not being poor.

Father became as uncomfortable to be around his hometown as he was to have his family around him in Pittsburgh. To be sure, he hosted the family to Pirates games at Forbes Field, sitting in the box seats of one of his clients, and to performances of the Civic Light Opera, held under the stars in the Pitt football stadium. The songs of

Victor Herbert and Sigmund Romberg—"Overhead the moon is beaming . . ."; "Deep in my heart, dear . . ."—drove my fantasies for years; my introduction to elegant living was Father pointing out the lighted windows in the expensive apartment buildings in Oakland on the drive back to Beaver Falls. But his attitude to his family was different when he was with us downtown in the Golden Triangle, his daily stomping grounds. One time he took my mother, sisters, and me to lunch at the Carlton House, where the maître de stopped me from entering because I didn't have a jacket. A hatcheck girl came to my rescue, taking me to her long, narrow closet to find a jacket that halfway fit. Father must have taken it as an affront, that he wasn't important enough to have a silly rule waived for a teenage boy. But what stuck was realizing that he was embarrassed. Not for me, but because of me.

There was the time I was grousing about the house on an early morning, complaining about this and that because I had to get up and go to school. Father addressed me in the bathroom mirror as he combed and brushed his hair flat with Wildroot Cream Oil.

"You know, Ditty, it takes the same amount of energy to be pleasant as it does to be unpleasant. It's all in your frame of mind. The thing is, you'll find that if *you're pleasant, people like to be around you and you're further ahead in the long run. Think about it." Which I did and decided he was right. The result was that I became one of those instant-awake, cheerful-in-the-morning people who drive wives and co-workers nuts.*

Something he undoubtedly should have told me about was the birds and the bees, but talking to his son about such a subject was obviously beyond him. I had to find out on my own one night sitting on the front steps of Joe Mulroy's house. We were talking about an earlier game of baseball in the street and I made some comment about Tootsie Muntean getting hit in the balls. Joe explained that it was an anatomical impossibility. Imagine my surprise.

After Barbara died, Shirley tried working in the office at Ambridge for a while, but it didn't pan out. Her heart was geared toward her wedding, which somebody decided should be as soon as possible, a testament in somebody's mind, I guess, that life in the family went on even though Babsie didn't. When Rusty returned from his tour with the Army in Germany—full of phrases such as Ich weiß nicht *and* auf wiedersehen *that he used every chance he could—Father laid plans to bring the boy into the firm. Father had always made it a principle to hire liberal arts students, rather than accounting majors. The theory was that the important thing was to have a well-rounded education, that the accounting courses could be picked up later, though admittedly Father was probably thinking about courses other than Driver's Ed and Competition Backstroke, part of Rusty's preparation for his chosen vocation of a driver and swimming instructor. Everyone agreed, though no one said out loud, that Rusty would be a real test of the theory.*

In Shirley's World According to Father, Father would not only pay for the wedding; he would pay for the honeymoon as well. While Rusty finished up his courses in accounting, Father planned to have the newlyweds bedded down on the third floor, above my parents' bedroom. Eventually, when Shirley and Rusty asserted themselves and declared they needed a house of their own, Father provided the down payment.

Father realized that he had neglected Shirley over the years, and he was trying to make it up.

De didn't come back for Barbara's funeral, though he wrote later as if he had:

The day we left you by your grave,
I wouldn't spare one tear.

For De, her death and the circumstances around it formed the basis of his theory of art. They are at the core of his poetics and his philosophy. In his essay "Finding a Poem," he writes that her death made him realize that "man alone has the choice to withdraw from the reality in which he lives, and so has the power to die, either metaphorically or literally." In Heart's Needle, he put it into verse:

Of all things, only we
have power to choose that we should die;
nothing else is free
in this world to refuse it.

Images of his dead sister fill his poems about the family, and what he learned from her death is implied throughout his body of work. But in his poems she appears alive only once, briefly, as a child. It's probably true to say that, because of who he was—the consummate artist, consumed by his sizable talents and his private vision of the world—nothing in her life was as interesting or as important to him as her death.

My father based his life on control, both of himself and of the world around him. He was a manipulative man, diplomatic and charming as the situation demanded, but always with an agenda. He believed that people added up like figures on a balance sheet, could be totaled and subtotaled. That was important—things had to add up. Balance out.

Unfortunately, things kept getting out of hand. It was as bad as walking the dogs. His wife was growing older and less attractive. He liked to walk the dogs, at least the idea of it, and it got him out of the house, away from her in the evenings. For one thing, there were all those pretty young secretaries at the office, dressed up every day as if for a party. But then Sam would sit down to scratch a flea while Buff pulled in the opposite direction toward the curb. His secretary, whom he had been screwing for years, was getting tired of waiting for him to leave his wife as he always said he would, was pressing him for a commitment. Sam would go running

around behind him in pursuit of a leaf, twisting his arm, while Buff would charge out to the end of the leash, then come doubling back through his legs and almost pull him inside out. On top of everything else, now his plumbing was going on the fritz, his erections going soft before their time. Sam would wrap his leash around his legs and begin humping his ankle. "Sam! Stop it!" Buff would jump up on him and knock him in the balls. "Get down! Get down!"

On his infrequent visits home, De kept telling him that there were other ways to do things. When Father told his oldest son he didn't think he could get an erection even if Marilyn Monroe lay naked in front him, De told him he was sure Father could find women who would be glad to help him get it up, urged him to leave his wife and find the love he wanted. And incidentally, De didn't have trouble with his dogs; he beat them.

One Sunday morning when I was very young, Father took me out to the front steps with a copy of Alice in Wonderland *and said, "This is one of the great books of the world and I'm going to read it to you." In this photograph taken that morning, I'm*

*not sure what else is going on to make me look so troubled, because that experience
is one of my fondest memories of my father. A lesson like that stays with a child.*

*Later on, he taught me another lesson. It was one of the last times I saw Father
and Mother together, when they came to visit me the year after I graduated from
Berkeley and I was living with the hippies in San Francisco. Father, for reasons of
his own, tried to drink me under the table while the three of us had dinner amid the
Victorian bordello splendor of Ernie's. Normally, he probably could have succeeded,
but this evening I was burning it off too quickly. He slouched in his chair, slurring
his words after his fifth Manhattan.*

*"Ah, Dickie-Wickie. You know, when you were a baby we used to have a lot
of nice times together. I remember once we were out in the backyard together, just
the two of us, and you were sitting on my lap in the hammock. We were swinging
back and forth, and you really liked being with your father, your dear old dad, you
laughed and laughed. But then the rope broke and we dropped straight down to the*

ground, really hard, but I kept you on my lap so you weren't hurt at all, even though I really cracked my tailbone, the darn thing still hurts to this day. And your mother came running out of the house crying, 'My beautiful baby! My beautiful baby!' and snatched you away from me. She never even asked if I was okay, you were the only one she was concerned about. And you know, I never resented you for that."

I figured that just about said it all; I didn't think it could get more pointed than that. But I forgot that they had been playing this game a long time. We left soon after that and I weaved down the red velvet steps of the restaurant, feeling the effects of the alcohol and my father's smile. While he went to the men's room, Mother took my arm.

"You'll have to excuse your father, I'm afraid he's drunk. The poor man. And of course you know what he said back there isn't true at all. He always resented you."

At the time I took solace in the sheer mastery of such interplay. It reminded me of a similar instance a few years earlier during one of their visits to Detroit. After a particularly strained evening at De's, Mother took me aside, pressed $50 into my palm, and said, "I want you to get yourself something nice. But sometime I'd like it *if you'd sit down and write me a letter and tell me exactly where we went wrong as parents." I responded to that particular bit of business by moaning and running out into the night, proud on some level of my mind to have a hysterical scene to match those of my brother.*

Such episodes seemed to confirm all that De had taught me about my parents, the deadliness of their emotional tricks, the manipulation of feelings that sap the strength right out of you. And all that is true, of course, such emotional tricks and manipulations are to be avoided at all costs, either from others who would do unto you, or as you might do unto others. But seeing such emotional manipulations through a Freudian lens turns out to be the easy part. It's seeing the terribleness below that level that is at the heart of the matter. The realization that my parents, each in their own way, were trying to tell me something. That each in his or her own way was saying, "I hurt. Please love me." And the further realization that there was nothing I could do to help them. Ever.

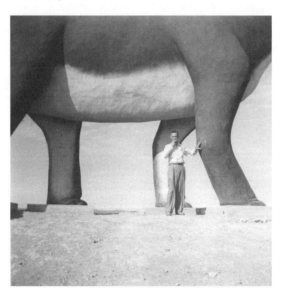

At a time in my father's life when he should have been reaping the rewards of his success, some things he had failed to deal with earlier began to catch up with him. His senior partner in the firm, one of the few men Father had allowed to get close to him, read the handwriting on the wall—it spelled son-in-law—and realized who was slated to take over Snodgrass & Company if and when Father ever retired.

Accordingly, he left to start his own firm and took half of Father's clients, the best half, with him. Then Father's brother—my uncle Stew, who had thrown me out of his house for thinking of becoming Catholic—had a heart attack on the steps of the Beaver Valley Country Club—he lived right across the street, handy for his nightly poker games in the clubhouse—and died. Father, busy trying to hold his own offices together, had no time or energy to devote to Stew's, so the partners from the Beaver Falls office bought Stew's half of the business and started a new Snodgrass accounting firm. On top of all this, his longtime secretary and lover left for another job and another guy.

After years of balancing figures, nothing in his life added up. And that wasn't the worst of it. After years of control, his body began to have a will of its own, and it wasn't on his side. After years of ordered addition and subtraction, multiplication and division, his cells started on a cancerous rampage through his careful organs.

I used to tell friends and curious acquaintances that my father died a disappointed man: he had one son who was a poet, and the other who was a construction inspector. It was always good for a chuckle, but I'm afraid not too far from the truth. He was trapped in a way: as he told Mother, "I guess if you raise them to think independently, you can't get mad at them when they do it." But he was mad, I think, angry. And irreparably sad.

When he learned he had cancer, he said he wanted two more years. Would fight for them. He figured he needed that time to prepare his son-in-law to take over the firm, to make sure Rusty knew how to handle clients, to get him to understand how to manage the other employees. Then what Father had built up would be secure, Shirley and his grandchildren would be provided for. Mother taken care of for life.

I won't go into details of the operations. After smoking two packs of Pall Malls a day for years, his insides were blackened. He told the doctors to take what they had to, so long as they left his head in place so he could think. Two more years. His legs went numb and he didn't have the strength to lift the supportive boots and braces. His stomach, his intestines, were straight pipes. Every breath hurt. Finally, with the cancers (there were more than one) attacking his lymph nodes, they had to take the left shoulder—not just the arm but the entire assembly to the neck. For two more years.

Little Barbara, his favorite of Shirley's children, took one look at him and said, "Poor Grandpa, he can't pick up little girls anymore."

After his final operation—when the doctors opened him up, took one look, and sewed him back together again—Mother arranged for a hospital bed in the living room, with nurses around the clock. Mike, father's cat, the one who had singled him out of a crowded train station one rainy night, took up residence on the bed and hissed whenever they tried to change the sheets. Father and Mother watched television together in a new routine, holding hands, their favorite program reruns of "Twenty Thousand Leagues Under the Sea." They laughed when the TV repairman came in and sat unknowingly on the chest that covered the portable potty. On a straight chair across from the bed, they propped the oil painting, done from a photograph, that the office had commissioned of him. The man he used to be. Probably the man he wanted to be. How he wanted to be remembered.

He lasted twenty-four days from the time they brought him back from the hospital. Toward the end he was drugged beyond comprehension most of the time, but two things seemed to have meaning for him, according to Mother. One was a

letter from his youngest son in San Francisco, who wrote that he was proud that the man was his father. The other was a copy of the latest book by his oldest son, a book of translations from the German poet Christian Morgenstern entitled Gallows Songs. He clutched both articles all day when they arrived, releasing them only when someone took them away, then forgot about them. Understandably enough. Neither son made the trip to see him.

For a time after Father died, De and I tried to time our visits back to Beaver Falls so we'd be there at the same time, for moral support, or so we told ourselves, against the emotional tricks and games of our mother—the self-anointed Brothers Snodgrass, the Poet and the Construction Inspector, home to do battle with the Wabbits. But I found as time went on that my visits there had other meanings, new interpretations, as I learned more about the family. The differences between De and me became more pronounced as I started to photograph the house and developed my own perspective, my own focus on the house. It didn't help, of course, that one time

when he sent me some of his latest poems for comment, I told him, as diplomatically as I could, that I thought he was starting to imitate himself. After that, all my correspondence with him was through his then wife.

Even before her husband died, my mother became something of a character in town and, on her own, lived her own life. Which consisted in good part of sifting through the things her family had left behind over the years, still with the idea that someday she would sell the house. On Sundays, after she taught her Golden Rule class at the church, she cooked dinner—always a roast—for Shirley and Rusty and their half dozen kids, whether they wanted it or not. She knew her two sons criticized her, but she also knew each son, for his own purposes, needed her—one as the source of blame; the other as a source of images. As with so much else, she learned to live with it—until it seemed enough.

Among the memories of my later visits home, there's one incident that keeps coming back to me. When she realized it was the night of a full moon, she led me outside to the front steps, where she reenacted for me an old wives' tale she learned as a child on the Great Plains, holding up an empty purse and crooning hopefully to the moon, "Fill it up! Fill it up!"

The Stories

Part Five

Going Away

1959

I pushed open the back door and stood for several minutes in the kitchen, getting used to the harsh light that filled the house at night, listening to its sounds. Beside the stacks of dirty dishes on the drainboard, a television set showed the eleven o'clock news, the sound blaring though no one was in the room. The camera panned over a crowd waiting outside the entrance of a West Virginia coal mine, the spotlights picking out isolated, worried faces in the darkness. From the entrance of the mine came a party of weary rescue workers, their faces black from coal dust, their eyes exhausted, as the announcer said the rescuers thought they heard tapping from the area of the cave-in but their attempts to dig another shaft kept collapsing. A woman in a formless coat was shown being led away, her head buried in the shoulder of a friend, hysterical with grief. The image shifted to a commercial for used cars.

Gabriel, the ancient neutered cat, came in the doorway of the kitchen, acknowledged I was home, and returned to the dining room. I moved to the entryway between the two rooms in time to see his gray tail disappear around the edge of the buffet. Every light in the downstairs was on—the cut-glass chandeliers, the imitation candles in their sconces on the walls, the lamps made from metal statues of courtiers and explorers and knights in shining armor. The television set in the dining room was tuned to the same station as in the kitchen, but the image was filled with snow and barely visible. Mother sat at the table, her back to me, across from the set, periodically

277

watching the ghostly figures as she pinned her hair into sausage-like curls over the top of her head. The noise from the set in the kitchen echoed the one on the dining room table, creating a hollow, empty sound. On the table between her and the television, not quite close enough to touch, Mike, the black kitten, lay sprawled on a copy of *Woman's Day*, watching Mother's hand dig in the box of bobby pins, then raise to the top of her head.

The card table Father used as a desk when he worked at home was sitting in front of the blue overstuffed chair across the room, but he wasn't there. In the mirror above the mantel, I could see him sitting in the living room, stretched out on the couch, watching the rerun of a cowboy series. The sound of the set in the other room rumbled among the others. As I watched, Gabriel appeared around the edge of a chair in the living room, and Father and cat looked at each other. Father said something to him, and the cat responded, but what they said was lost in the noise of the house.

For a moment I considered leaving again, tiptoeing out the back door the way I'd come in, getting in the car and driving around town some more. But I had been driving since seven-thirty that evening, up and down the main street of town, out Route 18 to Wampum for a pizza, down to West Bridgewater for a Coke at Jerry's Drive-in. I had said good-bye to all my friends, been to all the old places. There was nothing left to do.

I stepped into the dining room and tossed the car keys into the pile of things on the buffet. It occurred to me that I'd be leaving them there now, that I wouldn't need them anymore. Mother looked up and smiled.

"My sweet."

I nodded and went around the table, draping my windbreaker over the back of a chair. My usual place at the table was taken up with the portable TV—it also occurred to me that she had already found my replacement—so I sat beside it. Up close, the snow completely obliterated the television. I fiddled with the knobs and the rabbit ears; the picture cleared. The image showed the damage done by an unexpected flash flood in Pittsburgh.

"So that's what I've been watching," Mother said.

"I thought you'd be surprised."

"I think I liked it better the other way." She adjusted one of the curls on top of her head, watching the screen. "I should get somebody to come look at that set."

"It's okay. You just have to tune it."

"Maybe so," she said, not believing it for a second. She put her arms down long enough to add another word to the *New York Times* crossword puzzle from last Sunday's paper, then opened another bobby pin with her teeth and stuck it in her hair. Mike the kitten made a halfhearted attempt to play with the pen, but Mother moved it out of range.

The sound of the competing television sets was deafening. I heard the theme music rise to a climax in the living room. Father jumped up from the sofa and came high-stepping through the downstairs, elbows pumping, heading for the kitchen. The two dogs, Buff the terrier and Sam the Pekingese, trotted along behind him in single file, hoping there was food involved with whatever was happening. Father worked his eyebrows and grinned to me as he passed. I heard him in the kitchen filling the kettle for coffee.

"Well, did you say good-bye to everyone?" Mother said.

I nodded, and tried to look interested in a spool of thread. Mike's tail flipped back and forth on the table in front of me. I put the spool on it and she flipped it away.

"I'm sure they're all sorry to see you go."

"That's what they said."

Father came in with a glass of water and took a couple of Nembutals from a bottle on the mantel. The theme music swelled from the other room. He snapped back his shoulders as if he heard a clarion call, raised a finger to indicate he was on a mission, and hurried back to the living room, followed by the dogs.

"Are you sure you have enough clothes?"

"What?"

"I'm afraid you don't have enough clothes. You know we'll get anything you need."

I started to protest, to argue, to say of course I had enough clothes and if I didn't it's a fine time to worry about it now, to say of course I knew they'd get me anything I needed, anything I wanted—but decided it was useless. I got up from the table. Mother rested her hands on her lap.

"I only want to help."

"I'm going to the bathroom."

She searched my face for meaning. I looked away and went upstairs. In the bathroom I took out my brother's latest letter from my back pocket and sat on the closed toilet lid to read it one more time.

Tues. midnight

Brother-man,

This needs be short. Things here are going crazy! The lawnmower caught fire while mowing the grass and we almost succeeded in burning down the countryside, as well as the house. I went out to chop wood and almost put the axe through my foot. Sounds like I'm certainly trying to do myself in, all right.

But I did want to write you, now at this time. So you're really going to do it, you're going to get out of there! Hooray for you! I can't tell you how pleased we are. This is a gigantic step for you, and I'm not surprised at all that you're scared and confused about the future. Keep in mind there's time later for particulars, where you'll end up, what you'll be doing. Right now it's enough that you've overcome their attempts to drag you down, to pull you into the snake pit of their lives. You are on your way now to making your own happiness. Keep on the track!

I wanted to write you now because I'm sure at the last minute they'll try every trick in their book to put the screws to you, to make you doubt yourself, to undermine your efforts to become your own person. Damn their eyes! Don't let them do that to you! You are fighting the holiest of all wars, the right to be yourself. And your enemies will stop at nothing until they possess you, destroy you, see you buried. Remember they are the truly dead. We make our own lives.

Take care, old engine. Keep pulling.
All my best,
De

I refolded the letter and stuck in my pocket and sat for a while, studying my shoe on the edge of the throw rug. I realized I had been looking at it for the past five minutes. I flushed the toilet and went back down the stairs.

Added to the ruckus of the televisions was the piercing whistle of the kettle boiling in the kitchen. Father came trotting through the downstairs hall again on a commercial break, followed by his retinue of dogs. He looked up at me on the stairs.

"Head 'em off at the pass! Head 'em off at the pass!"

"Head 'em up and move 'em out!" I offered.

"Don't shoot, Sheriff!" he called, already in the kitchen.

I was sitting at the table again when he swung through on his return, this time holding a coffee cup and saucer.

"There's pie out there," Mother said without looking up from her crossword.

"Thank you." Father kept on going.

"And some ice cream in the basement refrigerator."

Father was gone.

"Did you hear all that?" she asked me.

"No, I'm still upstairs."

"Smarty. Well, it's there if you want it. Why don't you turn that off, I'm not watching it."

I turned off the sound on the television on the dining room table beside me; the sets in the kitchen and the living room thundered on. As Jack Parr mouthed jokes and a man stuffed trained poodles in a trunk, there were the sounds from the living room of horses galloping through the underbrush, wagons creaking, and gunshots among lowing cattle. Mother continued to watch the set as before, as if it all made sense to her, occasionally adding a word to her puzzle.

The theme music swelled to a close in the living room; the picture in the dining room showed the virtues of a vegetable chopper. This time the dogs were in front of Father in the parade, stumbling over themselves and each other as they kept an eye on him over their shoulders. He tried to pump his elbows with false enthusiasm, but the Nembutals were starting to take effect and his eyes were clouding. He went again to the kitchen, and Mother and I both cocked our heads to listen to the crinkle of cellophane and his voice saying something to the dogs. Our eyes met and we looked away.

"He's very tired," she said, not necessarily to me.

He returned moving carefully among the dogs that wiggled about his ankles. In one hand was his coffee cup; in the other was a small white plate with half a dozen Oreo cookies smeared with peanut butter.

"What's the matter, Helen, don't you ever feed these boys?"

"Not chocolate and peanut butter, I don't," she laughed.

"These poor fellows are starved." He sat down at his regular place at the head of the table and gazed down at the dogs. The terrier looked back at him; the Peke danced on his hind legs. Father grinned appreciatively and popped one of the cookies into his mouth.

"Don't you want one?"

"I don't think so."

"You don't know what you're missing."

"Maybe I'm better off that way."

"That's why you should listen to your poor old father."

"My poor rich father."

He ate another cookie and looked at me dreamily.

"You see, you're an investment to me. I've put a lot of money in you over the years, and I'll be putting a lot more money into you in the future, now that you're going to college. It's the same as if I was investing in a small business or some stock. It's my job to make sure my money's working for me, that I'm getting my money's worth. Full return for the dollar."

"What happens if you don't get the right return?"

"I'm a businessman, aren't I? I'd have to look around for other investments."

He was proud of his analogy and rewarded himself with another cookie. His blue eyes were moist and heavy as if he were drunk.

Mother was troubled. "What your father means is that we're interested in your future and what happens to you, and we want to make sure you have everything you need."

"I think the boy understands what I mean."

"Yes," I said. "I think the boy does."

Father was pleased with what he thought he heard. He got up, almost asleep, and moved across the room to the blue overstuffed chair at his work-table. Gabriel was stretched out in the chair. Father tried to ease him over so they could both sit there, but the cat moved to the center of the card table, stretching out across one of Father's ledger sheets.

Mother laughed. "It's a wonder he doesn't shake his paw at you. You disturbed his rest."

Father petted the cat affectionately, then leaned back in the chair. "Gabriel understands. Us older fellows have to take care of each other."

"They get along like two strange bulldogs in an alley," I said, repeating

Father's favorite saying to describe the relationship between the two of us. I don't think he heard me.

"You have to take care of the older ones, you know. They won't be around forever."

Gabriel looked at me and flicked his tail to make sure I got the inference.

"Well, if you go, just make sure you leave the money." Another old family joke.

Mother thumped her comb on the table. "I don't know about you, but I plan to be around for another thirty years. At least."

Father looked at her through slits. "I don't doubt that in the least."

"I don't see any reason why I shouldn't. Be around for another thirty years."

Father leaned back so far that his head touched the glass doors of the bookcase behind him. If he slouched any further, I was afraid he might slide off onto the floor.

"Your mother always does what she says she will."

Mother thumped her comb in agreement. Then she picked up a pen and starting scribbling in the borders of the newspaper. A note to herself about something.

"Your mother was always the strong one in the family."

"That's because I had you, dear."

"Piffle." Father gazed at us from far away under his eyebrows.

Mother watched her pen draw hash marks across the face of a model selling perfume. "It's true. When we were in college, the dean of women called me into her office one day and said she didn't think it was proper for us to hold hands on campus. We were quite the scandal in those days. And I told her, 'Miss Wallace, he walks so fast that if I don't hold on to him I'll lose him.'"

She stopped her scribbling and looked up. They smiled to each other across the room, my mother sitting at the table with her hair in bobby pins, my father nodding asleep in his big blue chair. Above on the mantel were the photographs of their children: my brother, a distinguished poet; my dead sister; my other sister with her firstborn child named Hope; and me. I was going away to college. I sensed my life would change irrevocably. And when I left the next day, I made sure I had copies of those photographs, to remind me in years to come who we were. Who I had been. But it is the image of my parents that night, smiling at each other across the cluttered dining room, across their many years of marriage, in the house that Father always called *Your Mother's* and that Mother always called *Ours*, that stayed with me in my mind, haunts me still, more precise than patterns of gray in a photograph, stronger than words.

Brothers in Arms

1965

I

The Greater Pittsburgh Airport was nearly empty this late in the afternoon on Thanksgiving Day. Coming through the terminal I looked for my brother, but all I found was my brother-in-law, surrounded by three of his children. Rusty and I shook hands and exchanged pleasantries; the children huddled on the other side of his legs, afraid of this stranger. De and I had arranged our flights so we'd arrive at approximately the same time. I wondered if he was delayed, but Rusty didn't say anything and I didn't ask. I collected my suitcase and we started through the tunnel toward the valet parking. I was about to inquire when I saw him coming toward me along the walkway, an imposing figure in his fur-lined storm coat, fur hat, and heavy patriarchal beard. I tipped my Stetson at him; he threw his astrakhan at me. And the Cowboy and the Russian locked forearms and embraced.

"Brother-man!"

"Hello, bro!"

"How goes it, laddie?"

"About like that. How's it with you?"

De gave me a meaningful look over the tops of his glasses as if I should know better. We punched each other on the upper arm.

"The car's down here," Rusty said, fearing for the corruption of his children and herding them in front of him. The Cowboy and the Russian trailed along behind. While Rusty arranged for the car, we watched a gaggle of stewardesses waiting for the shuttle bus to the Holiday Inn, their tailored miniskirts cut to mid-thigh. When a perky blonde bent over to pick up her overnight case, De and I looked at each other, looked at the black evening sky, and tightened our mouths.

"I think it's a good thing we left the wives at home," I said.

"Oh, absolutely. No need to get them involved in this mess."

"When did you get in?"

"About a half hour ago. I had to take a walk."

"I brought a bottle." I nodded toward my suitcase.

De sashayed a few steps around the loading area. "You are a good man."

The station wagon arrived and we climbed in, De beside Rusty in the front, me beside the oldest of the girls in back, and the two little ones lying in the flat space at the rear beside our suitcases. As Rusty wheeled through the terminal, up the ramp, and out into traffic, De glanced over his shoulder at me, then faced straight ahead.

It was almost night as we headed down the hills and into the valley, toward Beaver Falls. The streets of the mill towns were curiously empty and still with the holiday, though the mills and factories continued to send up their smoke and steam along the river; at Aliquippa, the blast furnace blazed orange against the lowering cloud ceiling. A few of the houses along the narrow streets were already decorated for Christmas, with strings of multi-colored lights tracing the outline of a porch or a doorway and a decorated tree in the window. A cardboard Nativity scene was spotlighted on the small corner yard of a church. The little girl beside me sat as close as she could to her door, staring at my Spanish boots. Behind me, the other two children giggled and sang to themselves:

> Jingle Bells, jingle bells,
> Santa Claus is dead.
> Someone took a forty-four
> And shot him in the head.

"Cut it out kids," Rusty said. "Be quiet."

"How's Mother?" I asked.

"She's doing okay. In fact, she's doing very well."

"I'll just bet she is," De said.

"She's a remarkable woman," Rusty said.

"No question about that," De said, and tilted his head in my direction.

It was as I remembered it, thought it would be—the big orange-brick house sitting on the corner at the top of College Hill, every light in the house, even in my old room in the attic, burning away as if there was a party, though the storm windows were on for winter—maybe they were left on year-round now—the curved windows at the corners overlaid with angled glass, the mullions like bars. At the top of the terrace steps, the cement planters sat tipsy along the walk, the flowers from last summer, or maybe the summer before, draped over the rims. The cement lions, the paint cracked and flaking, appeared vaporous like old ghosts.

De and I collected our suitcases from the back and Rusty followed us inside, mercifully leaving the kids in the car. The house was in the best shape I had ever seen it, even when I lived here—everything with a place, everything put away, though the amount of furniture and trinkets still made it close and cluttered. There was nobody here.

"Mother was really sorry she couldn't pick you up herself."

"That's crazy," De said, waving his hand to brush the idea or Rusty away. He started pacing aimlessly between the living room, dining room, and hall, looking at things but not really focusing on what he saw. Rusty stood near the front door, watching him come and go. I just stood.

"She left the white Cadillac for you," Rusty said.

"For me?" De said. He stopped and looked at him incredulously.

"Well, for both of you, I mean. She's got the black one with her."

"The black one?"

Rusty grinned, happy to explain. "Mother started driving Father's black Cadillac when she had to go up to the hospital in Pittsburgh all the time. She was afraid the white one might break down when she was coming back late at night."

"Oh sure," De said, looking at me as if to say, *You getting all this?* "Oh sure."

Rusty maintained his smile, not understanding for a second what was going on.

"She said she'd like you to come down as soon as you can. And there's a ham in the refrigerator."

I realized De and I were both pacing now, meeting off center in the doorway of either the dining or living room. It was several minutes before we remembered Rusty was still there. We thanked him and shook his hand, and he left us alone in the house. I took on Rusty's role as audience. As he paced, De went suddenly bug-eyed.

"Have you ever seen anything like this place?" he said.

"It's your world, and welcome to it."

He looked at me suspiciously, then turned his attention to Mother's collection of Indian cowbells and bells of Sarna, hanging from braided cords in the hallway, and the display of Amish trivets hanging on the wall in the dining room.

"I'll *bet* she started driving his black Cadillac," he said. "I'll just *bet* she did. If you look around here carefully enough, you'll probably find his balls bronzed like a pair of baby shoes somewhere in all this junk."

We looked at each other and started to giggle. In seconds we were howling, me sitting on the floor holding my sides, my brother waving his arms and doing a little dance under the hallway teardrop chandelier. The black cat, Mike, appeared from under a chair, took one look at the raving lunatics, and ran for the safety of the upstairs.

"What the hell was that?" De asked in mid-step.

"Ghosts."

We stopped and looked at each other. "I guess we better get down there."

We ate pieces of cold ham and Roman Meal bread standing in the kitchen, then went upstairs. I took my old room in the attic; De took the guest room on the second floor. All the furniture in my room was covered with large plastic sheets. I freed the bed and chair from their wrappings and opened my suitcase. When I heard De finish in the bathroom, I called down to him.

"Hey, what am I supposed to wear?"

"Wear what you've got on, I guess. That's what I'm doing."

"Yeah, but you're already wearing a suit."

"Well, I don't know." He stood at the bottom of the stairs, studying the rows of family portraits that lined the walls above the wainscoting. "Do you realize how many of these people are dead? It's like a trophy room."

"Come on up, I got something to show you."

"More craziness?" he said, following me into my room and looking around expectantly.

"Nope. Escape." I dug around in my suitcase and pulled out a bottle of Courvoisier. We toasted each other with water glasses, and again, and again, before dancing down the stairs, trading four-bar drum solos on the banisters, out of the house and into the night.

De didn't want any part of driving the white Cadillac; he didn't even like riding in it. I drove us down College Hill to the main part of town, parking on a back street across from a large corner house that glowed from spotlights on the lawn. The house was yellow brick, but there was a colonial flavor to it from the white trim and small pillars on what had once been the front porch. Gigantic carriage lamps hung on either side of the doorway to a new addition. The spotlighted sign on the lawn said *J. Orville Scott Funeral Home.*

The night air was moist and cold. The pavement carried a slight sheen from the mist that drifted along the quiet streets. We waited for a car that rolled through the stop sign, then crossed over.

"After you."

"Oh no, after you."

"I insist."

"Shit."

Inside the door the attendant in black must have recognized my brother, for he led us without comment into the front room. Perhaps a dozen people were there. Mother was dressed in pink, our sister Shirley in royal blue. We all kissed, patted, nodded, cooed. Mother took her two sons by the hands and led us across the room to Father. After I was satisfied that whatever was stuffed and painted inside the satin-lined box had nothing to do with me, I drifted off and began a detailed survey of the flowers in the room, reading each note carefully, amazed at how few of the names I recognized. De wasn't so lucky. Mother held on to his hand and related the fine points of funeral cosmetics to him for several minutes before he could break away. We met at the doorway. He staggered more than he walked.

"What are we supposed to do?" he whispered.

"I don't know. Stand here and look grieved."

"I've got to piss."

He wandered down the hall and left me on my own. I was a prime target for ladies in flowered hats. After several botched attempts, I hit upon a combination of a slight tilt of the head, down-turned mouth, and glassy-eyed stare that kept well-wishers at a distance. De came back in a few minutes.

"Are you okay?" he asked.

"Yeah. I'm practicing looking sorrowful."

"You look like your underwear's too tight." After we both giggled softly he said, "We've got to cut this out, this is serious."

From the middle of the room came the muted laughter of our sister along with several other ladies from the church. They were discussing the problems encountered with the last covered-dish dinner. When someone new entered or someone left, the talk became restrained again. Otherwise, the conversational level was about the same as a pleasant though not exciting cocktail party, with the guest of honor taking a snooze against the wall.

The claque of local businessmen who had held court in the enclosed front porch finally gave up, and De and I took over residence on a couple of folding chairs with a view of the street. We brought each other up to date on our respective jobs, wives, plans for the future. I had been to worse parties. We avoided most people by simply lowering our heads whenever someone looked our way. But a man and woman my brother's age came out on the porch and watched us for several minutes at a respectful distance. I finally called De's attention to them with a nod of my head.

Bob and Alice had gone to school with my brother. They didn't know it but they appeared obliquely in one of De's poems.

> *In the cellars where the sewers*
> *Rise, unseen, the pale white*
> *Ants grow in decaying stacks of old newspapers.*
> *Outside, the streetlamps appear, and friends of yours*
> *Call children in for the night.*

I remembered Bob as a worried young father sticking his head out his back door to yell at us older kids for picking on his bratty son; I remembered Alice as a sunbathing redhead stretched out on a chaise lounge in a bathing suit. She was plumper now, but De and I were both interested in her easy smile and crossed legs.

"I'm an egg man now," Bob said, sitting on the edge of a wooden folding chair.

"And I'm the egg man's helper," Alice laughed.

"It's great. We get to ride around together in the car all day, and a lot of the people invite us in for coffee. I work longer hours now than I used to on the bread truck, but I'm my own man."

"Are you still married, De?" Alice said.

"Uh, yes, but not to the same woman."

"Well, I figured that." She studied me studying her. "I remember you as a little boy without his pants."

I had no answer to that. Or none that I could say in front of her husband. Bob and Alice went away and the Brothers Snodgrass went inside. The party was breaking up. Mother was smiling until she saw her sons, then grew serious again. She asked us to join her one more time with Father, and I spent several minutes noting the marvels of modern casket construction. She was proud to walk from the room on the arms of her two sons.

We decided that one of us should ride back with Mother, and De opted for the black Cadillac rather than try to take the controls of the white one. As long as I was alone, I took a spin through town to listen to the radio, up and down the main street, the same route I cruised for hours in the evenings during my last two years of high school and the year before I left for college. I even remembered the speed to maintain, seventeen miles per hour, in order to hit all the green lights the length of Seventh Avenue. When that proved unsatisfying, I floored the big car up Steffens Hill and raced myself out to Darlington, coming back along the rim of the valley. When I got back it was nearly midnight, but the house was still as lit up as J. Orville Scott's.

Mother was sitting in an overstuffed chair in the living room, with a carton of cottage cheese sprinkled with sesame seeds. She was looking in the direction of the blank television set.

"Would you like me to turn it on for you?"

She looked at me and smiled. "What?"

"The television."

"It is nice, isn't it? It's a nice big screen. It was such a help to Father, when we brought him back from the hospital."

I decided to let it be. Mother had taken off the jacket of the pink suit;

her blouse was pulled out of her skirt and the buttons were buttoned wrong. The sesame seeds gave her false teeth some trouble.

"Can I get you something to eat?" she said.

"No. I think I'll just go on up. I'm pretty worn-out from the trip."

I kissed her on the mouth, the first time in years, and she patted my arm.

"Get a good night's sleep, dear."

The door to De's room was almost closed, but I could see him stretched out fully clothed on top of the bed, reading. I knocked lightly.

"You busy?"

He held up the paperback. *Bawdy Lyrics of the 13th Century.* "They're not bad. Some of them are marvelous."

"You want a nightcap?"

"I like the way you think."

We climbed to the third floor as quietly as possible and closed the door behind us. I poured doubles into the water glasses and we touched rims. De straddled the chair to my old desk; I took the bed. We didn't say anything for a long time.

"How do you think she's doing?"

"Mother?" De laughed. "She's as strong as an ox. This is the best she's looked in years."

"Yeah. Even the house is clean."

"She should be happy. She's finally got everything she wanted."

I sipped my cognac. When I didn't say anything, De went on.

"She's got his black Cadillac. She's got this big house all to herself. She'll get enough money from the estate to set herself up for life. It's a wonder she's not out dancing in the streets."

"I guess."

It was obviously not the answer, not the agreement, he wanted or expected.

"Don't kid yourself," he said. Then he looked at me over the tops of his glasses. "If you need any help with this, if you need to talk about it . . ."

"No, I'm okay."

"Because here it is, it's all laid out like Father in his casket. Everything we ever talked about. All their games, her tricks, the lies . . ."

I nodded. "Yeah. I'm really worn-out . . ."

He drained his drink and got up quickly, as if he were somehow embarrassed for me. Or worse, disappointed in me. I made a halfhearted attempt to smile. At the door he turned and studied me for a moment to see if I was friend or foe. Then he went downstairs. I got undressed and lay naked in the darkness, finishing off another water glass of cognac, afraid my brother had written me off as a lost cause. I finally fell asleep when my black window turned a safe and familiar gray.

2

I slept only a few hours. And when I woke I thought of my father, who wasn't going to wake that day, or ever again. As I got dressed for the funeral, I thought it would be a good story to tell De, to show him I wasn't a traitor in his war against my parents, even when one of the combatants was dead, that I was still on his side in the conflict. I checked myself one last time in the mirror above the dresser, to make sure that it was me, to make sure I was all there—it was me, sure enough, I was going to be all right—and headed downstairs.

De was leaning against one of the newel-posts at the foot of the stairs in the second-floor hall. I couldn't tell whether he was about to laugh or cry.

"You're not going to believe this!" he hissed.

"You okay?"

"I'm okay. I'm just fine. You'll just have to see this for yourself."

He pointed toward Mother's bedroom door and hurried downstairs. I stood there, wondering what it was I was supposed to see for myself, when Mother came from her bedroom. Dressed in white. White dress, white shoes, white stockings, white hat on her head.

"Would you zip me up?" she said, turning her bare back to me. "De was going to but he seems to have disappeared."

I looked for a way out, found none, and fumbled with her zipper, being careful not to touch her skin. When I finally got it fastened, I gave an audible sigh of relief.

Mother looked at me over her shoulder and giggled. "Thank you, kind sir."

She went over to the full-length hall mirror to adjust her hat. I found myself staring at her. She saw me in the mirror; she turned around and smiled.

"I know a lot of people won't understand why I'm wearing white, but I don't care. Black is a sad color and I think this should be a time of rejoicing. We are supposed to be Christians, you know; we are supposed to believe your father has moved on to a better world. He suffered so much at the end, he was in so much pain. And he was a good man, no man ever deserved his heavenly reward more than he. I'm sure your father would want me this way. He always said I looked very nice in white."

She thumped me twice in the chest with her knuckle as she passed to go back to her room. I went downstairs. I found De standing in the kitchen, eating a slice of cold ham and washing it down with ice water. He took one look at my face and doubled over.

"She's your mother, not mine," he said, washing his greasy fingertips under the faucet. I unwrapped a stale cinnamon granola bar.

"And I was feeling a little funny about wearing my boots."

"Compared to her, I wouldn't give it another thought."

Over our heads, Mother came down the stairs flat-footed. De and I looked at each other, shrugged, and went into the dining room to meet her. She was digging through a pile of white cotton gloves on the buffet, looking for two that matched. Her white plastic purse sat on the table.

"I'll be ready in a minute."

"No hurry," De said. "No hurry."

"Can't be late for Father's funeral." She suddenly stopped what she was doing and bent over, one arm braced on her knee, her mouth gaping. I thought she was crying or having an attack, but the sound that finally came out was a laugh. "In a way it would serve him right if we were late for his funeral. You know, he always said I'd be late for mine."

She went back to rooting through the gloves, found two that satisfied her, put on a pair of earrings with her initials. She clamped a large initialed bracelet the size of a manacle on her wrist, then gave a sharp nod of her head.

"We're off!"

De looked at me, looked at his hands, and threw them down at his sides.

The funeral home was going through the transformation from display to ceremony. Rows of chairs filled the main room; a small alcove to the side was curtained off for the family. I made another tour of the flowers to see the new arrivals. The sweet smell of the room was overpowering.

There were a few last-minute visitors. They had closed off the refuge of the porch, so De was left to stand by himself near the door. In his black suit and full salt-and-pepper beard, he looked like an Orthodox priest waiting to officiate at the service. Mother in white socialized through the last tears of the visitors. The people from Father's office in Pittsburgh stood in an awkward group to one side; I noticed that his longtime secretary, the woman who at one time thought she would become my stepmother, wasn't among them. As I watched, a tiny stick of an old woman tottered across the room, leaned down close enough to kiss Father in the casket, then turned around and crowed happily.

"That's Bruce! That's Bruce! He was a student of mine in school. I knew him as a little boy, such a cute little boy. Bruce. And now he's dead. He's dead and I'm still alive! I lived longer than he did, I lived longer than he did!"

A fat woman in a veil came over and lifted her away and out the door. I looked for De but he had disappeared. He only materialized again, noticeably pale, in time for the service.

De and my sister Shirley sat on either side of Mother during the service; somehow I got shunted down toward the end of the row. It was a toss-up as to which one got the most stares: Mother in white, or the appearance of the famous local poet. There was a good turnout of people from the town, business associates of the firm. I remember I had trouble agreeing with anything the minister said in his eulogy.

By the end, De looked visibly shaken. When the room was empty and the family started toward the cars, De lagged behind. I took Mother's arm to help her down the steps. She turned around, looking for her firstborn. He trailed along, looking at his feet.

"Poor De, your father meant so much to him."

"It's better to leave him alone," I said, thinking he needed to be left with his thoughts. After we got Mother loaded into the car, I had a chance to speak with him.

"You okay?"

"She's wearing Father's underpants," he hissed.

I was afraid my brother had finally lost it.

"That's what she told me in the middle of the service. She said she didn't have time to wash any of hers, so she put on a pair of his jockey shorts. She thought it was better than not wearing any at all, though she considered it. She said it made her feel warm and close to him. Do you believe that?"

He looked at me as if he finally had proof of everything he believed in, everything he blamed her for. All I could do was shake my head. I was having trouble not laughing myself—it struck me as a pretty funny image. When I didn't say anything or share in his outrage, he turned away.

The cortege consisted of the hearse, the funeral home's two limousines, two-late model sedans, and one old beat-up Chevy coupe. In addition to the family and the people from the firm who felt they had to attend, the only person from town to accompany the body to the cemetery was Ted Krzemienski, my best friend from high school, to whom Father had once loaned money for college. The cemetery was at the north end of the valley, on the hills overlooking Beaver Falls. They had the ground open for him when we arrived, but the mound of dirt was covered with artificial grass so it wouldn't scare anyone. We left the long box sitting under a tasteful little green tent, safe from the light rain. The men from J. Orville Scott got us back to the funeral home in one hour flat and unloaded us around the corner so we wouldn't see they needed the cars for the next service on a busy day.

Back at the house, the neighbors and church ladies had prepared food, baked ham and fried chicken, Jell-O salad and the concoction called heavenly hash—canned fruit cocktail mixed in whipped cream. De and I took turns going up to my room to take the last pulls from the bottle of Courvoisier. When everyone else was finally gone, her three children sat with Mother for a while, listening to stories of Father's last days, his operations in Pittsburgh, the way the home nurses kept trying to spirit him away to hotel suites at the William Penn—she didn't know for what purposes. She showed us the dents on the living room wall from his last convulsions as he lay in his hospital bed. Each time she teared up, De looked increasingly withdrawn and angry, as if he thought the display was somehow directed at him. He finally left the room and went upstairs. I stayed a while longer but at last retreated to my attic room and collapsed in a fitful sleep.

I startled awake a little after ten at night. The room was dark, the only light coming from the streetlight at the corner, the headlights of the passing cars. I looked for ghosts; I wondered if I had heard the sound of Father's bed knocking against the wall in his convulsions. I pulled on my boots and went downstairs. All the lights were on again on the second and first floors. From Mother's room came the sound of her deep sleep. De's room was empty. I found him in the dining room, sitting in the red plastic rocker, looking through an old *McCall's*. Beside him on the floor was the stack of magazines he had already been through.

"Let's get out of here!" he said. The chair creaked and groaned for half a minute, filling out to its original shape, after he got up.

We got our coats and headed into the night, up Fourth Avenue toward Morado. Our breath clouded with the cold; the streetlights were shrouded from the mist. We walked briskly, and it was good to be with him; I hoped that we were close again. For the last ten years he had been the most influential person in my life. We had bummed around together in New York, Detroit, San Francisco, and those were special times for me. Now the Brothers Snodgrass were abroad in the night again, this time haunting the streets of their hometown.

"Did you get some sleep?"

"Yeah. A little. How about you?"

"A little."

His hands were wedged deep in the pockets of his long coat, his astrakhan was set at a rakish angle. Drops of moisture were forming on his beard like jewels. The little stores along the street were black and desolate, except for DeAngelis' where a man in white was making doughnuts for the following day. I stopped in the middle of the sidewalk and extended my arms to clown.

"Fathers and teachers, you ask me what is hell? And I maintain that it is the inability to find anything to eat except baked ham and heavenly hash."

He laughed a little and walked on. I hurried to catch up. He was increasingly distant and remote. We passed the park at 37th Street, and I wondered if he was going all the way to the north end of town. Then he circled around the grade school, through the playground, and into the darker back streets, along Sixth Avenue toward home. The branches of the trees, bare for winter, threw rough shadows on the small trim houses.

"When are you going back?" I asked finally.

"Tomorrow. I've got to get out of here." As an afterthought he said, "How about yourself?"

"I'm going to stick around for a few days."

"What for?"

"I don't know. Just to be here, I guess."

He looked at me suspiciously. "You've got to take care of yourself, you know. There's nothing you can do for anybody here."

"I might be able to change a few light bulbs for her," I said, trying to make a joke. When he didn't say anything, I added, "No, I know what you mean."

He was lost in his thoughts. For several blocks I trailed a half step behind him along the broken sidewalks. Then he stopped and looked at me. He was trembling.

"Can you believe what she said to me?"

"What about?"

"That she was wearing Father's underpants to his funeral. The idea that she'd tell me a thing like that in the middle of the service."

I laughed uneasily. I started to walk again but he wasn't moving.

"And then to sit there when we got home and try to tell us that he was happy to be in that house at the end. That's the last place he wanted to be."

"Well, we don't know, he might have—"

"It's obvious, what are you talking about? She finally had him right where she wanted him: drugged, maimed, totally in her control at last. She got him, all right. She paid him back."

I knew what he was saying, knew what he believed, but I wasn't so sure. Not that I had a viewpoint of my own. I wasn't sure of anything anymore, much less trying to decipher what went wrong with someone else's life. None of the answers I had tried so far in my twenty-seven years, including my brother's, had worked for me. Standing there among the web of shadows from the bare trees, confronting the certainties of my brother, I could only pump my shoulders, give a little laugh through my nose like a couple short bursts of steam.

"She did it to him!" he said, increasingly angry and frustrated. "Can't you see that? She destroyed him. She wanted him there, trussed up and helpless, just like she's done to everything else in that house."

"Come on, De," I laughed awkwardly, wanting to move on. "You don't know that. . . ."

I thought he might try to hit me. He drew up into himself, his face twisted, his eyes glaring at me, his body shaking with rage.

"Don't you dare talk to me that way! Don't you ever talk to me that way again!"

"All I'm saying, brother, is that I may not agree with you on all of that. I don't think we can ever know enough of the story to—"

"You're blind if you can't see the way she is. You're blind and a fool."

He brushed by me and walked quickly away down the empty street. I watched as his figure diminished in and out of the shadows from the street-lights, then I followed behind, at my own pace, listening to my footsteps shuffling through the dead leaves, back to the house.

And to All a Good Night

1975

I finish my notes for the story I decide to call "Nightjar" and look to the dormer window. Black. It is after midnight; the traffic is gone from the hill. The only sound is the nightjar, the nighthawk, still chasing insects above the solitary streetlights. When I came upstairs from talking to Mother I was still hungry; now I'm ravenous. I heard her earlier moving around on the second floor; now the house is still. I tiptoe to my bedroom door, open it slowly, and peek down through the banister railing to the second floor; the hall lights are still on—they are rarely off, day or night—but her bedroom is dark, she must be asleep. I figure this is my chance. There is a photograph I've wanted to take, one of the statues that she's made into a lamp, but I haven't had the opportunity. Most of the photographs I take in the house are with natural light, what there is of it, filtering in through the drapes and Venetian blinds, a chiaroscuro that I hope provides a poignancy and melancholy to the imagery. But this lamp requires the harshness of its own light, its own irradiance in the cluttered room. I take my camera from its traveling case, mount it on the tripod, and hoist my accessories bag on my shoulder. Oh so carefully, I ease down the steps, keeping to the side of the treads to minimize the creaks and groans, to the second floor and then on to the first. Every light is turned on here as well. I stand in the front hall as if I've accomplished something.

I leave the camera on its tripod in the living room and go through the dining room to the kitchen, looking for a snack. The refrigerator is still full to overflowing, but unless I'm interested in cottage cheese—I'm not—there's nothing to eat. The cookies in a plastic container on the counter are soggy; the crackers in the several open boxes are stale. I remember there's a freezer in the basement and go down the stairs. There was a time, as late as when I visited the house in my twenties, when it bothered me to go down to the basement at night. When I was a teenager, it bothered me to go down to the basement at all, night or day. But now it isn't scary; there is only dirt and bad smells. Empty boxes, stacks of rotting newspapers, the storm windows stacked like a hall of mirrors. Trussed up to the ceiling with clothesline are the bicycles and wagons and pedal cars we used as children, protected from the dampness only to be thrown away when Mother dies. The freezer is as crowded as the refrigerator upstairs—packages of frozen meat, frozen vegetables, a flat white cake my brother-in-law is saving for the volunteer fire department. There are half a dozen containers of ice cream, all open. The substance inside has thawed and refrozen; I taste some on my finger but it is grainy and fibrous. I close the freezer, decide I'm not hungry after all, and go back upstairs.

My fears of the house were not limited to the cellar. Not too many years ago I would have been uncomfortable alone even in the dining room at this time of night. Once while visiting the house with my wife, I ran up the stairs after dinner into the darkness of the second-floor hall and felt an abrupt change of temperature. My body turned cold, and I knew my father, dead several years, stood beside me in the shadows. I didn't tell my wife of the encounter, but later, lying in bed on the third floor, we both felt a presence enter the room, look at us for a moment, then leave. We slept the rest of the visit with the light on, and my wife refused to visit the house again. Just last year, left alone in the house for an evening while Mother went to the church, I sat in the living room watching television and struggled to keep from screaming.

There was the time on a visit here, the year after Father died, when I came in late after doing my many trips up and down the main street. My sister Shirley was here keeping Mother company for a while, and I sat on the arm of a chair in the doorway to the living room to be sociable as they watched Johnny Carson. Suddenly, the ropes of Mother's collection of the bells of Sarna rang violently; out of the corner of my eye I saw the half dozen ropes leap as if slashed with an arm. I looked at Shirley, who said calmly, "Oh yes, they do that every once in a while." Later, after Shirley had gone home, Mother said, "You know, sometimes I can hear Barbara and Father talking in another part of the house. I suppose it would bother some people, but I always find it a comfort. It's like we're all together again."

But there are no spirits in the house now, or rather, the spirits that are here now are benign, melded into the walls and furniture and bric-a-brac. There are no monsters here, either, no soul-crushing, personality-sucking, life-destroying dragons—or Wabbits, as the case may be—no villains, as my brother believed. As I believed, until I saw the house and the family with my own eyes. I understand that my brother had to think what he did, believe what he did, for his work, for his life—possibly for his sanity—but the unbearably sad part is that there can be two different realities, in fact as many different realities as there are individuals to perceive them, perhaps infinite realities. I knew I loved his poetry and respected his achievement, both in its own right and for changing the course of mid-twentieth-century American poetry, though I came to disagree with some of his determinations; I knew that circumstances dictated that our brother love was more in one direction than the other, that he wanted, needed, an acolyte more than a brother, and when that brother eventually had thinks of his own, he was no longer as useful. I also knew I would miss him.

Back in the living room, I set about to take the photograph I had noticed earlier. The center of the image is the statue of an explorer, Magellan or Ponce de León perhaps, in full regalia with cape and sword and plumed hat, pointing the way to some distant point under a large white glowing lampshade. He stands among the clutter atop the baby grand piano, with the tapestry of courtiers and their ladies on the wall beside him; in the background on top of various bookcases are a companion lamp-statue of an explorer surveying the horizon, the Three Wise Men left over from Christmas, a Chinese sage, and a rearing Greek horse. In the upper right-hand corner is a winged convex mirror reflecting the room and sending the eye back to where it started. It isn't the best image I'll take in the house, but in the series it will say something perhaps about lost directions, misguided adventures, in addition to the haunting glow of the shade. On the ground glass, the image rings true.

The scene is impossible to meter, the values are at the extremes of light and dark, I'll have to develop the film with a radical contraction, D-23 split developer, minus 5 or 6 to compensate. I run through the calculations as I wait through the long seconds for the exposure, when there is an unearthly snarl behind me, a growl as if from the bowels of the earth. In my mind's eye I see a hellhound, my father's snarling ghost, the house itself come alive and vindictive. I turn slowly to find Mother asleep on the couch, half covered by a light throw on which is a pattern of hunting dogs. How did she get there? She must have been there the whole time. And I never saw her? How did I miss her? Her mouth is a gaping hole, her teeth sitting on the coffee table beside her head, her cheeks collapsed, the picture of death. I remember my earlier fantasy of plunging the knife into her breast; I flash on Raskolnikov hacking to death the old landlady to free his soul. I also think of the photograph it would make. I have taken a few other photographs of her asleep, but this would be damning, the image ludicrous, amusing and pathetic at the same time. But instead of taking it, I go over and gently tuck the coverlet in around her shoulders. As I reach to cover her feet, Merry Anne, lying beside her ankles, looks up at me, purrs once, and goes back to sleep.

I straighten up and look down at the two of them. Mother must prefer to sleep here on the couch rather than be stuck away in her bedroom. These are her things, this is her world, the reminders of her life; she knows there will soon come a time when she will no longer be with them. My eyes travel to the wall-sized mirror behind the couch, to the image of the middle-aged man standing over the couch before the clutter of the room. He smiles at me, and I find I'm smiling back. Quietly, I gather up my camera gear and head back upstairs to my room, to get ready to leave in the morning.